Bruce C. Sanders

By William G. McLoughlin

BILLY SUNDAY WAS HIS REAL NAME
1955

MODERN REVIVALISM FROM
CHARLES GRANDISON FINNEY TO BILLY GRAHAM
1958

BILLY GRAHAM: REVIVALIST IN A SECULAR AGE
1959

ISAAC BACKUS AND THE AMERICAN PIETISTIC TRADITION
1967

THE MEANING OF HENRY WARD BEECHER:
An Essay on the Shifting Values of Mid-Victorian America, 1840–1870
1970

THE MEANING OF
HENRY WARD BEECHER

The kingdom of Heaven is a leaven

—HENRY WARD BEECHER

The Meaning of Henry Ward Beecher

AN ESSAY ON THE SHIFTING VALUES OF MID-VICTORIAN AMERICA, 1840-1870

William G. McLoughlin

ALFRED A. KNOPF
NEW YORK
1970

This is a Borzoi Book published by Alfred A. Knopf, Inc.

Published in the United States by Alfred A. Knopf, Inc.,
New York, and simultaneously in Canada by Random House
of Canada Limited, Toronto. Distributed
by Random House, Inc., New York.
Library of Congress Catalog Card Number: 77-111239
Manufactured in the United States of America
First Edition

This book is dedicated to my daughters,

JEREMY, GAIL, *and* MARTHA,

who are teaching me about the shifting values

of mid-twentieth-century America

This church [Beecher's Brooklyn church] is simply the most characteristic thing of America. If I had a foreigner in charge to whom I wished to reveal this country, I would like to push him in, hand him over to one of the brethren who perform the arduous duty of providing seats for visitors, and say to him: "There, stranger, you have arrived; this is *the United States, the New Testament, Plymouth Rock, and the Fourth of July—this is what they have brought us to."*

—JAMES PARTON, *Famous Americans of Recent Times* (Boston; 1867)

It seems to me that I discern, arising in studies in Natural Science, a surer foothold for these [evangelical] views than they have ever had. Insofar as theology is concerned, if I have one purpose or aim, it is to secure for the truths now developing in the sphere of Natural Science a religious spirit and harmonization with all the cardinal truths of religion which have thus far characterized the Christian system.

—HENRY WARD BEECHER to Theodore Tilton, 1867

God's use of Nature as a revelation . . . has led me to my childhood faith again.

—HENRY WARD BEECHER, *Norwood*, 1867

A hollyhock is a moral and accountable being.

—HENRY WARD BEECHER, *Norwood*, 1867

PREFACE

> *His work was to secularize the pulpit, yea, to secularize religion itself, and make it as common and universal as the air we breathe.*
>
> —JOHN BURROUGHS,
> on Henry Ward Beecher

Henry Ward Beecher is treated as something of a joke by most Americans and many history books. He is the classic example of a pompous ass who got caught off base. Even though the jury could not agree in 1875 as to whether or not he had actually committed adultery with the wife of one of his parishioners, it has seemed all too fitting a climax to his career. The fact that for the last twelve years of his life, following this trial, he went on to even greater heights of popularity, seems to have been forgotten. It is assumed that, like Aimee Semple McPherson, he went into eclipse after his scandal and probably was never very significant before it.

This book is not an attempt to make Beecher appear a neglected hero of American history. But it does attempt to explain how and why such a man achieved such fame, popularity, and fortune in the half-century after 1840. To try to do this in terms of a biography, however, would be, if not impossible, at least not worth the effort. The biographical details of Beecher's life (here summarized in the first chapter) are not the essence of it; if anything, they derogate from his significance. What is significant is what he said, why he said it, why so many people believed it, what it meant to them, and therefore why Beecher seemed to most middle-class, churchgoing Americans of his day a very important man.

In order to do this, it is necessary to read what he wrote and to understand how he arrived at the theological and philosophical position which he preached so successfully to so many people for so long. He was far more than a pastor of a well-to-do suburban church. He was for much of his life an editor and weekly columnist of religious and secular newspapers with hundreds of thousands of readers. He published over thirty books. He spoke regularly, for large fees, on lecture platforms around the country. In the latter part of his life he averaged over 125 lectures a year—more than twice a week—as well as conducting his own church's affairs and giving regular Sunday sermons. Perhaps no fact better testifies to his spiritual leadership of the country in the Mid-Victorian Era than President Lincoln's choice of him as the principal speaker at a formal government ceremony in April 1865, when the American flag was raised once again over Fort Sumter. The occasion symbolized the reunion of the nation, and Lincoln believed that no one better than Beecher could find the words to suit that occasion.

It is becoming increasingly fashionable in biographies to apply the psychoanalytic approach of Erik Erikson as a means of explaining how certain men, in solving their own ego-identity problems, become spokesmen for the identity crisis of the age in which they live. Leadership is thus the application of the leader's personal identity resolution to the needs of his time. Erikson himself has used this approach to write brilliant, though controversial, biographies of Martin Luther and Mahatma Gandhi. Others have used it to explain Sir Isaac Newton, Kemal Ataturk, and Jonathan Edwards. But I am not a psychoanalyst and, as I have said, this is not a biography. I have here and there quoted a few statements which seem to me possibly to have psychological significance. But if Beecher's problems were those of his age, someone else will have to prove it. I have tried only to show that his solutions were adapted to his age.

One other point needs to be made at the outset. It has been customary for scholars to quote at random from Beecher's many volumes and to assume that his ideas did not change very much once he had acquired his reputation. But unfortunately Beecher felt obliged to say something about almost everything that happened in the world about him, and he was such an intellectual sponge that he picked up every cliché and catch-phrase of the moment and spewed them out at random. Furthermore, in his later years America began to face some major new problems—particularly in the organization of labor unions and strikes, the formation of the great trusts, and the rise of the multi-millionaire captains of industry—which he, a child of an earlier era, was not equipped to cope with. Concerning these problems he made ridiculous statements which, quoted as representative of his career, make him appear a moral idiot. That is why it has been so difficult to take Beecher seriously. Historians have seen him as a spokesman for the Gilded Age, a mouthpiece for the Robber Barons, when in reality he was a representative of the generation which preceded.

This essay (and I would hesitate to call it more than that) is an attempt to place Beecher back in the context where he properly belongs and in which he made his reputation and his contribution: the period from about 1840 to 1870. Consequently, I have seldom if ever quoted anything he said or wrote in his very prolific years after 1870—not even from his Yale lectures on preaching, which most scholars consider his most mature and valuable work. For my purposes the key work in the Beecher corpus is his novel *Norwood*, published in 1867. It was in this fictional effort to depict his philosophy of life and the practical application of his theology that he, for the first and only time, put down in a systematic way his over-all view of life and its meaning. I have begun by quoting from his first published work, *Lectures to Young Men*, which consists of addresses delivered in 1843, and have then proceeded to the various essays, lectures, and sermons of the years that followed—particularly his *Star Papers*, the essays signed with an asterisk which he wrote as a newspaper columnist in the 1850's and 1860's for the New York *Independent* and the New York *Ledger*. It was in these newspaper essays that he worked out, haphazardly and almost without premeditation, the basic ideas which ultimately came to dominate his thought. I would contend that it is these ideas, first laid out in an orderly fashion in *Norwood*, which constitute whatever claim Beecher has to historical importance.

The governing aim of the present work is to explain how the products of Beecher's theological and intellectual evolution corresponded to (or were correlated with) the major social, economic, political, and religious shifts in American society in these years. For the meaning of Henry Ward Beecher, if I have got it right, lies in the story of the great cultural shift in American values between the Age of Jackson and the Gilded Age—a generation which until now has had no name because it has not been thought to exist, but which recently scholars have decided to resurrect and to call the Mid-Victorian Era.

WILLIAM G. MCLOUGHLIN

Providence, Rhode Island
January 1970

CONTENTS

PROLOGUE
From Anxiety to Assurance in the Age of Victoria 3

I
"Liberator" or "Reactionary"? 9

II
Science and Religion 34

III
Through Nature to God 55

IV
It's Love That Makes the World Go Round 84

V
The Protestant Ethic and the Spirit of Affluence 98

VI
Art for the People, Culture for the Masses 119

VII
Transcendental and Darwinian Elitism 134

VIII
Social Engineering in a Democracy 152

IX
The North, the South, and the Civil War 185

X
White Supremacy and Anglo-Saxon Destiny 221

EPILOGUE
A Popular Prophet: "Thoroughly American" 243

NOTES 261

INDEX *follows page 276*

THE MEANING OF HENRY WARD BEECHER

PROLOGUE

From Anxiety to Assurance in the Age of Victoria

The earth has . . . its declared uses as an interpreter of God, a symbol of invisible spiritual truths, the ritual of a higher life, the highway upon which our thoughts are to travel toward immortality, and toward the realm of just men made perfect that do inherit it.

—HENRY WARD BEECHER
Star Papers, 1855

Unlike the Mid-Victorians in England, Americans felt no anxiety over the fall of medieval society and the rise of democratic society. They had already been through that revolution. Nevertheless, their sense of anxiety was acute in the years 1840 to 1870, and especially so for those living, or brought up, in New England. For in New England there had been a more tightly knit social structure, including an established church system and a clear definition of classes, long after the Revolution. The "dynamic, free-wheeling" new order introduced by the Jacksonian Era was exhilarating, but it was also frightening—especially so when religious doubts were undermining the fundamental faith which had united the nation. A new faith in science—far more convincing to many practical Americans than the older faith in dogma—was the most unnerving aspect of the period.

Like Matthew Arnold in England, Henry Ward Beecher threw his weight against the growing feeling that "there is no high, correct standard in intellectual matters; that everyone may as well take his own way."[1] And like Arnold, he offered "Culture" and the "taste" of a civilized elite as the basis for standards. Similarly, he threw his weight against the doubt that man could ever achieve a clear and accurate knowledge of God and His moral law. But since he recognized the failure of the old dogma and epistemology to sustain faith, he accepted and taught the new epistemology of Kant, Coleridge, and Hegel—the epistemology of Romanticism. "It is to be considered," he wrote in 1855, "that God found a reason of pleasure in every individual thing which he has made and that an education on our part, toward God in nature, consists in developing in ourselves a pleasure in every single object which exists about us."[2] And then, having shown Americans how to find God in Nature, it was easy to accept the evolutionary theories of Social Darwinism as an explanation of how God operated in Nature. Beecher's great achievement was to amalgamate Romanticism, religion, and science —the epistemology of Kant, the Gospel of Jesus, the teleology of Spencer. And then, as the final binding tie for these various elements, he superimposed a firm faith in the national destiny of Anglo-Saxon America.

Culture, as the Mid-Victorians understood it, asserts the reality of Platonic ideals of ultimate truth and beauty; transcendental philosophy explains how we can know and verify their existence. By means of personal religious experience in Nature, men could overcome the doubts fostered by the waning of faith in Calvinist dogma, Lockean psychology, Paley's natural theology, the philosophy of the Scottish Common Sense School, and the literal infallibility of the Bible. More important, the idealistic or transcendental epistemology of Romanticism made possible a permanent adjustment of the conflict between science and religion because it simply asserted the ultimate harmony of both. Science in the world of matter *must* conform to moral truth in the realm of spirit because God is the Creator and Sustainer of both. In probing the mysteries of Nature and its laws, we are simply coming to know and understand how God works. The thought that God is not only above but *in* Nature is not only awe-inspiring but reassuring. Evolution is God's way of doing things; Nature is "the auxiliary of revelation," as Beecher put it. The Bible contains the same truths which we find in Nature, albeit sometimes phrased in cruder form, suitable to the undeveloped state of man in the period when the Bible was written.

Beecher and the Americans of his generation had none of that sense of relativism which came to later English Victorians like Pater, Huxley, and Tyndall, and which in America found expression in the pragmatism of William James. In the midst of a period "of dissolving creeds and clashing theories," when "the taint of doubt" hung heavy in the air, Beecher and his followers were confident that Truth did exist, that moral values were secure, that the human mind (or soul) could attain to certain knowledge of God. Thus, out of conflicting "hope and dismay, optimism and anxiety," American Mid-Victorians steadily worked themselves toward a resolution in which hope and optimism prevailed. The essential feature of this revolution was a faith in progress; and Beecher's great contribution to this crisis of faith was his ability to convince the

American evangelical public that progress was more than scientific achievement, it was the redemption of the race through "the law of development and growth."

Beecher preached what he liked to call "the religion of eloquence," and while he admitted candidly that "I suppose I do slop over sometimes," his sermons, lectures, and newspaper articles nevertheless evoked for almost forty years an astonishing response from middle-class Americans across the nation. In the pages that follow, I have attempted to explain his role in the shaping, reconstruction, and reassertion of the beliefs and values of that great mass of Americans who feared that science and materialism were about to undermine the pillars of moral law and let loose a new era of barbarism.

It has been the custom for too long to break the study of American history at the year 1860—to see the Civil War as a great watershed irrevocably separating the Age of Jackson from the Gilded Age. Of course, there is a great difference between the mood and outlook of 1870 and that of 1840; but for the historian of social and intellectual life the important question is how and why that change took place—how does a culture maintain itself in periods of great change and challenge? That is the purpose of this study: to explain how Americans made the great shift from Calvinism to Liberal Protestantism, from rural to suburban living, from transcendentalism to Social Darwinism, from belief in the omnicompetence of the average man to the hero worship of the Horatio Alger captain of industry, from an age of reform to an age of complacency, from an age of egalitarian simplicity to an age of conspicuous consumption and the leisure class.

Looked at in these terms, a veritable revolution took place in American life and thought between 1840 and 1870. And yet, whoever thinks of Henry Ward Beecher as a spokesman for revolution? The solution, of course, lies in defining the difference between revolution and evolution—a transformation in which the Civil War, like the American Revolution earlier, played a crucial, catalytic role. But the war needed an interpreter and so did the social revolution. Henry Ward Beecher was to this revolution what Thomas Jefferson was to the earlier one.

CHAPTER ONE

"Liberator" or "Reactionary"?

Mr. Beecher's radicalism repelled those who were interested in maintaining the established order.

—LYMAN ABBOTT,
Henry Ward Beecher (p. 80)

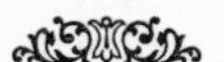

Henry Ward Beecher was considered something of a radical in his own generation. He was described as a "liberator" by the generation which followed, and he became a conservative or reactionary to the generation after that. In a sense, it all depends upon which stage of his long career one chooses to emphasize. As a young preacher in Indianapolis in 1840, mouthing his father's Calvinistic theology and attacking Roman Catholics, Beecher was certainly a reactionary. As an old and respected pastor in the wealthy New York suburb of Brooklyn Heights in 1885, he was, as one historian has said, "the summit of complacency" and social conservatism. But in the high noon of his career, from 1850 to 1870, there is much to be said for Lyman Abbott's claim that he was a radical, an innovator who did much to foment and sustain change in American social thought.

Beecher's radical reputation rested on his antislavery pronouncements, his support of armed emigration to "Bleeding Kansas," his denunciations of the five points of Calvinism, his espousal of women's rights, his auctioning of slaves to freedom from his pulpit, and his willingness to give freedmen the right to vote. His reputation as a liberator was bestowed by those Modernists or Liberal Protestant ministers who admired his concept of an immanent God, his ecumenical pan-creedalism, his acceptance of evolution and of higher criticism of the Bible. His reputation as a conservative derived from his opposition to labor unions, his espousal of the Social Darwinian principle of survival of the fittest, his admiration for successful businessmen, his Anglo-Saxon racism and chauvinistic nationalism.

All three of these descriptions are accurate, based upon solid factual evidence. Yet they are all wrong, and partial. All reveal more of the prejudices of the age which made them than of Beecher's own personality or significance. No one has yet explained why it was that just as Henry Clay, John C. Calhoun, and Daniel Webster, the three great orators of the Jacksonian Era, were departing from the scene in the early 1850's, a Congregational minister in Brooklyn emerged as the most popular orator in America—and held that position for over thirty years. Beecher's contribution to American social and intellectual history remains as moot to this day as the question of his adultery with Mrs. Elizabeth Tilton.

Part of this difficulty inheres in the fact that Beecher's chief realm lay in the spoken word. Despite the dozens of volumes of his printed sermons, lectures, prayers, and essays, the most significant quality of his personal appeal has disappeared forever. It is still possible to reconstruct the ideas which lay behind this charismatic appeal; but to do so requires that we take account of the social and intellectual framework of an entire age: the Mid-Victorian Era of 1840 to 1870.

One historian has summed up this period as an age of anxiety and doubt.[1] Another has described it in terms of a shift "from boundlessness to consolidation."[2] A third sees in it a steady drift away from Jacksonian democracy, a revival of an organic theory of society and of the institutional conservatism which went with it.[3] There are many ways to portray what happened in America between 1840 and 1870: in terms of the rise of urban industrialism, of a new ethnic pluralism, of the impact of Social Darwinian thought, of a critical loss of confidence or a reorientation in the value structure. But what is important is the temper of the American people, the intellectual flexibility which enabled them to shift their religious and intellectual ground and reconstruct their values in order to meet and cope with these changes. Obviously America was a very different place in 1870 from what it had been in 1840. How did Americans make the mental leap from one world to another? How did they manage to keep their ties with the past as they faced such a new and different future? A consideration of Beecher's career and the ideas he espoused provides one of the most effective ways to answer these questions, for he was, by common agreement, the most popular spokesman of that era.

To understand Beecher, we have to understand some of the vital aspects of his life. Born in the small Yankee town of Litchfield, Connecticut, in 1813, Beecher was the son of one of the most prominent religious spokesmen of pre-Victorian times. Although Lyman Beecher never acquired as prominent a national reputation as his son was to attain, he was nevertheless one of the giants of his day. Any psychological study of Henry Ward Beecher must reckon with his long effort to work his way out from under the shadow of his father in terms both of their personal relationship and of Lyman's reputation.

Lyman Beecher was most famous as a revivalist who thundered against deism, Unitarianism, Catholicism, and all the sins of intemperance, gambling, dueling, theater-going, Sabbath-breaking, and novel-reading associated with the term "Puritanism." He also waged a losing battle on behalf of the Federalist Party and for the maintenance of an established, tax-supported church system in New England (though he later decided that voluntarism was a blessing in disguise). A pupil of President Timothy Dwight of Yale and an intimate friend of the great Yale theologian Nathaniel W. Taylor, Lyman Beecher ardently preached that renovated form of Calvinism known as the New Haven or New School Divinity—later described by his son as "alleviated Calvinism" because it tried to take the sting out of predestination. While this new theology was successful in saving New England from deism and Unitarianism, its redefinition of Jonathan Edwards's conceptions of divine sovereignty and freedom of the will split the Congregationalists and the Presbyterians throughout the nation into two warring camps. As a young divinity student, Henry Ward Beecher suffered the humiliation of seeing his famous father tried for heresy and escaping only by the most dexterous logic-chopping. It is the great irony of Henry's career that the theological position which he later advocated was to be hailed by many Unitarians as a general endorsement of their own views. How his father would have hated that!

Lyman Beecher also achieved prominence in the first third of the nineteenth century as a leader in the many benevolent reform societies established to promote moral and social salvation. A founder of the American Bible and Tract Society and the American Education Society, he was a vigorous fund-raiser for home and foreign missions and for the education of the ministry. Almost single-handedly he launched the temperance movement in New England, and he fought vigorously against public immorality in every sphere from profanity and Sabbath-breaking to dueling and theater-going. But because he was a New Englander, he could never see eye to eye with the other great revivalist giant of his day, Charles Grandison Finney, who was equally devoted to these same causes but who, as a frontier preacher in the "burnt-over" district of western New York and Ohio, practiced an extravagant form of revivalism which Beecher considered barbarous and preached a doctrine of abolition and of perfectionism which Beecher thought dangerous. The elder Beecher clashed with one of Finney's most famous converts, Theodore D. Weld, when Weld was a student at Lane Seminary, of which Beecher was president. In 1834 Weld persuaded almost the entire student body at Lane to support the immediate abolition of slavery, and when Beecher opposed this view, the students left Lane to continue their training under Finney at Oberlin College.

Henry Ward Beecher grew to manhood not only under the domination of his father's enormous vitality and ego but also in competition with his twelve brothers and sisters, many of whom were destined to become outstanding writers, scholars, and preachers—notably Catharine, Harriet, Charles, William, Thomas, and Edward. Though not the youngest member of the family, Henry was usually treated as a baby and acted like one; he was constantly under the care of his sisters, and some measure of the shock he felt when he was crowded out of the litter by new siblings can be seen in his first known letter (written at the age of five in reference to his stepmother):

> Der Sister,
> We ar al wel. Ma haz a baby. The old sow has six pigs.[4]

A shy, self-conscious, emotionally insecure boy, his most poignant childhood memories were of loneliness and fear.

He never overcame the shock of his mother's death when he was three and his father's remarriage a year later to a woman who thought children should be seen and not heard. "Although I was longing to love somebody," he wrote later, "she did not call forth my affection and my father was too busy to be loved."[5] Even in his greatest moments of crisis he never felt that he could go to his stepmother for help: "I think it would have been easier to lay my hand on a block and have it struck off than to open my thoughts to her."[6] Beecher's longing for maternal love, nurture, and solace is evident in countless phrases and similes in his sermons and books—comparing his mother to the Virgin Mary, for example, and likening Christ's love to that of a mother. In his novel *Norwood*, the young hero "desires the truth as an unweaned child yearns for its mother's breast," and later in the story the whole nation, on the eve of the Civil War, turns to God for succor like an infant to its mother: "By Faith they laid their hearts upon the bosom of God, till they felt the beatings of that great Heart whose courses give life and law to the Universe."[7]

His father's Calvinism, even though slightly "alleviated," was still sternly wedded to the doctrines of predestination and total depravity, and a clear-cut conversion experience was demanded from all his children in order to assure him that they were among God's elect. All the Beecher children suffered from the overwhelming fear that at any moment God might strike them down and the Devil drag them off to Hell. When one of Henry's little playmates died without having experienced conversion, this terror came too close for comfort. He could not bear to think of his friend writhing in Hell, where he might soon join him:

> At intervals for days and weeks I cried and prayed. There was scarcely a retired place in the garden, in the woodhouse, in the carriage house, or in the barn that was not a scene of my crying and praying. It was piteous that I should be in such a state of mind and that there should be nobody to help me and lead me out into the light.[8]

He put his guilt feelings even more dramatically at another time when he said: "I wanted to be a Christian. I went about longing for God as a lamb bleating longs for its mother's udder."[9]

In 1826 his father moved the family to Boston in order to fight Unitarianism on its own ground. After a miserable year at the Boston Latin School, Henry decided to rid himself of his intolerable psychological burdens by running away to sea. But his father cajoled him into going to Mount Pleasant Academy near Amherst "to learn navigation" before embarking on such a career. He never had the courage to renew his rebellion until his father sank into senility twenty years later.

When Henry finished preparatory school, his father sent him to Amherst College, both because he thought a boy of his emotional instability might do better at a small country school and because he did not think Henry was bright enough for Yale. By all accounts Henry was a "backward" young scholar—"a poor writer," said his sister Harriet, who tried to help him, "a miserable speller, with a thick utterance and a bashful reticence which seemed like stolid stupidity."[10] What was worse, he was totally unable to memorize and recite, which was the whole basis of education in those days. "I have not a single pleasant recollection in connection with my schoolboy days," he once said, and in 1855 he wrote one of the most scathing indictments of country education in "the little old red schoolhouse" to appear until the days of John Dewey.[11]

In fact, however, he was by no means so stupid as his teachers thought. When he found something he enjoyed doing, he did it well. But he simply could not do it along the established pedagogical lines. One of his greatest pleasures was to play with words. The following episode occurred when he was ten or eleven and studying grammar at his sister Catharine's female seminary in Hartford—the only boy in the class. His teacher took him aside and pointed out that he did not seem to grasp the definitions and distinctions of grammar and syntax:

> "Now, Henry, *a* is the indefinite article, you see, and must be used only with a singular noun. You can say, *a man* but you can't say *a men*, can you?"
>
> "Yes, I can say *amen* too," was the ready rejoinder. "Father says it always at the end of his prayers."
>
> "Come, Henry, now don't be joking! Now decline *he*. Nominative, *he*, possessive, *his*, objective, *him*. You see *his* is possessive. Now, you can say 'his book' but you can't say 'him book.' "
>
> "Yes, I do say hymnbook, too," said the impracticable scholar with a quizzical twinkle. Each one of these sallies made his young teacher laugh, which was the victory he wanted.
>
> "But now, Henry, seriously, just attend to the active and passive voice. Now 'I strike' is active you see because if you strike you do something. But 'I am struck' is passive because if you are struck you don't do anything, do you?"
>
> "Yes, I do—I strike back again!"[12]

The incident was no doubt played up in retrospect, but it was recalled many years later as a remarkable bit of mental agility by the supposedly backward young student.

The years he lived in the town of Amherst, from 1827 to 1834, were highlighted by three crucial events. First, in 1829, he underwent a religious experience which enabled him to claim membership in his father's church, thereby getting him through one of the most critical *rites de passage* required of adolescents of that era: When "there arose over the horizon a vision of the Lord Jesus Christ as a living Friend who had the profoundest personal interest in me, I embraced that view and was lifted up."[13] Then, in 1832, he discovered the new science of phrenology, which provided a foil to the rigid evangelical theology of his father and professors. And at the same time he discovered that he had a certain talent as a debater and orator. He became captain of the college debating club, and with his friend Orin S. Fowler (later one of the country's leading exponents of phrenology) he began giving public lectures in the various towns and villages near the college. He was less interested in the practice of measuring bumps on the head than in the psychological assumptions which underlay this science. For phrenology emphasized an optimistic belief in man's ability to improve himself by the cultivation, through exercise, of his "faculties" or talents. In preaching "self-improvement," it opposed the superstitions of predestination and strongly supported the belief in freedom of the will. Thus, it led him toward a belief in human perfectibility which the Calvinistic doctrine of total depravity rigorously denied.

Henry saw no direct conflict between phrenology, as a science of the mind, and Christianity, as the world of the soul. But he was clearly attracted to an outlook which enabled him to be himself and to influence others through scientific knowledge, a medium quite different from the power of the Holy Ghost. "Not only is [phrenology's] nomenclature convenient," he later wrote, "but what it teaches concerning craniology and physiology furnishes valuable indications of individual character."[14] This was the beginning of his theological rebellion—though he did not realize it then.

Nevertheless, the force of his father's will, and his stepmother's hope that he would become a missionary, led him to enter the ministry. In 1834 he went west to Cincinnati, where his father had moved in 1831 because the dangers to religion from the barbarism of the West offered a more important Christian battleground than the Unitarian vicinity of Boston. Henry (then called "Hank") entered Lane to study theology under his father and other "New School" professors (including Calvin Stowe, who later married his sister Harriet). While he considered immediate abolition to be folly and had no desire to join Weld and the "Lane rebels" at Oberlin, he did display his devotion to civil liberties in 1836, when he patrolled the streets of Cincinnati as a specially deputized constable with loaded pistols, to protect the city's Negroes from threats of racial riots. The extent of the danger has been debated, but the bravado was typical. Throughout the 1830's Beecher, like his father, was a supporter of the efforts of the American Colonization Society to return freed slaves to Africa.

In 1837 Beecher took his first pastorate in the little town of Lawrenceburg, Indiana, twenty miles east of Cincinnati, and in that same year he married a New England sweetheart, Eunice Bullard, whom he had courted at Amherst. As it turned out, she resented the poverty and hardships of a small-town pastor's life and gradually developed into a hypochondriacal shrew who made his life miserable.

After some difficulties over his ordination, he left the Old School Presbyterians and persuaded his congregation to join the recently exscinded New School branch of that denomination. Though he was not particularly successful in Lawrenceburg, he received a call to a more well-to-do church in Indianapolis and moved there in 1839. Here he developed a new interest which he cultivated all his life—horticulture. So adept did he become at growing prize-winning flowers and vegetables that in 1845 he was asked to write a column on horticulture for the *Western Farmer and Gardener*.[15] Somehow his green thumb made him feel a deep kinship to Nature, a subtle harbinger of his eventual romantic view of Christianity.

A political supporter of Henry Clay in these years, Beecher at first opposed the Mexican War, but then supported it. It is significant that he long hesitated to preach openly about slavery.[16] Many years later, in 1872, he instructed ministerial candidates at Yale on the necessity of approaching controversial topics cautiously as young pastors. His admiring biographer, Lyman Abbott, put the matter this way:

> For some years, apparently, he did not deal with the question [of slavery] directly. His first reference to it was incidental and by way of illustration. He pictured a father ransoming his son from captivity among the Algerines in such a way as to enlist the sympathy of his hearers with the white slave against the negro slaveholders. 'They all thought,' he afterwards told the Yale theological students, 'I was going to apply it [the illustration] to slavery; but I did not. I applied it to my subject and it passed off: and they all drew a long breath. It was not long before I had another illustration from that quarter. And so, before I had been there a year, I had gone all over the sore spots

> of slavery, in illustrating the subjects of Christian experience and doctrine. It broke the ice.' It was not until toward the close of his Indianapolis ministry [in 1846] that he preached directly on slavery.[17]

Beecher was to use this circumspect approach to difficult questions throughout his career; he did not readily risk losing love and esteem—though he liked to think that he did.

Beecher's first public fame as a preacher came in 1843 when he gave a series of Sunday evening lectures to his congregation on the moral and spiritual dangers facing the youth of the nation. They were published in the local paper and highly acclaimed, and later appeared as his first book in 1844. They merit attention here in order to indicate how orthodox Beecher was at this time in his approach to religious and moral questions. As Lyman Abbott later observed: "Mr. Beecher's preaching at this period of his life was preeminently revival preaching," based upon his father's form of evangelical Calvinism.[18] While Beecher never openly repudiated these lectures, because with a certain segment of his following they established his ties to the religion of his father's generation, almost everything he wrote in later years was effectively a repudiation of them.

Entitled *Lectures to Young Men*, these addresses purported to deal with the most pressing social and moral issues of the day; and in the eyes of rural, Midwestern folk in the 1840's they probably were. The most controversial of the lectures was devoted to the evil of prostitution, "the scarlet woman." The other major topics were idleness, gambling, intemperance, theater-going, stealing, cheating, scoffing at religion, libertinism, licentiousness, horse-racing, circus-going, and fashionable or luxurious living.

The cure for all of these evils, Beecher said, was a change

of heart, a spiritual rebirth or conversion to Christian living —a conversion which only God, acting through the Holy Spirit, could bring about. There is no mention in these lectures of the great social issues of the day—nothing on politics (except to deplore demagogues, dishonest office seekers, and card-playing judges), no discussion of slavery (except to say that the hard-working slave is often morally better off than his lazy master), no mention of economic issues (except to point out that fortunes based upon honest industry do not disappear overnight in a panic the way speculative fortunes do). Nor is there any mention of the conflict between science and religion, any discussion of religious doctrine, any philosophizing upon the moral and spiritual symbolism of Nature, scarcely anything that could be called romantic. The emphasis is strictly upon personal immorality and individual reformation. The essence of the message is the Protestant ethic, pure and simple: Industry, sobriety, thrift, and piety are the roads to salvation and success.

A careful reader may find some aspects of Beecher's later outlook latent in these sermons. But they appear strangely out of focus. For example, he noted that New Englanders were less prone to some of the worst aspects of indebtedness, gambling, and political chicanery than Westerners; he implied that "knavish propensities are inherent" in the children of knaves and probably cannot be bred out of them; he maintained that "health is the platform on which all happiness must be built"; he mentioned the quality of "Ideality in Milton," which was the essential ingredient of genius; and, of course, he emphasized the danger of sultry passions: ". . . imagination is closely related to the passions, and fires them with its heat." The Negro received little discussion (except as a gambling type), but the superiority of the white race is explicitly asserted in his discussion of how the Indian "savages" are doomed to go down before "the skill of civilization."

The nearest he came to discussing God in Nature was to note that God had made so many aspects of Nature beautiful that it is a pity men feel it necessary to go to circuses:

> Men shall crowd to the Circus to hear clowns, and see rare feats of horsemanship; but a bird may poise beneath the very sun, or flying downward, swoop from the high heaven; then flit with graceful ease hither and thither, pouring liquid song as if it were a perennial fountain of sound—no man cares for that.[19]

But there is no hint of his later claims that birds carry spiritual messages from God and that Nature is itself the embodiment of His spirit.

The whole tone of the book is that which we have since come to associate with fundamentalism: It exhibits an aggressive, harsh, anti-intellectual, authoritarian, small-town morality in which fear and threats predominate—fear of God, of Hell, of torment on earth and hereafter for those who fail to live up to the letter of God's moral laws:

> When at length death gnaws at your bones and knocks at your heart, when staggering and worn out, your courage wasted, your hope gone, your purity and long, long ago your peace—will he who first enticed your steps now serve your extremity with one office of kindness? . . . you have a DEPRAVED HEART.[20]

As for the corrupters of youth:

> We denounce them; for it is our nature to loathe perfidious corruption. . . . We lift our heart to Him who beareth the iron rod of vengeance and pray for the appointed time of judgment. Ye miscreants . . . The bolt shall yet smite you! . . . And, as borne on the blast thy

> guilty spirit whistles toward the gate of hell, the hideous shrieks of those whom thy hand hath destroyed shall pierce thee—hell's first welcome.[21]

The social outlook of the book was also predominantly small-town: The farmer is superior to the businessman; village life is superior to city life; parents should tell their children to be blacksmiths (an honest trade) rather than urging them to be merchants (where they will become greedy for profits, learn to cut corners and to cheat their customers). Inherited wealth is a danger, and by and large the poor man in his hut is happier than the rich man in his mansion.

Like most evangelicals in the 1840's, Beecher thought that the essence of Christian philanthropy was embodied in the noble work of the missionary, tract, and benevolent societies, and in these lectures he warned the young against the sins of avarice and miserliness—"the miser's master-maxim—CHARITY begins at home." For such mean-spirited persons, he wrote, "it certainly stays there."[22] The usual rural fear of city slickers, intellectuals, bon vivants, and "witty" men pervades the sermons. The anti-intellectualism is evident not only in his praise for simple men leading simple, honest lives but in his warning concerning the implicit danger for any soul who tries to argue with a cynic, scoffer, or wit. As for culture, art, taste, and refinement, the lectures are one sustained diatribe about the dangers of novel-reading, theater-going, and high society. Even "Shakespeare is sometimes gross. . . . He began wrong, but grew better"—especially in bowdlerized versions. "The language of many of Shakespeare's women would be shocking in our day." The French novelists and playwrights are the worst of all. Most of this lewdness came from foreign sources, thank God: "Novels of the French school and of English imitators are the common-sewer of society."[23]

Beecher was still strongly under the influence of his father's Calvinism at this time, and the book's main theme was the total depravity of man and the absolute necessity of a miraculous conversion by the sovereign grace of God. But probably the most typical quality of this volume, apart from its antagonism toward big-city life, was the pervasive fear that the nation was becoming rootless and forsaking all of its moral and institutional values: "Many who are not in danger may incline to turn from these pages; they live in rural districts, in villages or towns, and are out of the reach of jockeys and actors and gamblers. This is the very reason why you should read. We are such a migratory, restless people that our home is usually everywhere but at home."[24]

This, then, was the predominant mood and temper of America in the early Victorian Era, at least among evangelical churchgoers. Because today we associate the term "Victorian" with London, we tend to forget that throughout the whole age of Victoria Americans were predominantly a rural, small-town, agricultural people. And for many American evangelicals *Lectures to Young Men* remained the best book Beecher ever wrote. After 1870, however, these were the evangelicals who joined the fundamentalist movement and preferred the revival sermons of Dwight L. Moody to those of the aging, but ever more liberal, Beecher. The surprising and significant fact about Henry Ward Beecher's career was that he managed to maintain his hold upon so large a segment of the evangelical public, West and East, even after he had departed quite radically from the conservative stance of this first book.

In 1847 Beecher reversed the trend of the times and went *east* to grow up with the country. He received an invitation to become pastor of the Plymouth Congregational Church in Brooklyn Heights, and having set his roots in that suburban community, he found the soil so congenial that he never pulled them up again. Brooklyn Heights at this time was becoming an increasingly fashionable residential area for the expanding metropolis of New York. Well-to-do middle-class businessmen, who found the city too crowded and the cost of land in upper Manhattan unduly high, were moving across the river to build luxurious new mansions, with fine lawns and gardens, in which to raise their families while they commuted by ferry to their offices in Manhattan. Many of these, and especially those who were attracted to Beecher's church, were born in New England, and they were as devout in their evangelicalism as he. But, like him, they were besieged by doubts and fears about many aspects of contemporary life.

As evangelicals they were worried about the challenge to Scriptural inerrancy being made by geologists, paleontologists, and biologists, as well as by the higher critics in philology, archaeology, and linguistics. On the other hand, they admitted that the old Calvinistic faith and its metaphysical justification in the Scottish philosophy no longer satisfied them either intellectually or spiritually. They found deism too coldly scientific, too materialistic or mechanistic, and had never heard of the positivism being advocated in France at that time by Auguste Comte. However, they were deeply touched by the romantic fervor for Nature in the poetry of Wordsworth and Robert Burns. Emersonian transcendentalism was obviously too heretical and extreme, though much of what Emerson said in his *Essays* seemed very true.

Beecher's Brooklyn congregation was also worried about its growing affluence, about the cupidity and corner-cutting practices of competitive business enterprise in the city, where shrewdness and bluff were often more useful than simple country honesty. These suburbanites were sufficiently sophisticated to question the narrow morality of their small-town upbringing, but not sufficiently so to know what moral values to put in its place. They wished their families to live in comfort and respectability, but they were anxious about the dangers of luxury, fashion, wasteful consumption, idleness, self-indulgence, and public displays of wealth. They wanted their children to be well educated, cultured, and refined, but they did not want them to abandon their evangelical Christian faith.

In addition, these rising middle-class suburbanites had all of the usual social and political fears of their class: fear of foreigners—especially of Irish and German Roman Catholics; fear of political corruption and demagogy; fear of mobs which would not respect private property; fear of being socially, politically, and culturally inferior to the European nations which many of them were now wealthy enough to visit for themselves. (Beecher himself made his first grand tour of Europe in 1850 and joined other American bourgeois provincials in his awe and admiration for the art, architecture, culture, and antiquity of European civilization.) They feared most desperately of all the dissolving bonds of society and of political order evidenced by the great social and geographical mobility of the nation, the increasing sectionalism, the barbarism of frontier life, the aristocratic arrogance of the slaveholding South, the wild-eyed fanaticism of socialists, abolitionists, and other outlandish reformers.

And yet, beyond and despite all their anxieties, they maintained a strong will to believe, an ardent belief in progress, and a sincere attachment to the basic credo of the American democratic faith.

Although Beecher's Brooklyn congregation was slowly swinging into the antislavery camp by 1847, it was utterly opposed to abolitionism. Beecher quickly developed a marvelous facility for threading his way among diverse views and yet seeming to be uncompromisingly dedicated to liberty and equality. He found the appropriate political stance on slavery in the Free-Soil and, later, the Republican Party. (His congregation gave him two months off to campaign for John C. Frémont in 1856.) The proper approach was to combine "moral suasion" with brotherly love toward the misguided Christian brethren of the South. If this meant opposing the Fugitive Slave Act and arming the New England emigrants to Kansas, Beecher explained such positions as defensive rather than offensive in nature. If slavery would keep in its own backyard, the members of Beecher's congregation were willing to trust God to bring the South to its senses in His own good time.

Beecher was an immediate success in Brooklyn and soon was writing regularly for prominent New York newspapers, which in those days devoted as much space to moral instruction as the tabloid papers now do to comic strips. Beecher had a way with words and was temperamentally in perfect rapport with the feelings of his middle-class audience in every sphere of moral, religious, political, and economic thought. He had to grow considerably in sophistication and self-assurance, but with his father fading fast into old age and his own small but gratifying successes in Indianapolis behind him, he finally was able to let himself go.

Over the next quarter-century he developed various lines of argument for helping his congregation cope with all of its problems—and his congregation rapidly became the whole of the evangelical North. By 1855 he was giving fifty public lectures a year and thereafter averaged one hundred or more per year until his death. The view expressed in 1875, that if Beecher were convicted of adultery, the whole cause of Christianity would suffer—"the scandal would tend to undermine the very foundations of social order"—was not entirely farfetched.[25] The middle class needed to believe in Beecher because it desperately needed to believe in the solutions he had provided for their doubts and fears. He was "a beneficent power for good in the community," and even his most hostile biographer, Paxton Hibben, says of him that up to that time "his life had been a singularly useful one."[26]

Psychologically it may be significant that Henry Ward Beecher's fame rose as Lyman Beecher's declined; but it is also true that Lyman Beecher's theology and social philosophy were out of date and badly needed redefinition. Most of what his children did and wrote ran contrary in some way to what Lyman had stood for. Henry, far from suffering from the rising fame of his siblings, was able to use it to bolster his own rebellion; it gave him courage to stand at last upon his own feet. He found himself in finding that his oratorical talents and emotional sympathies elicited from his auditors the kind of adoring response, the love and warmth, he had always longed for. His congregation became for him a family of which he was at once paterfamilias, fair-haired boy, and prodigal son. "I like above all things in the world to be loved," he had said at twenty-seven.[27] Now his wish came true.

After 1850, volumes of his sermons, prayers, lectures, and newspaper articles began to appear almost annually. He injected himself with gusto into all of the political issues of the day and found that the old taboo against ministers meddling in politics (which the Jeffersonians had labored so hard to instill, especially against men like Henry's Federalist father in New England) had now disappeared. In an age of doubt a gifted, "chosen," anointed minister of God was a man whose voice was sought on every issue. Someone was needed to interpret God's will to man, and Beecher seemed to have a prophetic talent for striking the mystical chord which quieted men's fears and lifted their hopes. He squared what was with what ought to be. And the American people were deeply grateful to him.

Concerning Beecher's later career, it is not necessary to go into detail here. He worked for Lincoln's election but was ready to let the South secede in peace until the flag was fired upon. Then he became a zealot for crushing the rebellion and restoring national honor and union. On a visit to England in 1863 he made a number of speeches which many thought at the time were influential in swinging British public opinion from a pro-Confederacy to a pro-Union position (though it seems in retrospect that certain fortuitous military victories were far more effective in this regard). Beecher received one of his most famous accolades in 1864, when that Brahmin arbiter of national taste, the Autocrat of the Breakfast Table (and an arch-Unitarian), Oliver Wendell Holmes, Sr., published an article in the *Atlantic Monthly* praising his work in England and calling him "our Minister Plenipotentiary." Beecher also parlayed a couple of brief encounters with Lincoln into a personal "friendship" which paid enormous dividends when the wartime President was martyred. Lincoln attended a Sunday service in Beecher's church in February 1860, and talked with him once in Washington in 1864, but there is no record of any other meetings. Nevertheless, the fact that the President chose him to deliver the major address when Old Glory was raised once again over Fort Sumter was probably more than a personal favor. It was a unique acknowledgment of his importance as an expositor of the Northern evangelical mind.

After the war Beecher briefly favored the "soft" reconstruction policy of Andrew Johnson—one of the few times he was out of step with his audience. But ten years later he was able to claim that everyone had been out of step but him. Endorsing Grant in 1868 and 1872, and hoping he would run again in 1876, Beecher supported "God and Garfield" in 1880 and then astounded his friends (but once again proved his public sagacity) by switching to Cleveland in 1884. Although the suit for adultery brought against him by Theodore Tilton in 1875 seriously undermined his standing with some, the fact that the jury could not agree on his guilt (the vote was nine to three for acquittal) and that he continued to have the loyal support of his wife, his congregation, and his Congregational brethren of the cloth, helped to tide him over the crisis.

His public endorsement of Herbert Spencer in 1878 and Charles Darwin in 1882 (though he had implicitly espoused their views in his writings much earlier) helped make Beecher a hero to the rising generation of ministers who considered him one of the leading fighters for a more liberal Protestant theology. At the same time, his dislike for trade unions and labor agitators made him appear to more conservative laymen as a champion of the same old Protestant ethic which Americans had always believed in (at least since Benjamin Franklin). At his death in 1887, Beecher was widely eulogized as one of the great men of his day, and even hostile historians have had to acknowledge that he played no small part in shaping the era he epitomized so well. "Beecher was as much the embodiment of nineteenth century America," wrote one of the best scholars of the era some years ago, "as Walt Whitman."[28] But it seems hard to imagine Whitman sitting in one of Beecher's pews, even when they both lived in Brooklyn.

He did have one thing in common with Whitman besides long hair, and that was his massive inconsistency. Whitman is well known for saying, "Do I contradict myself? Very well then, I contradict myself." When Beecher was told that what he had preached one Sunday was contradictory to what he had preached the previous Sunday, he replied, "Oh, yes! Well, that was last week!"[29] Or, as he put it another time, "Life is a kind of zig-zag."[30]

It would be easy to make a long list of his inconsistencies both in general principles and on specific issues. For example, he was clearly a New England chauvinist, proud of his Puritan heritage and convinced that New England was the brains and heart of the nation; yet he repudiated almost all of Puritan theology and generally considered himself as much an American, or Brooklynite, as Whitman. He was an ardent nationalist; but he opposed a strong, centralized government. He fervently proclaimed himself a democrat, a believer in democracy as the highest and purest form of government; yet he preached just as often that men of taste, refinement, education, and character were a superior type who deserved to rule over those of lesser endowments. He was an individualist who maintained that the family, church, and school were the vital institutions which held society together; he was a nationalist who advocated Anglo-Saxon unity, and a believer in free will who thought that heredity, training, and environment molded all men. He praised the unsuccessful revolutions of Europe in his time, but argued that the Negro slaves should not be encouraged to revolt because they had no chance of succeeding. He declared that slavery had perverted the Southern whites and destroyed their claims to be Christians; but he thought the freed slaves would be better off entrusted to their former masters than to an army of occupation. He maintained that the cities were the centers of civilization and the big businessmen the fittest of the race for survival; but he also considered cities dens of iniquity and businessmen greedy, corrupt, and materialistic. He regarded poverty as a sign of sin, while he continued to argue that the honest poor were far happier than the idle rich. He expressed the view that the Bible must be adapted to the discoveries of science, yet insisted that God was still master of the universe and worked miracles daily. He declared that only men of exquisite taste and refinement could be artists, but he also rejoiced that art in America was under the control of the masses. He argued that John Brown was right but he was wrong and William Lloyd Garrison was wrong but he was right.

How then is anyone to make any sense out of a man like this? To say that Beecher was not a systematic or logical thinker is merely to beg the question. Nor does it help to quote his own rationale that he purposely preached no doctrines but "only Christ" and that in soul-winning, "He is the best fisherman who catches the most fish." Somewhat more to the point was his argument that "you can gain men easily if you get around their *prejudices* and put truth in their minds, but *never* if you attack *prejudices*."[31] But essentially what lies behind his inconsistency is what lay behind that of Emerson and Whitman. He was part of the romantic rebellion against the Age of Reason. The underlying premise of his whole approach—whether to preaching, theology, or politics—was that imagination is more important than intellect, the heart than the head, and that men are governed not so much by their rational faculties as by their feelings.[32] Is it worthwhile, then, to try to analyze or make logical sense out of an orator who sought primarily to appeal to the feelings?

Henry Ward Beecher did make sense to his age. His words were listened to and quoted. They moved men and women. If we do not insist too much upon a strictly logical order in dealing with the popular mind of an era, it is possible, at the very least, to trace its responses and to make some generalizations about them. Nor is this simply a matter of saying that his inconsistencies were, and to a large extent still are, those of America itself. For there were a series of crucial issues on which decisions had to be made and on which Beecher did take a stand, however equivocal he might have been on specific details.

On the whole, his decisions or choices were progressive, forward-looking, in line with the advanced thought of his age. Though his claims to radicalism cannot be sustained, his claim to be a liberator can. But the critical judgment which has to be made in each area is the extent to which his progressivism was such only in terms of the generational revolution that occurred over the years 1840 to 1870, and the extent to which it was genuinely forward-looking from the perspective of the century which has elapsed since. And in either case, what do his stands tell us about the important reconstruction in American values which did take place in those critical Mid-Victorian years?

CHAPTER TWO

Science and Religion

I began to read Spencer's works more than twenty years ago. They have helped me through a great many difficulties.

—HENRY WARD BEECHER, 1882

The major problem of the Mid-Victorian Era was the reconstruction of American religious and national faith. Americans were caught between the death of Calvinism (whose epitaph Oliver Wendell Holmes, Sr., had written in *The One Hoss Shay* in 1850) and the birth of Modernism or Liberal Protestantism, which can be dated roughly between 1867, when Beecher published *Norwood*, and 1872, when he gave his sermons on preaching at Yale.

This crisis of faith had many aspects. Some of them were the consequence of a loss of faith in the future of the nation, a loss of belief in America's divine mission, arising from the various economic, sectional, and political crises which seemed to portend the failure of the great experiment in democracy after 1850. But a more direct challenge arose in the questions which science raised about the literal infallibility or plenary inspiration of the Bible. As a pietistic, Protestant people, Americans believed that God's will was revealed to man in the Bible; this had been the basis of hope and faith since the arrival of the Pilgrims. All else might fail, but the truth of God was securely bound in that book. Lyman Beecher's generation had fought off the first challenge to Scriptural truth when he and others successfully rallied Christians against the heresies of Thomas Paine, Ethan Allen, and Thomas Jefferson, and the deistic attack upon Biblical infallibility. Perhaps Lyman Beecher's most famous and enduring address was his sermon "The Faith Once Delivered to the Saints," delivered in 1823 against the renewed onslaught of Unitarian rationalists.

But in Henry Ward Beecher's generation the challenge to revealed truth was based not upon Enlightened Reason but upon cold, hard scientific evidence: the results of geological examination of rock strata and the fossil bones embedded in those rocks; the philological investigations of old documents and the intensive textual analyses which exposed mistranslations in Scripture; the archaeological discovery of ruins and inscriptions which brought the dates of Biblical history into question. In addition, science was giving man new control over his environment, new control over disease and pain, a new sense that he was master of his own fate because he could master Nature instead of being enslaved to it. Men became less willing to accept the mysteries of the Bible and less submissive to the unfathomable will of God, because they found less need to be submissive to the world in which they lived. "It is not long since pestilences, plagues, and many special forms of disease, such as leprosy, and many varieties of convulsive disease [such as St. Vitus's dance] which affected the nervous system, were regarded by the medical faculty, and by the church itself, as the results of spiritual causes," wrote Henry

Ward Beecher in 1859. "I remember in my own day, very long sermons to prove that the cholera did not depend on natural agencies, but that God held it in his hand and dropped it down upon the world."[1]

But there was something even deeper than all of these challenges to the spiritual faith of that era. This was an unconscious yearning to find in religion a more direct appeal to the feelings. We have become so accustomed to associating the early years of the nineteenth century with the frenetic emotionalism of camp meetings and revival preachers that it seems difficult to imagine that there was any starvation of the emotional side of religion in America. But it all depends upon where one looks. As early as 1825 some students at Harvard experienced keen disappointment "when, at the usual stage in the college curriculum we were promised 'metaphysics' and were set to grind in [Dugald] Stewart's profitless mill. . . ."[2] The student who wrote this was Frederick H. Hedge, later one of the leading Christian transcendentalists. While the revolt of Emerson and his friends around Concord against the "corpse cold" theology of Boston churches in the 1830's may be seen as a reaction against Unitarian rationalism, there is plenty of evidence that Calvinists were equally upset with the theology which they were learning and preaching.

James Marsh, president of the University of Vermont, who introduced Coleridge to American readers in 1829, was—though a Calvinist—clearly part of the transcendentalist movement.[3] When Francis Wayland became, in 1827, president of Brown University, a Calvinistic Baptist institution in Rhode Island, he was required to teach moral philosophy to students as bored with it as those at Harvard. He, too, became disgusted with the Lockean rationalism of the Scottish Common Sense metaphysics which was the staple diet in the textbooks on that subject, and eventually, in 1835, he published his own textbook, *The Elements of Moral Science*. In this he gave new emphasis to the institutions or the moral sense of man so as to give more weight to the feelings of the heart than to the ratiocinations of the brain in man's search for ultimate truth. "There is a world without us and a world within us which exactly correspond to each other," and through the faculty of taste "we are conscious of the existence of beauty and deformity." By cultivating our taste and refining our intuitions, we can come closer to perceiving the perfect beauty of God in the world he has created: "Much of the happiness of man depends upon intellectual and moral cultivation."[4] Wayland frequently quoted literature (mostly Shakespeare and Robert Burns) in this text on "moral science," because he wished to touch the hearts of his students as well as improve their minds.

By 1850 the same rebellion against the Lockean rationalism of the Scottish School was evident even in the citadel of neo-Edwardsian Calvinism, Andover Theological Seminary, whose students generally regarded the "alleviated" Calvinism of New Haven as too liberal. Edwards A. Park, who taught theology at Andover, argued that "somewhere" Calvinistic theology "must be wrong" if it could not "strike a responsive chord in the hearts" of men and women, "stir our own souls, reach down to our hidden responsibilities and evoke sensibilities" too long dormant. Something, he said, in the sermons of even the best Calvinists of the mid-century had somehow given "an abiding impression" to churchgoers across the land "that the divine government is harsh, pitiless, insincere, oppressive, devoid of sympathy with our most refined sentiments, reckless of even the most delicate emotion of the tenderest nature."[5]

In *The One Hoss Shay* Holmes put his finger on the failings of the reigning theology of the day: "Logic is logic, that's all I say." And when Henry Ward Beecher sought to show how an intelligent, discriminating, well-educated man could be turned into a "scoffer" or a "materialist" by the preaching be heard in New England pulpits in the 1840's and 1850's, he invented a fictional character named Judge Bacon who said:

> It was a poor exchange that the Puritan made when he bargained off imagination for logic, emotion for metaphysics, moral consciousness for proof. A genuine Yankee Puritan thinks that he can prove anything. . . . I'm tired of logic and argument and doctrine and discussion.[6]

What Judge Bacon wanted (but did not have the "ideality" to get), and what most evangelical churchgoers wanted by 1850, was a religion which appealed to their emotions. To Beecher it was a great tragedy that Jonathan Edwards had to repress the poetic side of his imagination because of the Puritan insistence upon logic and reason.[7] He was ready to agree with many Mid-Victorian churchgoers that the pulpits of New England were "candlesticks whose candles won't burn—learned men, but can't speak, like deep wells and a pump that won't fetch water."[8] And if New England's pulpits, the font of the nation, were so dry, what must be the state of religion elsewhere?

A psychological biography might see much of Beecher's liberalism as a rebellion against his father. But it reflected the rebellion of a whole generation of Americans against the teachings of their fathers. This rebellion was far advanced in New England, and throughout the Northeast, when Beecher returned from Indianapolis to Brooklyn in 1847. Nonetheless, Beecher advanced toward a new theological position slowly and cautiously. It was twenty years before he openly stated his liberal position, and then he did so in the form of a novel, behind whose fictional characters he could hide himself from any attacks—a form of deviousness his father would never have indulged in.

Not that he could not be bold on specific issues when he chose. In 1859, for example, he attacked the doctrine of total depravity. And when he was called to account by a Calvinistic newspaper for this heresy, he defended himself in characteristic fashion by distinguishing between truth and dogma, between facts and doctrines: "We do not hesitate to say now, that we regard it [total depravity] as one of the most unfortunate and misleading terms that ever afflicted theology."[9] The term is "an interloper," it is "not to be found in the Scriptures" or "in the Catechisms and Confessions of Faith of Protestant or Catholic Christendom." Of course, he went on, there is no doubt about "the deep sinfulness of universal man" and "we do believe in the exceeding sinfulness of sin"; but "We have no sympathy with those theologians who use Time as a grand alley and roll back their speculations six thousand years, knocking down and setting up the race in the various chances of this gigantic theologic game. . . ." His approach, he said, was direct and practical: "There is the human heart right before my eyes every day, throbbing, throbbing, throbbing! Sin is not a speculation but a reality. It is not an idea, a speculative truth, but an awful fact, that darkens life and weighs down the human heart. . . ."[10]

Beecher's answer to the contemporary crisis of belief was to preach to the throbbing human heart, to reaffirm its faith in Christianity, and yet to do so without undermining the equally profound faith of Americans in science, education, and learning—in short, to harmonize religion and science not through metaphysical speculation (as his father and Nathaniel W. Taylor had done) but through appealing to emotional experience. The problem was that the revival preachers of the day were defining religious experience in terms of a direct, supernatural confrontation with God in the miracle of conversion. And this experimental crisis was, by theory and practice, so cataclysmic, so shattering, so traumatic as to produce what in modern terms would be called "hysterical" psychological reactions. This was hardly suitable to a sophisticated, fashionable, Eastern suburban church, however satisfactory it may have been on the frontier.

Horace Bushnell had tried to face this problem as early as 1846, contending that there was a "deficiency and incapacity of language [as philosophical logic or speculative theology] to serve as the medium of religious truth."[11] But his own speculations had been too recondite for most churchgoers and too heretical for most of his ministerial brethren. Though Beecher did not agree completely with Bushnell, he was influenced by his work; it is clear that he too was trying to bridge the gap between Nature and the supernatural in terms which can only be called transcendental. Beecher and Bushnell were, on different levels, advocates of that new, Romantic Christianity which began to flourish in the 1830's and which eventuated in the 1860's as Liberal Protestantism. That is why John W. Buckham claimed in 1919 that "Next to Horace Bushnell, the greatest liberator of American theological thought was Henry Ward Beecher."[12]

Neither Beecher nor Bushnell liked the irrational and anti-intellectual aspects of frontier revivalism; neither thought the spasmodic fervor of revivalism was beneficial for the Church as an institution; neither liked appeals to the animal emotions as a means of working people into spiritual states of exaltation. Both were therefore advocates of Christian nurture, of institutionalized Christianity, of an organic view of society as opposed to the anti-institutionalism, individualism, and perfectionism of Jacksonian revivalists like Charles G. Finney or Jacksonian reformers like Theodore Weld and William Lloyd Garrison. Beecher and Bushnell, both pastors of fashionable metropolitan churches in Mid-Victorian America, were largely responsible for harnessing the emotional energy of Romanticism to conservative ends, making it a means of social control, of law and order, in the face of what seemed a dangerously disintegrating social system.

It is not surprising, though it is perhaps ironic, that Henry Ward Beecher was praised in 1860 as a leader of liberal thought in America by the official organ of Boston Unitarianism, the *Christian Examiner*. The Boston Unitarians knew a social conservative and a liberal theologian when they saw one, but they did not put their praise in social terms. The *Examiner* reviewed two of Beecher's books, *Life Thoughts* and *New Star Papers*, in an article entitled "The Liberal Religious Movement in the United States." Beecher may have felt some embarrassment at finding his theological position compared in this article with that of Theodore Parker, Henry W. Bellows, and Thomas Whittemore, but the praise was well meant. Beecher, like these other theological liberals, said the reviewer, was seeking to "harmonize the advanced thought of the age with a working and living faith." Unlike the unlearned frontier Baptists and Methodists, "he has not the prejudices against learning and philosophy" which blind and narrow religious thought. "He could not be a bigot if he would."[13]

Perhaps most important, "Mr. Beecher is emphatically a man of the people." Though not a logical or coherent thinker, "He reaches a large class of persons who would not otherwise be brought into direct contact with living and progressive ideas." The Unitarians were particularly pleased to hail Beecher as a force for their kind of liberalism because "The whole drift of his preaching and writing is in opposition to the fundamental idea of Calvinism." But, as we shall note later, the Unitarians also were pleased that, however liberal his religious ideas, his social theory was intensely conservative. Beecher was, to paraphrase a famous statement that Franklin D. Roosevelt once made about himself, "that kind of a liberal because he was that kind of a conservative." Liberal conservatism is the keynote of Beecher's philosophy, as it is of most of American social and intellectual history.[14]

Beecher's adroitness at balancing himself upon the fence between liberalism and conservatism (or Unitarianism and Trinitarian orthodoxy) is evident in his efforts to deal with the issue which was central to the conflict between religion and science in that era, the issue which had cut Theodore Parker off from Unitarianism in 1840—namely, the nature and necessity of a belief in miracles as an essential feature of Christian faith. Or, as Parker had put it, the effort to differentiate "the transient and the permanent in Christianity." Beecher could attack the doctrine of total depravity by denouncing the theological terminology in which it was phrased while accepting the psychological reality of man's universal sinfulness. But the reconciliation of the concept of immutable natural laws with supernatural intervention or interference with those laws required a somewhat different approach.

Beecher tried to outflank this issue in an essay published in 1859 entitled "Natural Laws and Special Providences." The substitution of "providence" for "miracles" was itself typical of his verbal dexterity. The crux of the essay was contained in these two reassuring sentences:

> The progress of science lays a surer foundation for a belief in God's active interference in human affairs than has existed without it. When maturer fruits of investigation shall be had, there can be no doubt that science itself

> will establish our faith in prayer, in miracles, and in special providence.[15]

But what proof did he have to give for this faith? First, he pointed out that in primitive times or among contemporary uncivilized tribes, people are governed by "superstitious notions" which are contrary to fact and which distort their lives. But as men grow more civilized and learn the laws of Nature, they come to see how benevolently our Heavenly Father has organized the universe in order to help his children. "God has not put us before nature to make us only its pupil, but also its master." Obviously science and God's will work in harmony in this respect. Scientists, by learning Nature's laws, and inventors, by utilizing them, are helping mankind to improve their lives and civilize the human race. Someday, perhaps, all of the laws of Nature would be known.

Some men, however, push this principle to an illogical extreme and "are ready to say that all things are effects of physical causes and that there is no immediate divine volition exerted upon natural laws." But anyone who says this is not a Christian; for

> The doctrine of the presence and actual interference of God in the world, producing effects which would not have fallen out otherwise, is taught in the Bible . . . as the argument and foundation of prayer, of courage, of patience, and of hope, and as a special development among others of the incarnation of Christ to bring to light the reality of God, who wrought invisibly in life and nature both before and since.

There are three things to be said of this marvelously wrought sentence. First, it begs the question at hand by pitting the Bible against science as a form of proof for miracles. Second, it begs the question by saying, almost incidentally, that God is present in the world and hence the question of interference is obviated. And third, it reduces miracles to the mystery of God's unfathomable purposes which we must accept on faith, with patience and courage, in the hope that whatever happens is for the best because God wills it. At the conclusion of the essay, for example, Beecher cites, as the kind of providential act which God performs ("because he loves to give needed things better than earthly parents love to give good gifts to their children"), the answered prayers of a parent caught on a train during a snowstorm; his child is fretful and hungry as the train struggles to make headway against the drifts, but God hears the prayers and finally the train gets through to the station. This is supposed to prove that "God administers natural laws—of the mind, the body, and the outward world—so as to produce effects which they never would have done of themselves."

Unchristian men may call it good luck, accident, or coincidence that the train got through, but Beecher called it answered prayer and claimed that God often acts directly in such cases. Similarly what men call *bad* luck can also be the direct result of God's action and is to be interpreted not as bad luck but as divine punishment for sins personal or national. The fact that God is present in Nature, and that he is kindly disposed to help educate and improve his children by rewards and punishments in this world as in the next, is hardly a startlingly new or liberal answer to the problem of miracles. Yet because Beecher faced the question (or seemed to) and came out strongly in favor of science without undermining faith, those who read this essay found reassurance where they had formerly had only doubts. "Not only would I cast no obstacle in the way of scientific research, but I hail it as the great almoner of God's bounty."

One other important point in this 1859 essay deserves mention. A major part of Beecher's discussion was taken up with the assertion that because man has learned to master Nature, it can be assumed that God, who is the master of the universe, is also the master of Nature and can manipulate it as He wills: "If we drive natural laws, cannot God do it?"

Beecher's argument here is, of course, tautological; it is simply faith based upon faith. But what he was trying to establish was not only that God is in Nature but that Nature is as dependent upon man as man is upon it:

> While natural laws, in a certain way, influence and control men, yet they are, in the effect which they produce, just as much controlled by man and just as dependent on him. If nature should abandon men, *they* would die and *it* would become poverty-stricken.

Here he seemed to assume, for the sake of argument, that nature might be amoral, red in tooth and claw. Let us suppose, he implied, that God lets the laws of Nature operate remorselessly. Does that prove that man is simply a helpless pawn in the grip of vast forces beyond his control? On the one hand, "Let nature forget us, and the heart would cease to beat. The pulsations of endless electrical currents would cease." But "on the other hand, let man forget nature, and the city would crumble and go back to a wilderness; the garden which had grown up from a thistle-ground would return to its native condition. . . . Nature needs man to keep her at work." So much for those who would exalt Nature at man's expense.[16]

It was a reassuring thought—but also a sobering one. Men must assert an iron control over Nature or it would assert such over them. The net result of this approach to harmonizing religion and science was to make those individualists and perfectionists who recklessly cared only about cultivating themselves seem totally irresponsible. For the laws which govern Nature were viewed as also governing human society, and therefore if individual men forgot the institutions which gave order and meaning to society, mankind would soon revert to a state of barbarism, just as would an unweeded, unfenced, and uncultivated garden. Mutual dependence—man upon Nature, Nature upon man, society upon order, the world upon control, the garden upon cultivation—this was the lesson Beecher drew from the new discoveries of science. But he had faith both in God's benevolent superintendence and upon man's will to mastery of his fate. Because God is greater than man and thus even better able to "drive" the laws of Nature; because He is in Nature and guiding it every moment and not a clockmaker God who exists outside the world He has made; because He has given man the power to discern the laws by which the universe works and the intuition to perceive His hand at work in them, there is no need to be fearful either that Nature will overwhelm us or that God has forsaken us or that science will lead us away from God. Our quarrel is not with God or Nature or science but with those of our fellow men who refuse to do their part in the mighty mutual effort to bring order out of chaos and perfect the universe.

Beecher's optimistic faith in science not only led him to welcome the new-found laws of geology, paleontology, thermodynamics, evolution, and microbiology but also the pseudo-scientific fads and frauds of his day, like hydropathy, phrenology, craniology, homeopathy, mesmerism, and Graham bread. "Through life," said his son, "Mr. Beecher was as free with pathies in medicine as of isms in religion, and used allopathy, homeopathy, hydropathy, electricity, or hand-rubbing as seemed to him at the time most likely to secure the coveted result."[17] Beecher was always insistent upon the basic importance of health in the pursuit of happiness, and he belongs to that long train of American positive thinkers extending from Benjamin Franklin to Mary Baker Eddy and Norman Vincent Peale. A volume has yet to be written upon the increasing neurosis of the Victorian Age, particularly its strains upon the dyspeptic businessmen and their fainting womenfolk. But it was undoubtedly a large measure of Beecher's appeal that he was the living embodiment of vigorous health and a preacher of good hygiene.

He was forced to defend himself against the charge that by praising phrenology he was endorsing a crackpot, dangerous, and infidel system. Most clergymen found it antireligious because it attacked all dogmas and creeds as superstition. But Beecher, having risen above creeds and doctrines, was not put off by this. "We are far from regarding Phrenology as a completed science," he wrote in 1856, but "we regard it as incomparably beyond anything which has been regarded as a science of the mind."[18] First of all, he found "its classification and divisions of faculties and its laws of combination and activity" very helpful in defining human character. "It simplifies many things which in other systems are obscure." Its theory that "mental traits can be discovered by the conformation of the head" (i.e., by the study of the bumps on the head) was "its least value" according to Beecher. Far more important,

> Phrenology assumes the brain to be the organ of the mind. It teaches that the brain is not a simple unity, but a congeries of organs; that special faculties employ several special portions of the brain for their manifestation; . . . The usefulness of Phrenology to a minister of the Gospel is to be settled by asking the question, Is it beneficial to a

> teacher and healer of the mind to know what the human mind is, and what are the laws of its action?

No one could doubt that it was. And hence "it is a mere impertinence to say that the knowledge of the human mind, or of Phrenology or the science of the mind, will not secure a man from mistakes. Nothing will secure a man from mistakes but Death." And so, adroitly, the charge was deflected, and the critic was asked to merely be open to new ideas, to be willing to take what he finds useful in science and discard the rest, but not simply to scoff at science because it might make a few mistakes. "There is a great difference between knowing nothing and knowing something," and the man who knew phrenology had made some start toward a better understanding of the brain and its faculties. Hence Beecher was perfectly free to admit that as far as he was concerned, he owed to it much of "the practical knowledge of the human soul" which he possessed and therefore he praised it for helping him "in bringing the truths of the Gospel to bear practically upon the minds of men."[19]

We can see what Beecher actually found so appealing in this pseudo-science by the description of it given by John D. Davies in his scholarly study *Phrenology: Fad and Science.* The phrenologist, he says, extolled the moral law, the free individual, and the mission of America; he opposed sectarianism and "emphasized each man's individual endowments and set of capacities by means of which he could lift himself." Only in America were men sufficiently free to develop themselves to their fullest capacities. "Like Unitarianism, Universalism, and Transcendentalism, phrenology taught that sobriety and virtue, chastity and self-improvement were the keys to the good life." While "it underscored the role of heredity" and the "varying endowments of men and their differentiation," nevertheless "it escaped the anti-democratic implications of this emphasis by neatly balancing against it the function of environment, the doctrine of the growth of the faculties through exercise," and the optimistic belief that God or natural law meant all men to improve and perfect the human race. "With the postulates of science it combined a moralistic deism and a religious teleology—like Silliman's geology it was a sort of 'Christian' science." Obviously such a "science" was just what Henry Ward Beecher and his age were looking for. "It might be said of phrenology . . . that it allowed its advocates to believe what they wanted to believe"; and that consisted in combination of the most usable of the past and the most advanced of the present.[20]

The same could be said of the interpretation of Darwinian evolution which Herbert Spencer provided for the Gilded Age, and which he had already adumbrated in his *Social Statics* in 1850, nine years before the *Origin of Species.* It is not clear when Beecher first read Spencer or just how much of him he ever read. Since by his own admission he "never read a book through,"[21] he probably obtained much, or even most, of his understanding of Spencer's views from the many magazine articles about them. One of Beecher's more admiring biographers maintained that he had accepted the principle of evolution as early as 1860; in a sermon of that year Beecher said: "The world has come uphill every step from the day of Adam to this."[22] Better evidence for his having read Spencer and Darwin (or read about them) lies in a letter he wrote in 1867:

> I regard the labors of naturalists as indispensable to the final adjustment of truth, and I would encourage such men

as Spencer to say whatever is given them, not because they bare the full truth but because they bring out the truth. . . .[23]

In 1882, during Spencer's triumphal visit to the United States, Beecher was asked to deliver one of the orations at a banquet to him. This address epitomizes Beecher's method of reconciling science and religion:

> I began to read Spencer's works more than twenty years ago. They have helped me through a great many difficulties. Whoever gives me a thought that dispels the darkness that hangs over the most precious secrets of life, whoever gives me confidence in the destiny of my fellow-men, whoever gives me a clearer standpoint from which I can look to the great silent One, and hear Him even in half, and believe in Him, not by the tests of physical science, but by moral intuition—whoever gives that power is more to me than even my father and my mother; they gave me an outward and physical life, but these others emancipated that life from superstition, from fears, and from thralls, and made me a citizen of the universe.[24]

It is almost pathetic to hear the great preacher exalting this pseudo-philosopher above his father because Spencer had freed him from the fears of his father's superstitions and given him a renewed faith in "the great silent One." But what is most characteristic is his statement that Spencer's books revealed God's will not by "the tests of physical science" but by "moral intuition." Neither divine revelation nor empirical science was the arbiter of truth in the end—only intuition.

Ultimately, in 1885, Beecher published his series of lectures entitled *Evolution and Religion* (originally delivered in 1882–3), in which he proclaimed himself "a cordial Christian evolutionist." But anyone who reads his sermons and essays will agree that he was more or less accurate in saying, in 1882: "Slowly and through a whole fifty years I have been under the influence, first obscurely, indirectly, of the great doctrine of evolution."[25] What he meant by this was that soon after 1850 he began to lose his old belief in predestination and the other deterministic and pessimistic doctrines of Calvinism and to emphasize that optimistic faith in progress toward the millennium and the Second Coming of Christ which had always been part of Christianity and which, in the Age of Jackson, were flourishing with even greater vigor—so much so that millions of Americans actually believed the predictions of the Baptist preacher William Miller that Christ would return on the night of March 25, 1844.

Beecher's sermons, lectures, and essays in the 1850's were filled with hope and optimism; he continually talked about human progress, the development of civilization, the advance of the human race. He equated this primarily with the history and destiny of the United States, but he applied it also to the general development of democracy and republicanism in Western society. "The earlier and ruder forms of society are the monarchic. The later and riper developments are republican in spirit, whatever be the form" (the qualification served to allow for English monarchic constitutionalism).[26] He wrote this in 1860, and that same year in a Thanksgiving Day address—although the nation was on the brink of disunion and civil war—he gave thanks for "the advance of Christ's kingdom in the whole aspect of the world," including "the whole human race."[27] He took particular care to note "the emergence of the common people to that degree of political power that makes it necessary now for the whole of Western Europe to ask their permission for the establishment of any throne or monarchy." The example he gave was the newly formed kingdom of Italy under Victor Emmanuel, a monarch "who almost reconciles republicans to kings." He went on to note the intention of the Czar of Russia to free the serfs. In earlier sermons and newspaper articles, in the 1850's, he had praised the revolutions in Hungary, Germany, Italy, and France as similar signs of progress.

But more closely allied to his early, though "obscure," belief in evolution were his frequent references to the laws of Nature, to God's universal laws of growth and development, which were perfecting the human race for its final reconciliation with God. "Our prosperity," he wrote in 1860, "had its beginning and continuance in Natural Laws. God's will in nature and in human society is the source of human strength and human wisdom." And even though civil war seemed imminent, he urged Americans to believe that "in the end, right political economy will work out prosperous national economy."[28] The reason "we have prospered in days past is . . . because we have known just enough to see the way in which natural law and God's kingdom were going and to follow them."[29]

For Beecher, as for most middle-class, churchgoing, Mid-Victorian Americans, faith in God and in Christianity was a faith in progress and in a moral law governing the universe. The conflict between Genesis and geology which troubled so many Mid-Victorians was no problem for Beecher: "I had early been interested in science and I was convinced God had two Revelations in this world, one of the Book and one of the Rock, and I meant to read them both."[30] It did not take much more than a persistently sanguine and pragmatic temperament to insist that science and religion were both essentially evolutionary, onward and upward: "I say to all those clergymen who are standing tremulous on the edge of fear in regard to the great advance that God is making today . . . you must be sure to meet the Lord when He comes in the air, when He moves in the providences of the world, when He is at work in natural laws . . . when He is shining in great scientific disclosures . . . and to see that the habiliments of Christ [in Nature and in this world] grow brighter and brighter, and nobler and nobler, from age to age, as He puts on righteousness and comes in all the glory of His kingdom towards us."[31] To some it was easier to see this after 1865 than in the decade before the war, but for Beecher the vision was never in doubt.

It was one thing to have an obscure faith in evolution and a strong hope in the Kingdom of God on earth even as it is in Heaven; it was quite another to rest Christianity simply upon this vague hope that science and religion, natural and revealed law, were in harmony—especially when these new scientific laws were so complex and difficult for the common man to understand. A scientist might see the glory of God's master hand underneath the complex laws of thermodynamics, electricity, or evolution; but what about the uneducated, average man? How did it help his faith in revelation? Beecher admitted that there was a great gap between the genius of science and the simple and untutored: "What do you suppose Baron Humboldt would have been to an Indian boy fifteen years of age, if he had come before him with all his astronomic, geometric, and geographic knowledge—with all his scientific knowledge—with all the boundless wealth of his great mind?"[32] Obviously the poor Indian boy would learn nothing about science or about faith from such a great mind. Similarly, "An ignorant and stupid man, standing in the scope of a natural law, makes nothing of it. An intelligent and wise man, by using it, makes the fields fruitful, covers the hillsides with thrifty orchards, and fills the valleys with beautiful gardens."[33]

The implications of this for the importance of education,

for a theory of elitism or rule by the *aristoi*, we will return to later. But in terms of the religious crisis of the times, what is significant is that scientific wisdom is not in and of itself sufficient to restore man's faith. In fact, it was more likely to drive simple men back to an anti-intellectual, literal belief in the Bible and sophisticated minds into materialism, naturalism, or skepticism.

What Christianity needed in order to survive as a living faith—now that the God of Calvinism was, with Beecher's help, dying—was some direct and simple way for the average man to find a direct, experiential relation with the God of natural law. Having decided that the frenetic emotionalism of the revival was not going to prevail among the rising middle class in the cities and suburbs of the East—not only because it was too vulgar and unrefined but because it was retrogressive, a return to barbarism and an injury to the organic life of the Church as an institution—the liberators of American evangelical Protestantism had no recourse but to adopt the transcendental, experiential approach of Kantian idealism as expounded by Coleridge, Carlyle, and Wordsworth.

In order to reconcile religion and science, the clergy had to romanticize Christian experience. In the end, this proved a dismal retreat from the true strengths of the Christian dialectic; but at the time, and for several generations thereafter, it appeared to be a brilliant maneuver which completely outflanked the menace of materialism. The way to find God was not through microscopes and telescopes but through the inward eye of reflection and the outward light of setting suns. For God had so constructed the human soul that it was capable of perceiving Him directly.

CHAPTER THREE

Through Nature to God

A hollyhock is a moral and accountable being.
—*Norwood* (1868 ed., p. 53)

Henry Ward Beecher was no theologian and never tried to write anything which could be called a systematic exposition of the theology he preached. In fact, he made a virtue out of attacking theological systems and deploring the doctrinal factionalism which had, by 1850, divided Protestant America into 150 different sects, each vigorously asserting that its own tenets and practices constituted the only true path to Heaven.

In 1867, however, Beecher did publish a novel, entitled *Norwood,* in which he set forth, as specifically as it was possible for him to do, just what he conceived the relationship between man and God to be, what life was all about, and how it should be lived. Here he drew together many of the ideas which he had developed gradually over the preceding twenty years and which had appeared in various half-digested states in dozens of sermons, lectures, and newspaper columns. The distance he had traveled theologically since arriving in Brooklyn can be measured only by contrasting *Norwood* with his *Lectures to Young Men.* In his first book he had spoken with the simple faith of the old rural evangelical Calvinism. In *Norwood* he produced what may well be the first fully developed statement of Liberal Protestantism to appear in popular form.

It would be possible to trace in a general way the various steps which Beecher took between 1847 and 1867 as he gradually shed his Calvinistic, revivalistic, small-town, evangelical outlook. Year by year through the 1850's and 1860's Beecher sopped up the culture and "advanced thought" of the East and became sophisticated. He was talking to a new audience in Brooklyn, an audience which considered itself far removed not only geographically but educationally and socially from the crude frontier civilization of the Midwest. The Brooklynites had prejudices and shortcomings, but they were very different from those of his congregation in Indianapolis.

The most fundamental difference, of course, was that the Brooklyn congregation had succeeded in the world. Its members were making money. They were building fashionable brownstone houses and mansions designed by professional architects. They dressed in the latest fashions from England and France. They prided themselves upon having refined manners, well-furnished homes, and cultivated minds. Many of Beecher's parishioners had been to Europe, and consequently he had felt obliged to go there too. His letters home, in 1850, reveal the terrific culture shock Europe gave this raw New Englander and Midwesterner: He wept when he saw his first ruins; he was transported into ecstacy by the museums and picture galleries; he grew lyrical over his visit to Shakespeare's home, where he noted with awe the names of the great and the near-great scrawled upon the whitewashed walls of the Bard's house, though he modestly contented himself with signing the guestbook. When he returned home, he began to read Matthew Arnold and John Ruskin and to write about culture and art as though he were as knowledgeable about them as about farming, horticulture, science, and theology.

Unfortunately there is no sign of his having read the works of the seminal philosophers of transcendentalism in either England or America—no references to Coleridge or Carlyle, Emerson or Thoreau, Kant or Cousin. But he did read the poetry of Wordsworth and Robert Burns, and he no doubt read *about* transcendentalism in the middle-class magazines found on marble-topped tables in the well-to-do homes of Brooklyn: the *Atlantic Monthly*, the *North American Review*, the *Nation*. Actually, however, Beecher and his parishioners lived at a level of sophistication considerably below that of the Boston Brahmins who edited and wrote for these magazines. The Brooklynites were new rich, not old rich. Their reading fare, and Beecher's principal writing outlets, were middle-brow secular newspapers like Robert Bonner's New York *Ledger* and Horace Greeley's *Tribune*, and middle-brow religious newspapers like the *Independent* and the *Christian Union*. Beecher served for many years (1848–70) as a contributing editor of the *Independent* and then for eleven years as editor of the *Church Union* (later the *Christian Union*).[1]

In short, for twenty years Beecher was engaged in making his way up the ladder of social and intellectual respectability, and as he did so, he absorbed through every pore the burgeoning culture, art, and refinement of his day. The Mid-Victorian *nouveaux riches* were hounds for culture and mad for self-improvement; Beecher, as one of their leaders, became an intellectual sponge, sopping up whatever was the popular interest of the moment in art, architecture, or literature. While he was anything but an omnivorous or careful reader, he picked up through newspapers, magazines and conversations the notions and ideals, the fears and hopes, of those with whom he associated and whom he felt an obligation to instruct and uplift.

Many hints of what Beecher was thinking as he worked himself out of the fold of Calvinism can be found in his sermons and essays in the 1850's—for example, an essay written in 1854 for the New York *Independent* entitled "Nature as Minister of Happiness." In this, after rhapsodizing about the beauties of a summer's day in the Berkshires (where he had at that time a summer home in Lenox, Massachusetts), he posed the question: "Is it Nature that has the power of conferring such religious joy, or is it Religion that inspires Nature to such celestial functions?" And he answered: "To a Christian heart it is both. The soul seeks and sees God through nature and nature changes its voice, speaking no longer of mere material grandeur and beauty, but declares through all its parts the glory of God. Then when Christ is most with us, do we find nature the most loving, the most inspired; and it evolves a deeper significance, in all its phases, and chants, with its innumerable voices, solemn but jubilant hymns of praise to God."[2]

A psychologist might speculate that Beecher's jubilation as he basked in the pleasures of his summer resort home was really the beginning of his own spiritual release from the insecurities and anxieties of his childhood. He was beginning to change from a nay-sayer to a yea-sayer. He had returned to New England, the scene of his unhappy and lonely childhood, a success. The world was opening up for him, and so it seemed to be opening up for all men. Beecher had come out of the shadows and into the full light of psychological and spiritual freedom. He had claimed to find a similar release when he was converted in 1829, and again in a second religious experience at Lane in 1835. But however real these earlier moments of emotional release, they were shallow and short-lived. Not until the 1850's did Beecher really feel free to be himself. And it was a glorious feeling, which he wished to share with all of those worried, doubting, anxious Americans who were yet locked within the imprisoning fears of a bleak Calvinism or a narrow materialism:

> The earth has its physical structure and machinery well worth laborious study; it has its relations to man's bodily want, from which spring vast activities of industrial life; it has its relations to the social faculties and the finer sense of the beautiful in the soul; but far above all these are its declared uses, as an interpreter of God, a symbol of invisible spiritual truths, the ritual of a higher life, the highway upon which our thoughts are to travel toward immortality, and toward the realm of just men made perfect that do inherit it.[3]

Thus in 1854 Henry Ward Beecher was beginning to perceive dimly the relationship between industrial progress, civilization, culture, self-improvement, natural law, and God's spiritual laws of human development. Having read Matthew Arnold, he was beginning to play with broad concepts like the Hebrew mind, the Greek mind, the Roman mind, the Puritan mind, and the conflicts between barbarism and civilization, culture and anarchy, dogma and literature. "No one who has made himself conversant with the representations given of the natural world by the Hebrew mind, but will feel the infidelity of our modern occidental mind."[4] The Western or Modern mind, as Beecher saw it in 1854, was apt to be rationalistic, logical, materialistic; the Hebrew mind was full of the wonders of God's glory, "the old prophet felt his sense kindled by the divine touch, and read the face of the heavens and of the earth, as God meant them to be read; how full of meaning and of majesty were the clouds, the mountains, the morning and the evening, the storms, the birds and beasts, the insects and the grass through which they creep."[5] All of this was grist for Beecher's philosophical and spiritual ferment.[6]

By 1866 he was ready to say that "We cannot come to the conviction of the divinity of Christ so well by the intellectual and philosophical method as we can by the spiritual and experimental method."[7] And the experimental method for him was that of experiencing God in Nature—the Liberal Protestant doctrine of divine immanence: "Nature becomes to the soul a perpetual letter from God, freshly written every day and each hour."[8] The essence of his new-found idealistic epistemology—which he felt he had imbibed far less from the transcendentalists than from the mystical side of Puritanism which he found clearly expressed in Jonathan Edwards—is evident in an essay entitled "Hours of Exaltation," written in 1857. The key passage contains these words, which Coleridge or Emerson might have set down:

> The roots of Nature are in the human mind. The life and meaning of the outward world is not in itself but in us. And when we have taken in all that the eye can gather, the ear, the hand and the other senses, we have but the *body*; we do not yet read and know the spirit and truth which cannot be received by the sense but by the soul.[9]

He may not have been reading Walt Whitman, whose *Leaves of Grass* had appeared only two years earlier; but as he wandered about his summer estate in the Berkshires or, later, on the Hudson River, he too was loafing and inviting his soul.

Yet he was no antinomian. He did not see communion

with God in Nature as an ecstatic bolt from the blue nor as a mystical dissolving of self. "One man communes with natural objects by many more faculties than another," and he made it clear that he required, for the highest sense of communion, a combination of sensation, reason, imagination, and religious intuition. "What a man sees in Nature will therefore depend upon what he has to see with." A man who brings nothing to Nature but his senses "will see the rind and husk of Nature" and nothing more. "If he bring reason along, he will perceive the connections and homogeneities of natural objects, their relations to each other and to us." But "if he add imagination" and "feeling," and then "religious feeling," and "if he hold all these up against the background of the Infinite, then indeed, to his unspeakable satisfaction, the heavens declare the *glory of God*, and the firmament showeth his handiwork."[10]

Obviously Beecher was not an Emersonian pantheist, or a mystic like Bronson Alcott. He wished to be a Christian transcendentalist. However, his transcendentalism was not egalitarian; the multiple endowments and sensitivities which he thought requisite to full communion with God experientially in Nature, implicitly assumed considerable prerequisites of education, training, and innate endowments which limited the highest spiritual experiences to a precious few.

It says something for the distance Beecher had traveled intellectually in twenty years that he was willing to write a novel when asked in 1865 by the editor of the New York *Ledger*. No doubt, the success of his sister with *Uncle Tom's Cabin* helped to goad him on. But he also knew that there was a vast novel-reading audience that he could tap by this genre, and he was sufficiently eager for popularity and enough of an egotist to try. It seems probable, also, that he thought he could work out in this story a great deal of the philosophy of life which he had been developing over the previous twenty years. And he may have especially welcomed the idea of putting all his thoughts down in some kind of order in a work of fiction, because this would leave him the option of denying responsibility for anything awkward his characters might say.

Unfortunately Beecher had none of his sister's gifts as a novelist. Moreover, by subtitling the book *Village Life in New England*, he misled literary critics then and ever since as to what he was writing. Most reviewers saw the book as one more in the new genre of local-color fiction, designed to portray the quaint customs and characters of Yankee New England. The *Biblical Repertory and Princeton Review*, completely missing the book's revolutionary theological significance, called it an "interesting and instructive presentation of a phase of New England character and life which is rapidly passing away."[11] The *Atlantic Monthly* quoted extensively from its scenes of Yankee wit and homespun philosophy, praising "its cordial and friendly humor, its pathos and sympathy, its generous and manly sentiments," but ignored the theological substance entirely.[12] The *Nation* praised his "gallery of Yankee portraits," equating them with the best local-color writing of Harriet Beecher Stowe and Oliver Wendell Holmes, Sr., but dismissed the story as a typical sentimental war novel.[13]

The only critic to take its religious message seriously was Orestes Brownson, who reviewed it for the *Catholic World*. Brownson, having himself passed through Liberal Protestantism in his Unitarian and transcendental phases, was not taken in by Beecher's quaint Yankee portraits: "The persons or personages of his book are only so many points in the argument he is carrying on against Calvinist orthodoxy and for pure naturalism." But Brownson was as mistaken as the other reviewers. The purpose of the book was not to promote naturalism but to advance Romantic (or transcendental) Christianity of a very conservative form. It was the herald of the new era of Liberal Protestantism, a long-neglected key to a significant transition in the American religious mind.

Beecher made his purpose plain in a letter in 1866 to the editor of the New York *Ledger*, Robert Bonner, who paid him $30,000 for the privilege of printing the novel in weekly installments. Having commissioned the book, Bonner asked Beecher what it would be about, and Beecher replied:

> I propose to make a story which shall turn not so much on outward action (though I hope to have enough to carry the story handsomely) as on certain mental or inward questions. I propose to delineate a high and noble man, trained to New England theology, but brought to excessive distress by speculations and new views. . . .
>
> The heroine is to be large of soul, a child of nature, and, although a Christian, yet in childlike sympathy with the truths of God in the natural world, instead of books.
>
> These two, the man of philosophy and theology and the woman of nature and simple truth, are to act upon each other and she is to triumph.[14]

This was hardly a new theme in American and English literature. The problems of head and heart, science and religion, faith and doubt were central to much of Victorian belles-lettres. Hawthorne had dealt with the theme in various ways and places, most notably in *The Marble Faun* and in short stories like "The Birthmark" and "Rappaccini's Daughter"; Melville had treated it in *Moby Dick*, *Pierre*, and *The Confidence Man*. In England a host of prose works—*Sartor Resartus*, *The Ordeal of Richard Feverel*, *Yeast*, *Alton Locke*, among others—as well as Tennyson's *In Memoriam* and Arnold's *Dover Beach*, had tried to cope with the crisis engendered by a dying faith and the search for a new one to replace it. And in the decades which followed 1865, the number of such works increased manifold. Beecher, as always, had his finger on the pulse of the times, and though the book was not popular with reviewers, it was widely read by the public.[15]

What was unique about his approach was that it came close to being a perfect expression of the American resolution of religious doubt. In *Norwood* the last vestiges of New England Calvinism disappeared finally and forever, and in its place the new theology of liberalism at last emerged in terms which everyone could understand. The reason the reviewers of the leading Boston literary magazines were not impressed by it was that they were Unitarians who had long ago become liberals. To them, what Beecher was saying was old hat. But to middle-class evangelicals like his parishioners in Brooklyn, it was a marvelous revelation of just what they needed and wanted. In spite of the reviews, it became one of the better sellers of 1868. The year before, while still being serialized, it had been dramatized in a moderately successful play in New York, with Beecher's permission (though he did not go to see it). It appeared in at least four different editions between 1867 and 1887; this in addition to the thousands who read it as it appeared serially in the *Ledger*.

Superficially at least, the book is a love story concerning Barton Cathcart, the noble young man marooned on the shoals of scientific doubt, and Rose Wentworth, the large-souled child of Nature. The action takes place over the years 1830 to 1866 in a town not unlike Litchfield, Connecticut, or Lenox, Massachusetts (Beecher gives its location as fifteen miles east of Amherst and twenty miles north of Springfield). But the principal character is not the ostensible hero or heroine—it is rather the town doctor,

Reuben Wentworth, Rose's father. He is the spokesman for Beecher's views, and it is in his many conversations with the town's Congregational parson, the Rev. Jedidiah Buell, D.D., and the town lawyer, Judge Bacon, that the basic philosophy of Liberal Protestantism is developed. Bacon, as we have noted, is the "discriminating scoffer" who represents the materialism and incipient skepticism of the age, a believer in "the physical theory of mind." Barton Cathcart says of him: "Judge Bacon chills me. . . . His cold touch shocks me. I feel when he talks about religion as I should if my mother were dead and I saw a surgeon using her body for anatomical demonstrations." More horror than this would have been difficult for a Mid-Victorian American to conceive of.

Parson Buell, on the other hand, is almost as bad. A graduate of Yale, a doctor of divinity, he is an advocate of the corpse-cold "alleviated Calvinism" of Lyman Beecher and Nathaniel W. Taylor. Buell's greatest failing is that he lacks "ideality," he has no imagination or sense of beauty and no moral sympathy. In fact, he is almost as heartless in his way as Judge Bacon. When his wife is dying, Buell constantly badgers her about the state of her soul. The poor woman refuses to say that she is content to leave her husband and fly to the arms of Jesus. It plagues Buell to distraction that she "was willing to go but did not rejoice" in dying. "Day by day he held up to her the searching tests by which, since the days of Jonathan Edwards, the more earnest New England Christians tried themselves." Until finally one of the quaint Yankee characters, a blunt spinster named Agate Bissell (after the carpet sweeper) who is nursing the dying woman, finally can stand it no longer and blurts out: "Why do you worry the poor child, doctor?" The well-meaning but obtuse minister accepts the rebuke, but throughout the novel he is portrayed as totally ineffectual, an old-fashioned country preacher—more or less the kind of man Beecher had been in Indianapolis twenty years earlier and, if we look deeper, a reflection of old Lyman Beecher—well intentioned but totally incompetent to deal with the complex religious problems of Mid-Victorian America.

It is the Boston-born, Harvard-educated, European-trained medical doctor, Reuben Wentworth, who is the real shepherd of souls in Norwood. It is he who succeeds in answering Judge Bacon's barbs at Christianity, he who saves Barton Cathcart's soul from damnation, and he who, in the end, educates the parson and the reader as to the true meaning of Christianity in the year 1867. "It is remarkable, Doctor," says the befuddled parson, "that you, a physiologist, should incline to the spiritual faith, while Judge Bacon, of sound education and not given to the physical sciences, should hold, as I suspect he does, the physical theory of mind."

There are two important chapters in the book in which Beecher expounds the essence of Liberal Protestantism or Romantic Christianity. The first of these occurs early in the novel, when the doctor and the parson are conversing in the doctor's garden; the second deals with Barton Cathcart's conversion. The first episode begins when, having been told that Judge Bacon is a materialist because he has no ideality, the parson inquires naïvely of the doctor: "But you have told me that I had no ideality—whatever that may mean. How is it that the deficiency does not work in the same direction in both cases?" To which Wentworth responds frankly: "It does."

The parson is abashed; he has always considered himself a good Christian and faithful servant of God. But Wentworth does not spare him:

> You [and the Judge] may differ in regard to facts and convictions, but both of you insist upon reducing all truth to some material equivalent before you are subject to conviction. A truth which does not admit of a logical statement seems to you a phantasy. You believe not upon any evidence in your spirit but upon the semi-material form which language and philosophical statements give to thought.

In other words, the parson is a captive of theological speculation and logic. He does not realize that "Imagination is the very marrow of faith." Wentworth, however, having read Coleridge—or at least imbibed the central tenet of transcendentalism that the Reason (intuition or imagination) is a faculty superior to the Understanding (mind or intellect)—proclaims:

> I accept the facts which appeal to my senses as the lowest possible truth and as appealing to the lowest avenue of my mind. Nature is more than a vast congeries of physical facts, related to each other as cause and effect, and signifying nothing else.

Wentworth then launches into a popularized account of the new epistemology of Kantian idealism which Liberal Protestantism utilized to replace the realistic epistemology of Lockean and Scottish Common Sense philosophy. The heart of the new approach lay in the doctrine that God is present, immanent or indwelling, in Nature, and that the world of Nature is therefore essentially a world of spirit. And the crucial consequence is that, since God has given all men intuitive powers, He has made it possible for all men to have direct perceptions or experiential confrontations with Himself in the realm of Nature.

This approach had been used by the transcendentalists thirty years earlier to overcome the "corpse-cold" rationalism of Unitarianism. Emerson had seen clearly that the Unitarians, in reaction against Calvinism and the emotionalism of the Second Great Awakening, had reduced the life of the spirit to training, education, discipline. They had left out the heart of religion and thereby cut themselves off not only from God but from the common people. Well-educated Boston Brahmins might find satisfaction in the Unitarian creed of salvation by character, but the common man preferred a more simple and direct interaction between himself and God. Hence they had ignored Unitarianism for the revivalism of Lyman Beecher.

Unfortunately Emerson, himself a Harvard-educated Brahmin, had not been able to make transcendentalism sufficiently clear and simple for the average American to whom he wished to appeal. His followers were bright, highly educated, emancipated young men and women who seized upon the more individualistic and perfectionist aspects of transcendentalism in their revolt against the philosophy and institutional controls of their parents. Henry Ward Beecher's contribution to American religious development was to effect a workable marriage between the romantic, idealistic, individualistic aspects of transcendental philosophy and the conservative, well-ordered, institutional aspects of Christianity. While Emerson provided exceptional young people with a philosophy of self-governed, self-realizable freedom, Beecher offered the average, middle-class churchgoer a philosophy of (in his words) "regulated Christian liberty." However, the starting point for both was the conviction that man must go through Nature to God.

"See that clump of hollyhocks," says Wentworth to the puzzled Buell, as he points to the flowers in his garden, "white on yellow, and rose on crimson, so they stand, and the light falls on them alone, through that opening among the trees. They are transfigured! The light seems to palpitate upon them, and on the crimson blossom it fairly trembles! Is that mere materialism? Is there no moral around them?"

"You don't mean," asks the parson in astonishment, "that a hollyhock is a moral and accountable being?" That is precisely what the doctor does mean and just what Emerson had been saying to uncomprehending Americans for thirty years. "Does it not act?" Wentworth replies:

> Does it not send sheets of light to my eyes? Does not that raise up a thousand fancies and yearnings? Do I not, in its exquisite effects, almost see through matter and into the other life? And is not that clump, with its atmosphere of light, the instrument producing such effects? And when God created light and flowers, did he not know that power it was possible that they could exert upon human souls, and design that they should do it? They have a moral function, even if they have no moral nature.

Many Americans had read things like this in the poetry of Wordsworth—notably in his poem about the daffodils and his lines written above Tintern Abbey. But they had never seen such a theory seriously advanced as a description of Christianity. Yet here was the most prominent preacher in America—and a Beecher to boot—saying just that.

Buell, a Yale-trained minister, still thinking in such conceptual categories as Lyman Beecher had taught, can hardly believe his ears. This was preposterous: "It is mere fancy. It is not sober fact," he tells Dr. Wentworth. It is, as Andrews Norton, the pope of Boston Unitarianism, had said of Emerson's *Nature* in 1836, mere "mysticism" or pantheism, "the latest form of infidelity." Wentworth, however, is not to be frightened by such terms:

> Fancy is itself a fact, just as much as an argument, a leaf, or a stone. God made the soul to be played upon by its fellows, by a whole round of visible nature, by invisible things, and more than all by Himself. If shaking leaves stir up the soul, there was a power in them to do it, as much as in the soul to be agitated. I insist on a living, divine power in physical things. Why should men be so anxious to degrade nature?

The gnawing doubts of the Victorian mind, assailed by science and materialism, were thus simply answered by Beecher. Nature was not to be downgraded as the source of skepticism or deism or pantheism, but to be upgraded to what he called "an auxiliary" or "a coordinate of the Bible." In his father's day the God of Nature had been used by the deists as a weapon with which to attack Christianity; old Lyman Beecher had never understood Romanticism. In his Yale lectures of 1872 Henry Ward Beecher pointed out very clearly the difference between his generation and that of his father in this respect:

> I find a great many persons who say, 'I do not much enjoy going to church, but if I am permitted to wander out into the fields, along the fringes of the forests, and to hear the birds sing, to watch the cattle, and to look at the shadows on the hills, I am sure it makes me a better man.' Some others, like my dear old father, would say, 'That is all moonshine; there is nothing in it, no thought, no truth, and no doctrine of edification.' But there *is* truth in it.

Beecher knew his audience well. He knew the inroads that Romanticism and Nature worship had made into the popular mind, and he knew how inadequate the old evangelical Calvinism was to cope with it. But just to make sure that he did not alienate any devout Christian, he took pains even in his novel to show that he had no intention of downgrading Scripture or revelation. He offered a broad array of

Biblical texts which seemed to him fully to support his transcendental view of Christianity and which he had Wentworth quote to the parson:

> Dr. Buell, do you believe Scriptures? Do you believe that those very heavens above your head declare the glory of God; or only that they *did* four thousand years ago? 'The earth is the Lord's and the fulness thereof, the world and they that dwell therein!' now, today, here in this field,—yonder, over that meadow, just as much as in Palestine.

The Hebrew mind! The Old Testament prophets were the first transcendentalists:

> 'Thou crownest the year—Thou visitest the earth—Thou makest the outgoings of the morning and evening to rejoice. The Lord sitteth upon the flood; yea, the Lord sitteth king forevermore.' Do you think that I can believe this universal presence of God—in the sun, in the season, in the sea and on the mountains, in tree and herb, in clouds and storm, in summer and harvest, in the city among men and in the wilderness—and yet suppose that Nature has nothing more for the soul than the catalogue of scientific names and a recitation of the order in which phenomena happen?[16]

The best defense is a good offense, and Beecher clearly wanted to have his cake and eat it too. He wanted to preserve Biblical revelation and also to refute the speculative logic of Calvinism. He wanted God to be both in the world and above it.

The proof of this new theological pudding becomes evident in the struggles of young Barton Cathcart to find God. Herein lies the second crucial aspect of *Norwood*. Cathcart's difficulties begin, as with so many young men in the 1850's, when he goes to college and studies geology. Yet the attitude young Barton expresses is as much that of

Henry Ward Beecher against old Lyman as it is that of the young generation of the 1850's. Barton, be it noted, attends Amherst:

> Young Cathcart, during the last two years of his college course [roughly 1855 to 1857] had found his religious life passing from a state of acquiescent acceptance into one of eager questioning. His Reason was asserting its sovereignty. Should he believe because his parents and teachers did? Should he suffer himself, among so many sects, holding widely different beliefs, to be located without any deliberate investigation or honest judgment of his own? Was a man to be superscribed by his parents, like a letter, and sent to this or that church?[17]

The message of Emersonian self-reliance was getting through at last to American evangelicals. Cathcart, of course, will not desert Congregationalism, but neither will he accept the faith of his pious forefathers simply because the ancient and honorable of this world affirm its truth. "To this rebound of reason from youthful faith was added the influence of scientific studies, to which his taste had strongly inclined him." Barton is obviously one of those highly endowed natural aristocrats who will commune with God through a great many faculties. The path he is to tread in his quest for faith has already been mapped out early in the book—it is the same one that Dr. Wentworth had followed when he went to Harvard as a young man. Wentworth too had had "a strong taste for Natural Science," but "with an instinct as strong as that which leads an infant to its mother's breast for food, he turned from the dry descriptions and classifications [in the science text-books] to the living things themselves."[18] In studying Nature, Wentworth was guided not only by his reason but by "an instinct, the sensibility of exquisite taste." And to this was added "a moral sympathy," a divine intuitive sense "until he found himself united to the organized system of nature with every part of his being."

And so Barton, too, pursues his search, from reason to science to taste and moral sympathy. "But the result [at first] was far other than he had anticipated." He had started out to examine, "investigate and settle, one by one, the great truths of religion." But he found that reason was not enough: "He began to feel that convictions could not follow logic. The feelings must be consulted, and the imagination as well as the reason in re-establishing faith." Reason had the power "to bring into doubt every one of his childhood beliefs"; but only the feelings and imagination, in moral sympathy with Nature, could bring him from doubt to security again.

In his state of perplexity he naturally turns first to his pastor in Norwood for counsel. But the village parson gives him old and worthless answers which do not help. "Dr. Buell kindly but firmly pressed him with consideration of duty." It was his duty to believe on faith, his duty to his parents to accept the doctrines they had taught, his duty to the Church and the community to be a believing, upright, Christian man. But considerations of duty, like appeals to logic and conscience, were incapable of solving the doubts which reason and scientific investigation had raised. Duty said, "Accept the traditional answers"; but his feelings said, "Find the truth for yourself." Like the young Emerson or like Melville's Ahab, Cathcart is almost ready to believe that if he is the Devil's child, he would rather live for the Devil.

The solution, of course, lies in Nature, or rather, in seeking God in Nature rather than in the Church or its doctrines, or even in the Bible. But the way to find God in Nature is not through the "natural theology" of William Paley's *Evidences*; for that is mere speculation, mere reasoning *about* God. What Cathcart needs is a direct experiential encounter with God. Yet Beecher obviously cannot endorse the standard revivalistic definition of conversion, which was based upon the old concept of dualism—a miraculous intervention of a transcendent God breaking into the laws of Nature, the supernatural impinging upon the natural world. In 1867 this seemed contrary to both reason and science, not to mention Romanticism.

Beecher's answer, as I have intimated, was a combination of transcendentalism and Bushnellian Christian nurture. Barton had been educated in a Christian home and a Christian environment. His large nature and many faculties had been refined and developed by his parents and by the religious institutions of New England Puritanism. His reason had been enlarged by education. "With his mental organization and with the domestic influences which had from childhood been acting upon him, Barton Cathcart could hardly fail to be of a religious turn." And what he now needed was to become sufficiently sympathetic to the world of Nature to let it act upon, or interact with, his soul. He needed, as Dr. Wentworth tells him, to stop trying to puzzle out the answers to his doubts by using his Understanding and to rely instead upon Coleridgean Reason, intuition, imagination, feeling. Through these divinely given faculties, and only through them, could he open his heart and soul to commune directly with God.

Beecher is never quite clear, any more than most revivalists were, about the exact operation of conversion—that is, whether the infusion of grace came at the will of God or at the behest of the seeker. As he says elsewhere in *Norwood*: "I am inclined to think that the Arminian and Calvinist, when not under controversial fire, hold the facts substantially alike." As in the case of the supposed conflict of religion and science, "The issue is not necessary, is forced, is abstract, which divides them on this point."[19] As far as Beecher was concerned, grace was neither predestined nor irresistible. All that was needed was faith, an open, yearning heart, a willingness to ask and to receive what a benevolent God was willing, nay eager, to give to those who asked. It was as though there were electrical waves of grace emanating through the world at all times, and all the unconverted needed to do was to get on the right wave length to receive it; the receiver must be a finely wrought and delicate instrument to hear God loud and clear.

Finding no help from his pastor, Barton Cathcart then turns to Dr. Wentworth, who soon puts him on the right path. After speaking to Barton, Wentworth then explains the situation to the ineffectual Buell, who is fearful that Cathcart will become another Judge Bacon instead of a pillar of the Church: "We cannot," says the parson in despair, "endure to see a nature so noble made a castaway." Wentworth reassures him:

> He desires the truth as an unweaned child yearns for its mother's breast. It ought not to be difficult for such a one to find firm faith. His is a clear instance of that doubt which has widely sprung up in the track of physical science. It arises from the introduction of a totally new *method* of investigation. It must be met on its own grounds [that is, not on the old Edwardsian grounds, where the method was "agonizing," prayer, "law work," and "waiting on God"]. If the distinguishing doctrines of grace have their types and root in nature, as I believe they have, then evidence from that source will reach the trouble. The alphabetic forms of moral truth found at large in the world will serve to teach one at length how to read those clearer manifestations of the divine nature and of moral government, which are perfectly disclosed only in the life and teachings of our Saviour.

Grace is typologically rooted in Nature, and Barton must find in Nature's "alphabetic forms of moral truth" the laws of God which he cannot find in speculative theology or materialistic science but which are disclosed (though not believed by the unconverted) in the Gospels. Barton tries the transcendental "method" of finding truth which Wentworth has suggested and, in due course, he does have several religious experiences in communion with Nature which end his doubts and reaffirm his childhood faith. He describes one of these in his diary; it occurs while he is standing in the chapel tower at Amherst looking toward the setting sun:

> The scene that burst on me was wonderful. The heavens seemed to be drenched with rose color. All the west glowed with it. . . . Gradually it changed to flame-color and then the landscape was more wonderful still. Fearful it was. It seemed to be like a universal conflagration. . . . The whole world stood in an unnatural trance and the most familiar things looked wild and almost fearful.

He is explaining the incident to Rose Wentworth (to whom he has not yet disclosed his love), and she asks: "Did it leave no effect?" Barton answers: "In truth it did. It awakened all my mother in me."

"What?" she asks.

"My mother has the sense of infiniteness, a mysteriousness more than any that I have ever known."

If Rose is hurt, she does not say so. Barton, having seen the wonder, fearfulness, and mysterious infiniteness of Nature, later has a second encounter with God which fuses mother-love and mating-love. This occurs in moonlight as he looks out of his window in June about a year after his graduation. God's presence this time is not in setting suns but "bird-enclosed":

> I had fallen into one of those balanced states of mind in which is calm, and all the evening scenes tended to soften even to tenderness. A robin flew into the trees over against my room, and began the peculiar song which indicates the absence of its mate. It is the sweetest and most passionate of all their singing. And since I have learned that it is a call of loneliness for company, of love *for* love, it seems to me very exquisite, though very sad. . . . My soul was strangely affected. I almost ceased to be conscious of my body. Stealing up from the east, the moon threw a light on the valley. . . . I seemed alone, helpless, unhappy. I involuntarily called out, '*My God*, why hast thou forsaken me?' What followed I can account for only as a phantasy. I did not *think*. It was *seeing* rather! The whole heaven seemed full of ineffable gentleness. It seemed as if I was caught up into it, and felt borne in upon me a sense of God's care for me—his love, his wisdom in guiding me. A wonderful conviction seemed to flow in on me that I should surely be brought out of my darkness and that all this trouble of soul was like the trouble which a seed feels when yet underground—dying that it may sprout and live. Then, all unbidden, there sprang up in me such a desire to praise God as I never felt before or imagined. For the first time in my life I had a conception of *infinite* love.

After that, it is all smooth sailing for Barton. The seed of faith, called forth by love, slowly sprouts and grows, and soon he is able to say: "I do know there is a realm of truth. . . . It is an [in]expressible relief to feel a *certainty* that nature has a Master." The terrifying Mid-Victorian fear that God had forsaken man and left him alone in the grip of overwhelming, purposeless, natural forces, has been conquered: "Now I will seek Wentworth again, and see what he means when he says that the Bible interprets Nature and that Nature nourishes the truths of the Bible, and that they are parts of one development and in harmony." The key word here, as we shall see, is "development."

It is important to note that Beecher includes in this exposition of transcendentalized Christianity a good deal more of Scriptural revelation than Emerson and Wordsworth did. He finds in Nature not only the moral truths of the Oversoul but also "the distinguishing doctrines of grace." Moreover, he retains, in his conception of Barton's religious experience, that principle of an infusion of grace which was part of Bushnell's theology. Bushnell, for all his belief in Christian nurture, and Beecher, for all his belief in self-cultivation, both insisted that "a new inner sense"—the "sense of the heart," as Jonathan Edwards called it —could only come to man through the influence of the Spirit of God. Bushnell, like Beecher (and like Edwards), "located the root of the current decaying piety in the growing tendency to substitute a notional, speculative knowledge of God for an immediate experience of God."[20] And Barton Cathcart, when he later describes his conversion to Wentworth, says:

> There came, finally, one experience further. When I was most imbued with the truth as I found it in Christ, most tender in my feelings, I seemed to have, on various occasions, borne in upon me a tide of influences which I could account for on no theory of ordinary causation, and which I have come to believe was divine. The spirit was promised. To me it has been fulfilled.[21]

Conversion was still a miraculous influence from God, even though it differed markedly from the emotional experiences of the revival meeting. The seed of the old Adam still had to die and be reborn even though God was immanent in Nature. Beecher had changed the locus and origins of grace but not the essential feature of regeneration—a new birth through God in Nature.

Yet, for all his efforts to conserve this central tenet of evangelicalism, Beecher had rejected far more than he retained. Not only had he repudiated the speculative aspects of Calvinistic doctrine, but the literal infallibility of the Bible as well. Barton began his conversion process when he "analyzed the doctrines of the church and disputed many of them." Then, having shed this burden, he was led to explore the Bible for himself and, "Finding the extreme reactionary Protestant doctrine that the Bible was the sole fountain of religious truth, could not be true, he began to question the grounds of inspiration; then the reality of the truths revealed." His conversion re-established the reality of the truths, but not the superior authority of the Bible. As he tells Wentworth after his conversion: "I have not got beyond difficulties. I cannot answer certain technical questions arising in my mind respecting Revelation."

He explains how he got around this problem, however: "I have been sticking at a great many of the so-called difficulties of the scriptures"—meaning those raised by the higher criticism. Then he recalled Wentworth's having compared the Bible to a flawed will (that is, the last testament of a dying man): "What if, instead of regarding *possession* as the best argument in favor of the genuineness of the will, he should indicate his philosophy and shrewdness by picking flaws with the grammar, quarrelling with the messenger, instituting a special plea on the doctrine of probabilities in the case." How foolish that would be. So instead of questioning the Bible because of its technical flaws, he decided instead to "take possession of the contents rather than criticize them," for "to refuse it was as if a man should refuse oranges because the tree was crooked or the bark diseased or the thorns too long and too sharp." Fundamentalists might want to deny that the Bible was crooked, diseased, or thorny; but Liberal Protestants who could find God in Nature were ready to abandon the Letter for the Spirit.

Barton's conversion two-thirds of the way through the novel harks back to Dr. Wentworth's earlier conversation with Parson Buell about the direct perception of God in Nature. In that talk in the garden Wentworth had said that the Bible was like a textbook of botany "which does not contain living plants but only word-descriptions of them. If I would see the plant itself, I must go out of the book to nature." Or, in other words, "The Bible cannot contain the truth itself, only the *Word-forms*, the lettered symbols" of truth.

This was to be the approach of most Liberal Protestants in the next half-century as they faced the growing battery of technical flaws which the scientists and higher critics discovered in Scripture. Long before he wrote *Norwood*, Beecher had been telling his congregation not to be afraid of these assaults. "There are many men," he said in 1859, "who will trouble you with the dust of the Bible, its foundation knocked from under it, and the superstructure all taken down, but what you need is not curious speculation, but rich and pure living—deep-hearted piety, to build you up higher and higher in a true manhood!"[22] The solution to doubt was not a revivalistic conversion experience or a stubborn insistence that every word in the King James Version of the Bible was true; it was to mold your life upon Christ's example: "While, if you are perplexed and puzzled with various questions, you may investigate freely, see to it that no troubles in respect to external circumstances move you from that which is the marrow of truth—Christ your model, and a character shaped and fashioned according to his example."[23] This was what the Unitarians found so liberal in Beecher's preaching.

Beecher also made considerable concessions to the Liberal Protestant concept of the relativity of religious truth and the virtues of comparative religion. While he did not go so far as many liberals did in finding many of the essential truths of Christianity expressed in the other major religions of the world, he was ready to concede that religious faith was as subject to "the law of development" as any other aspect of human life and society. And he would not deride those earlier men who had worshipped other gods. In fact, Dr. Wentworth finds a certain innate wisdom in animism:

> I suspect that much of what we have been taught to regard as a stupid idolatry was regarded in its time, by intelligent worshippers, only as a kind of symbolism. Trees were supposed to *contain* deities. Fire was the element through which the gods manifested themselves. If I had lived before the days of Revelation, I should have worshipped the Sun or Trees.[23]

Beecher was not ahead of the most advanced thought of his time on this, but he was abreast of it. Few evangelicals in that heyday of missionary activity could look with anything but loathing upon the idolatry of the heathen in Africa, Asia, and Polynesia. But Liberal Protestants were soon to follow Theodore Parker and the transcendentalists into the syncretic realm of comparative religion.

There is no need to labor the point that Beecher was a liberator, a reconstructionist, who provided a very helpful transition for many post-Civil War ministers and church-goers as they moved from the old Calvinism and evangelical revivalism to the new Liberal Protestantism. The essence of his liberalism lay in his belief in a "living"—rather than a "speculative"—God, who is to be reached through the affections rather than the intellect. "Your God," says Wentworth to the fading Parson Buell,

> is historic—mine is living. Your God is in a temple—mine everywhere. You have excogitated and built up element by element, attribute by attribute, a conception of God to which by resolute concentration you direct your thoughts, without help in symbol, natural object, or any instrument whatever, but wholly by will-force. Now and then there will arise out of this stretching void some dim image or sense of Divinity. But even at that your conscience, not love, clothes him.[24]

What a volume for the future of Liberal Protestantism lay in that word "love."

Buell's problem, like that of the old Calvinists in general, was that he had "little help from your affections; less from ideality; none from taste and beauty; and really, you worship an *abstract thought*—a mere projection of an idea—not a whole Mind, a *Living Being*!" Help from the affections, from idealism, from self-cultivation—this is the real death of Calvinism in America. Holmes's *One Hoss Shay* in 1850 hardly counts as a funeral oration, since it was written by a Unitarian. Finney's rejection of Calvinism in the 1830's, like that of the itinerant Methodist circuit riders, was a frontier, not a New England, burial. Bushnell's rejection in the 1850's was too high-brow to be generally understood, and those who did understand it tried to unfrock Bushnell for heresy. But when Henry Ward Beecher, the most popular preacher in America, the son of Lyman Beecher, the voice of middle-class New England evangelicalism and Brooklyn Heights respectability, pronounced Calvinism dead in 1867, the corpse was beyond resurrection. It is true that there was talk of trying Beecher for heresy in 1882, after he had gone so far as to reject Hell itself, but the Congregational ministers of the nation overwhelmingly rallied to his defense and pronounced him orthodox. Calvinism did not, of course, die "all at once and nothing first," Holmes notwithstanding. It died in different sections of America at different times. But *Norwood* was its death certificate for the rising middle class of the cities and suburbs which controlled the destiny of the nation.

CHAPTER FOUR

It's Love That Makes the World Go Round

That mystic Law with which God has bound himself to his infinite realm—the law of Love.
—*Norwood* (Chap. III, p. 10)

Calvinism, even in its alleviated New Haven form, was essentially based upon the concept of a God of wrath, a sovereign God of justice and authority. The New Haven theology is often spoken of as "the moral government" theory of God, for it argued that Christ's death was not so much an act of divine mercy toward man as an act of divine justice to God. Christ died to atone for the sin of Adam, to provide a legal remedy, a suitable expiation, which would allow God thereafter to pardon men without giving anyone the idea that sin could go unpunished in the universe. God's moral government operated upon such a strict sense of righteousness that until someone had paid the penalty for original sin, God simply had no alternative—if His system of government was to be consistent—but to damn all mankind. God therefore sent His Son to die in order to right the balance of the scales of divine justice in God's government. It was all very logical, very Puritan; but, like the doctrines of predestination, total depravity, and irresistible grace, it seemed very harsh and unreal in 1850. It did not provide a great deal of comfort to those who wanted to believe that God was good, kind, and benevolent—a loving Father rather than a stern Judge.

The greatest achievement of Henry Ward Beecher, according to a prominent religious historian writing in 1939, was that "he rehabilitated the principle of divine love and made it really the ruling principle of his theology."[1] Beecher's rejection, in the 1850's, of the sovereign God of his father was clear and emphatic:

> God's sovereignty is not in His right hand; God's sovereignty is not in His intellect; God's sovereignty is in His love. 'I will have mercy on whom I will have mercy, and whom I will, I will harden.' He stands in the plenitude of all-comforting grace.[2]

Without attempting to decide how much credit Beecher himself deserves for this change in comparison to other theologians—like Horace Bushnell or Edwards A. Park or the Christian transcendentalists—it is evident that Beecher reached a very different and a much wider audience than any of those theologians who struggled so hard to say on a high plane of system and consistency what could only strike home at a much lower, and nonrational, plane. One can argue that the Methodists were preaching this way long before Beecher, but they too reached a different audience. The important point is that between 1840 and 1870 the reconstruction of Calvinism was taking place in many different places and social levels, and Beecher reached what may well have been the most influential of these.

The theme of God's love is not much in evidence in Beecher's *Lectures to Young Men* in 1844. But it became increasingly prominent in his writings after 1850, and it permeates the novel he wrote in 1867. The most interesting feature of his concept of divine love is that it included not only God's love for sinners but also man's love for his brothers, man's love for woman, a mother's love for her children. Once again it is easy enough to find psychological reasons for Beecher's personal concern about this. His own longing to be loved, his insistence that his real mother's love was the most important factor in his life, his fear of his father, his lack of love for his wife—these were all focal elements in his preaching as in his personal life. It is difficult to avoid the temptation to reduce Beecher's theology to these psychological terms.

"The memory of my mother as one sainted," he wrote, "has exerted a singular influence on me. After I came to be about fourteen or fifteen years of age, I began to be distinctly conscious that there was a silent, secret, and if you please to call it so, romantic influence which was affecting me. It grew and it grows, so that in some parts of my nature I think I have more communion with my mother, whom I never saw except as a child three years old, than with any living being. I am conscious that all my life long there has been a moral power in my memory of her."[3] His friend Lyman Abbott described him as often remarking that "through his feelings for this almost unknown mother, he could understand the feelings of the devout Roman Catholic for the Virgin Mary":[4]

> Do you know why so often I speak what must seem to some of you rhapsody of woman? It is because I had a mother, and if I were to live a thousand years I could not express what seems to me to be the least that I owe her. . . . no devout Catholic ever saw so much in the Virgin Mary as I have seen in my mother, who has been a presence to me ever since I can remember.[5]

The poignancy of his mother's death and something of its impact upon him can be seen in his sister Harriet's recollection:

> They told us at one time that she had been laid in the ground, at another that she had gone to heaven. Whereupon Henry, putting the two things together, resolved to dig through the ground and go to find her; for being discovered under sister Catherine's window one morning digging with great zeal and earnestness, she called to him to know what he was doing, and lifting his curly head, with great simplicity he answered: 'Why, I am going to heaven to find ma.'[6]

How many Americans of that time suffered similar tragedies or had similar oedipal and nurturant problems cannot be estimated. But in that day, when sex was never discussed with children, when overworked mothers with large families died often in childbirth or from illness, when wandering sons felt guilty about the mothers they left behind them, it seems fair to assume that Beecher found many in his audience who shared his feelings. His own personal cravings, yearnings, rhapsodizing, and rationalizations undoubtedly matched those of multitudes of his contemporaries.

No one who reads popular Victorian novels or poetry can miss the central themes of love and longing. No one who reads Victorian hymnologies can fail to see the great emphasis upon a God of love. No one who studies American social history can mistake the importance of the symbols of hearth and home, mother love, and premature death. It seems obvious enough that as America was expanding, as both geographic and social mobility split families up, isolating nuclear family units from grandparents and other relatives—in short, as American family life seemed to be disintegrating—the ideal of family life naturally took on increased importance. What had hitherto been taken for granted now had to be made explicit and even overemphasized. And death, which for the Puritans was simply a fact of life, for the Victorians became a tragedy. All histories and sociological studies of the American family in the Victorian era confirm this. And so do the popular art and poetry of the period: "Where is my wandering boy tonight?," the candle in the window, the variations on the theme of the prodigal son, the doctrine that all virtue is learned at Mother's knee, and that, as every man who made good is supposed to have said, "Everything I am or ever hope to be, I owe to my mother."

"Had you a mother that was a woman of God," Beecher asked an audience in the 1850's, "and was faithful? Do you scarcely dare to look back and think of the instructions which, upon her knee, you received? I have hope for you, not because you are good—you are base and most unworthy; but, O, the power of a mother with God—it is great. And I believe that for the children that are consecrated in the lap and bosom of maternal love, there is hope until they pass away, and the whole scene closes."[7]

Beecher did not hesitate to compare the love of a mother to the love of God and to insist that they were part and parcel of God:

> There is a love brighter than the morning sun, fairer than the evening star, and more constant than either . . . the love most unselfish and therefore most divine, that makes suffering itself most sweet, and sorrow pleasure—that love which the mother bears to the child—the mother that is in parentage. It is the only one that glows with any considerable resemblance to that great central fire from which it flows, for it is a revelation of the love of God. . . .[8]

Similarly in the realm of courtship, marriage, and sexual relations during the Victorian era, the theme of romantic love predominated. The theme was not "virtue is its own reward" but "love conquers all." Love, of course, required absolute purity, absolute chastity, absolute moral virtue. But love was more than all of these. And Christian love, the love of a Christian woman for a Christian man, this was the zenith of popular romance. Good women sometimes redeemed bad men, but no good man ever redeemed a bad woman.

Beecher spoke often of "the law of love" or, more fulsomely, of "the glory of that mystic Law with which God has bound himself to his infinite realm—the law of Love." In the face of myriad dangers seeking to dissolve the bonds of the home, of society, of humanity, the Mid-Victorians yearned for some overarching ideal or principle which could hold themselves and their world together. The answer was "Love"—Love in all its many forms, which became the cardinal theme of Liberal Protestantism for two generations after 1865. Love was its answer to the atomistic view of men in the Lockean social contract, to the self-interest of utilitarian ethics, to the naturalism of the mechanistic scientist, to the rugged individualism of Manchester school economics, to the greed of business and the chicanery of politics. And it was Beecher who gave the theme one of its first full-blown expositions in *Norwood*, the book which first expressed in systematic form his conception of the nature and destiny of man.

Virtually the whole alphabet of Nature begins with "L" in *Norwood*. For many of the aspects of the theme touched upon in the novel, his treatment merely represented the culmination of the direction his thought had been taking over the preceding twenty years. Nevertheless, when his views were expressed in fictional form, presenting love as the primary motivating force behind the saga of life, the difference between *Norwood* and *Lectures to Young Men* is striking.

Beecher deals with three different aspects of love in *Norwood*. First of all, the novel is concerned with the romantic love between man and woman; second, with mother love as the foundation of the family; and third, with God's love for the human race as the nexus of nature and the supernatural (which is why the mating call of the robin is the symbol of God's love).

We first come across a lyrical celebration of love on page 10 (1868 ed.), where Beecher is describing how Barton Cathcart's parents, Abiah and Rachel, fell in love. His description of mortal love sounds so much like a theological disquisition on regeneration that it seems almost as though Beecher were writing with tongue in cheek. But there is no evidence that he meant it to be taken as a joke:

> The most solemn hour of human experience is not that of death, but of Life—when the heart is born again and from a natural heart becomes a heart of Love. . . . Then for the first time, when one so loves that love is sacrifice, death to self, resurrection and glory, is man brought into harmony with the whole universe.

And so Abiah Cathcart, avowing his love for Rachel Liscomb, and having it returned, found that "his soul was overshadowed with a cloud as if God were drawing near. He had never felt so solemn."

To make the parallel between romantic love and spiritual regeneration even closer, some of the village characters, noting the peculiarly solemn look in Abiah's eyes, observe: "I shouldn't wonder, by the way he looks, if he had got a hope" ("getting a hope" being the New England expression for undergoing a religious experience which the person involved hopes signifies that he is one of the elect). Moreover, once Abiah obtains Rachel's love, he is from that moment "a different man":

> Every faculty was quickened, but most his moral nature. . . . Taught from his childhood to reverence God, he felt suddenly opened in his soul a gate of thanksgiving and through it came a multitude of thoughts of worship and praise. The world was recreated before his eyes. Nothing before was ever beautiful if judged by his present sensibility.

Beecher was perfectly well aware that this description of the change wrought in Abiah's soul by a woman's love was precisely the kind of change which most evangelicals described when they felt they had been converted at a revival meeting. What is more, Beecher actually compared Abiah's love for Rachel with his love for God: "He worshipped God with reverence. He worshipped Rachel with love; he came to her as one comes to an altar or a shrine. He left her as one who has seen a vision of angels." Further than this it was hard to carry human love without idolatry. But for Beecher, man's love for woman was as sacred as his love for God because it was part and parcel of it.

At one point Beecher adds a quasi-scientific factor to romantic attraction, a phenomenon which later generations referred to by saying "It's in the genes," but which Beecher called "the hidden nature of faculty":

> Lovers sit in the early ecstasy saying, Tell me *why* you love me? And then, when every reason is given that fancy can suggest, does not every one know that there is something deeper than all that is told?—That there is in the hidden nature of faculty an attraction of one for another which, when the conditions are once secured, acts as do the great attractions of the globe, drawing all things together centreward.[9]

It is difficult to find before this in American evangelical writing such an explicit statement of the romantic basis of love as distinct from the older contractual or sacramental basis. The transcendentalists had spoken thus, but they were infidels. And what a revolution has taken place in New England orthodoxy since the days of Anne Hutchinson when Beecher can state flatly: "There is a wisdom of feeling as well as of thought. The intuitions of moral sentiments seldom mislead us." This was what Edwardsians had condemned as sheer "enthusiasm." Beecher deplored "enthusiasm" in strictly religious affairs, but applauded it where love was concerned.

Nonetheless, love can be dangerous if it is not in harmony with "the intuitions of moral sentiments." Some kinds of love can even be evil—notably love which is prompted by "passion" and "sultry ardors," love which is rash and sudden rather than love which unfolds gradually from friendship to "brotherhood and sisterhood" and then imperceptibly becomes that "higher love" which George Bernard Shaw later parodied so deftly in *Arms and the Man*. Beecher provides the idealized portrait of Victorian higher love in his story of Barton and Rose. For most of the novel these two, though obviously predestined for each other by the hidden nature of their reciprocal faculties, are content to think of themselves as brother and sister. This, Beecher admits, "is the mask which bashfulness wears before it gains boldness enough to say love. It is a gentle hypocrisy, under which souls consent to remain and dream in hope by-and-by of a rapturous waking. It is the halfway house between friendship and ardent affection. . . . Love is war. The friendship of a brother and sister, unrelated, is a truce in which both parties are secretly preparing for the onset and victory."[10] Even the nonpsychologist cannot help pondering how much Beecher was rationalizing his own "sultry ardors" as he read these lines from his manuscript to his incipient mistress, Mrs. Tilton.[11]

"The passions," Beecher wrote in *Norwood*, "need the

rein and curb."[12] In order to stress the importance of "repressing" or "restraining" those passions which can wreck a brother–sister relationship by causing "gentle hypocrisy" to be abandoned and "war" declared too soon, Beecher portrays two suitors, both admirable in their ways, who fail in their pursuit of Rose Wentworth because they are too precipitous (as well as having the wrong genes). Barton, because he has the highest kind of "sensibility springing from manly pride," is shy toward Rose. He realizes that "his feelings had really not grown to a ripeness for disclosure" at the time these two rivals appear on the scene. "Where love is a mere passion, or where it is largely an imaginative sentiment, it is susceptible of sudden development."[13] But this is usually disastrous, at least with high-souled people.

The rivals are Frank Esel, an artist from Boston, and Thomas Heywood, a Southern gentleman from Richmond, Virginia, both of whom fall in love with the heroine the wrong way—the former from sentiment and the latter from passion. Both disclose their "unripe" and unhealthy feelings for Rose Wentworth and are rejected (though we are not allowed to see these traumatic scenes). Both of them thereby suffer emotional shocks which almost destroy them; they have touched the ark of the Romantic Protestant covenant and are stricken by God for their temerity. Fortunately both are noble and manly enough to admit their errors, and Rose emerges unsullied. Barton Cathcart, it might be noted, however, does seem somewhat overripe when he finally marries Rose at the age of thirty-three—though the loss of a letter declaring his love is to blame for this.

In one of the great anticlimaxes of the novel, when Rose learns of Barton's love at the same time that she learns of his supposed death in the Battle of Gettysburg, she bursts out: "At last I am free. No more checking. No more self-deceiving. No more suffering and misnaming of one's deepest life. No more shame for the heart's best fruit. . . . It is noble to love with an unsullied love."[14] Obviously she will never consider marrying anyone else. She can let go of the reins upon her passions only when their object has been removed. As Shaw put it some years later: "The higher love is a very fatiguing thing." Despite the divine or spiritual implications of this new concept of romantic love, the Victorian middle class approached it with all the formality of a minuet, even when they followed the infallible promptings of moral sentiment and feeling. No wonder Beecher remarked that if the passions need the rein, "moral sentiments need the spur."[15]

Three aspects of Beecher's conception of romantic love need to be stressed. First, true love is possible only in persons of a higher nature—the hierarchy of human sentiment or sensibility is as strict in matters of love as in matters of intellect or religion. Common folk are capable only of a lower form of love; true love is for the aristocrat: "Love is seldom seen in its full and perfect form. For that it requires a greatness of nature that does not come often; and two natures, both large and various, yet unlike, though not discordant, are still rarer. In ordinary life, the affection of love is a mere melody, the music of a single affection. But in its higher form love is many melodies wrought into a harmony."[16]

Secondly, love, like everything else in the universe, operates under the laws of growth or development: "it must yet, like summer flowers, have gone through a development from the seed or root to the blossom of the fruit." Or, to put it another way: "Love is a leaven that silently works through the whole economy of mind and soul and gradually pervades every part of the nature." That is why "it cannot be sudden."[17]

Norwood was written throughout to illustrate the principle of slow, evolutionary or organic growth from a lower to a higher form. And, as we shall note, this carries within it the notion of gradations not only in terms of human love and the organization of human faculties but also in terms of social classes, cultures, nations, and races. The elitist aspects of romantic love are part of that "whole economy" which pervades the universe. Beecher's God is a snob and, as we shall see, a racist as well as an elitist.

Thirdly, Beecher is careful here, as everywhere else, not to offend his evangelical readers by making love, even in its higher forms, superior to piety. He will not unequally yoke unbelievers. When Barton is struggling to overcome his religious doubts, he must add "to all the rest" of his torments "this secret horror, that I am separated by my miserable [doubting] state from Rose. She could never love me, could she see what a soul I bear. I would not deceive her if I could. Could a man of honor, if he was diseased, be so foolish as to hide it from a woman whom he honored—knowing that he would secure her hatred when she discovered it?"[18] Love apparently does not conquer all, or rather, there can be no true love between noble and refined persons unless they are both pure in their relationship to God and Nature. Thus, in the end, love is Providential, ordained and directed by God, like everything else. Barton's mother, congratulating him on not declaring his love for Rose before it is ripe, says: "you had almost followed the inspiration of your own heart, and not the openings of Providence. . . . Oh, my son, it is a sacred thing to love. . . . When God ordains, he will bring it forth."[19] With restrictions such as these, romantic love was safe from passion in America until the 1920's.

It is thus easy to see why the love of man and woman can be more or less equated with mother-love in Victorian literature, for both are too sacred to be discussed in terms of human passion. Beecher offended some reviewers by the coquettish and almost incestuous love play he depicted between Frank Esel and his widowed mother. Yet he was innocent of any improper intention. To him a mother's love was like God's love or the higher love of man and woman, devoid of sex. It was ethereal, angelic, noncarnal. "Not every angel even is given to know the full meaning and sacredness of a mother's and a son's innermost communion, in a love utterly without passion, without color of selfishness, deep as life and stronger than death."[20] Because mother-love pervades the home, Beecher takes special care in preparing to describe Mrs. Wentworth's room to the reader—"the heart of the home, the mother's room. The old temple had no such holy of holies."[21] Yet, by some strange Freudian slip, he never does describe that room. Instead he slips into a description of Agate Bissell's room, and Mrs. Wentworth remains a shadowy spirit in her own home.

The tie between mother-love and God's love we have already noted in regard to Barton's first religious experience in the Amherst chapel tower. The awesome beauty and mystery of Nature, while it awakened "new conceptions of Divine power" also "awaked all my mother in me." So we may assume that Christian nurture from a Christian mother does in fact plant the seed of love, that anguished "yearning for the mother's breast," which will ultimately find relief only in God's love. Herein lies the Mid-Victorian sublimation of sexual and oedipal guilt. Beecher's mother, who died when he was three, had forsaken him. Barton, in his hour of agony, awakened by the robin's yearning for its mate, asks why God has forsaken him. The result is union and communion with God.

Protestantism has no place in its theology or symbolism

for the Mother of God, but Mary Baker Eddy sensed what Beecher was talking about in the very years when he was writing *Norwood*. And so she devised the "Father-Mother God" of Christian Science, and its positive-thinking approach which sublimates all suffering, to cope with the oedipal anxieties of Mid-Victorianism. To the Freudian sociologist, all of this helps to explain what is called "Momism" in America. To the Liberal Protestant, however, it became simply the gospel of love, the "love that makes the world go round."

CHAPTER FIVE

The Protestant Ethic and the Spirit of Affluence

The family is the digesting organ of the body politic. The very way to feed the community is to feed the family.

—Norwood

Probably the most famous, or infamous, address ever made by Henry Ward Beecher—certainly the one most often quoted by historians in recent years—was his attack upon trade unions and strikes. This was a sermon delivered in 1877, during the height of one of America's periodic, almost decennial, depressions euphemistically explained away in terms of "the business cycle." The sermon, entitled "Hard Times," roundly denounced the railroad workers for going on strike when their employers had arbitrarily cut wages by ten to twenty percent:

> The necessities of the great railroad companies demanded that there should be a reduction of wages. There must be a continual shrinkage until things come back to the gold standard and wages as well as greenbacks, provisions, and property must share in it. It is true that $1 a day is not

> enough to support a man and five children if a man would insist on smoking and drinking beer. Was not a dollar a day enough to buy bread? Water costs nothing. [Laughter.] Man cannot live by bread [alone], it is true, but the man who cannot live on good bread and water is not fit to live. [Laughter.][1]

This passage is usually cited to prove two points: first, that Beecher, though a Christian minister, was really an exponent of the amoral Social Darwinian theory of the survival of the fittest; and second, to indicate how easily the old Protestant ethic of thrift, hard work, and piety was transposed during the Gilded Age into the Reverend Horatio Alger's success myth and Andrew Carnegie's Gospel of Wealth. The general impression is thus conveyed of Beecher as a spokesman for the well-to-do businessmen of the era, a man not only hardhearted but ultraconservative, even reactionary, in his attitude toward the great problems of urbanization and industrialization.

Now there can be no doubt that Beecher shared the view held until the 1930's by most Americans, as well as the U.S. Supreme Court, that trade unions were dangerous conspiracies in restraint of trade which sought to deprive employers of fair returns from their property, and employees of the right to freedom of contract—in other words, the right to work for whatever they could get. If Beecher is compared to such incipient leaders of the Social Gospel movement as Jesse Jones, Washington Gladden, George Herron, and W. D. P. Bliss, who were beginning in the 1880's to sense the real dimensions of the capital–labor crisis, then of course he must be labeled a conservative. But not many Protestant ministers sided with the Christian Socialists even after 1900, and Beecher, it has to be remembered, was born in 1813, not 1850. He was not a child of the Gilded Age but of the Age of Jackson. He reached maturity and fame in the Mid-Victorian Era of 1840 to 1870. His chief work was done by 1870.

But it is of some importance to note also that Beecher was far from old-fashioned or backward-looking in his approach to the Protestant ethic or to the problems of urban industrialism—especially considering his position as pastor of a flourishing, upper-middle-class suburb of New York City. In his own way he was very much in touch with the times—at least with the problems of the times as experienced by his congregation, and others like it throughout the nation. Of course his perspective was not that of the workingmen in the factories and the mines, and he did not understand their problems in the least. He did not even try.

However, he did criticize the businessmen of his parish for exploiting their workers, for being overly concerned with profits and property, for being too little concerned about corruption, dishonesty, and the generally materialistic values of a commercial society. The following paragraphs, written in the later 1850's, might have been composed by Walter Rauschenbusch in 1910:

> I look at the life and disposition of these [business]men who cry for the lullaby of love in the family, in the shop, in all the departments of life, and I find that they abhor love except on Sunday when I preach on that doctrine of God's moral government. But if I were to go to them at their places of business, and say, 'I understand that you take advantage of the circumstances of your workmen, and employ them at one quarter of what they ought to have, so that they can scarcely subsist on what you pay them; and as you wanted me to preach about love, I thought I would come and tell you what the doctrine of love is as applied to matters of this kind'; they would say, 'Religion is religion and business is business. Go home, and

> when I want you to come to my shop and preach to me I will let you know.' In other words, they want sermon love, poetic love, theoretic love, love that makes them feel good during the insurance day—for Sunday is the insurance day of the week! And they want me to talk of love because it subdues their fears, soothes their hearts, and makes them feel pleasant.[2]

Beecher knew his congregation and he knew what made them fearful and anxious.

His concern, however, was not to preach economic reform, not to increase anxiety, but to find some way to sustain the American faith in democracy, in the free and responsible individual, in a system of moral law against which God judged every culture and age. Because he saw the world around him changing so rapidly, he shared the fears, doubts, and anxieties of his middle-class parishioners about the stability of the nation and the meaning of all natural laws. He therefore sought desperately to reinterpret the old values and myths which had formed and sustained the nation—to readjust them to the needs of the times. And with regard to the Protestant ethic, he saw three particular problems which seemed paramount.

The first was the conflict between the town and the city, or between the virtues of rural life and the necessities of urban life. The second was the conflict between the ethic of work, thrift, and asceticism and the urge to utilize newly earned wealth for leisure, improved social status, and a more refined and luxurious way of life. And the third was the conflict between the older standards of stewardship or philanthropy which his father had utilized to build the great benevolent and missionary societies and a new standard of philanthropy—preached in England by Ruskin and Arnold and in America by men like Andrew Jackson Downing and Frederick L. Olmsted—according to which the best way for men of wealth to benefit society and civilization was to beautify life. These were the questions to which Beecher addressed himself and which his Brooklyn congregation employed him to answer. And to them he devoted a large part of his time and eloquence.

Beecher was, like most Mid-Victorians, terribly ambivalent about the virtues of rural life and the benefits or failings of urban life. Most city dwellers in the 1850's, including Beecher himself, had been born and raised in the country, and they looked back with considerable nostalgia on the experiences of their youth. As country people by origin they often found the city cold, formidable, unfriendly, and confusing. At the same time, they also found it exciting, stimulating, and challenging; if its difficulties were great, so were the rewards it offered. Similarly, the country, for all its peace and quiet, was often stultifying, dull, backward-looking, and boring. The people in country towns could be as narrow, nasty, petty and conformist as they were, at other times, friendly, folksy, and open.

In 1844 Beecher recognized the lure of the cities for young men, but he sought to frighten them away from leaving home:

> There is a swarm of men, bred in the heats of adventurous times, whose thoughts scorn pence and farthings and who humble themselves to speak of dollars; hundreds and thousands are their words. They are men of great operations. . . . They mean to own the Bank, and to look down before they die upon Astor and Girard. The young farmer becomes almost ashamed to meet his schoolmate whose stores line whole streets, whose stocks are in every bank and company, and whose increasing money is already well nigh inestimable.[3]

But this mania for success was sheer madness, for such commercial crises as those of 1837 and 1844 proved how hollow such speculative ventures could be (further confirmed subsequently by the great financial panic of 1857–8).

And even when a country boy might only think of making a modest living in the city, he would find himself cheated by those "who are skilful, indefatigable, but audaciously dishonest" and who "swarm in cities" looking for honest country boys to bilk.[4] These city slickers "dazzle our poor country boys," and "meanwhile the accustomed restraint of home cast off, the youth feels that he is unknown" and suddenly begins to indulge in all kinds of vicious activities he would not think of trying in his small home town.[5]

Even in his sermons of the 1850's, after he himself had become a familiar denizen of the Great Babylon of New York, Beecher still urged the young to beware of the city: "There is a whole deluge of white-faced, white-livered, imbecile, lily-handed men in the city, seeking wealth without toiling for it—seeking honor without achieving it—seeking place without deserving it."[6] For any young man asking how he could make his fortune, Beecher's answer was: "Go to sea!—we need sailors. Go out to work!—we need farm hands. Go into the shop!—we need mechanics. Do not congregate and house in the city, where when having made a few abortive attempts to be honest and succeed, and having failed, you will take the gimlet of craft and cunning and bore your way through life . . . to utter disgrace and ruin."[7]

Beecher frankly said that to make a success in the city was too hard to be worth it:

> I dread nothing more than to hear young men saying, 'I am going to the city.' If they ask me, as they often do when I am traveling about the country, what chances there are for lawyers in the city, I say, 'Just the chance that a fly has on a spider's web; go down and be eaten up!'

> If they ask me what chances there are for a mechanic in the city, I say, 'Good! good! there Death carries on a wholesale and retail business. . . .' If a man's bones are made of flint, if his muscles are made of leather; if he can work sixteen or eighteen hours a day and not wink, and then sleep scarcely winking—if in other words, he is built for mere toughness, then he can go into the city and go through the ordeal which business men and professional men are obliged to go through who succeed. . . . There are ten men that can succeed in the country where there is one that can succeed in the city.[8]

Beecher bemoaned the unfriendliness of life in the city, where no one knew his neighbor or cared what happened to him. Who goes to a city funeral? he asked; who even knew the name of the man in the passing hearse? "His life was not a thread woven with mine; I did not see him before, I shall not miss him now. We did not greet at the church; we did not vote at the town meeting; we had not gone together upon sleigh-rides, skatings, huskings, fishings, trainings, and elections. Therefore it is that men of might die daily about us and we have no sense of it, any more than we perceive it when a neighbor extinguishes a light."[9] "Cities are hateful";[10] cities are mad "whirlpools of excitement where men strive for honor and know not what is honorable; for wealth, and do not know true riches; for pleasure and are ignorant of the first elements of pleasure."[11] The "city seems always full . . . the crowd is always there, surging along the street, coming and going with endless industries."[12]

The principal failing of the city, of course, was that it was too far from Nature. Fortunately for the kind of people Beecher was addressing in the 1850's, it was then not difficult to "wander out of the arid city till we come to those crowned monarchs of the fields [the stately elms], we need not be ashamed to stand with lifted hands and bless our God for a gift of beauty greater than any man may build."[13] He praised those city dwellers who rented a home in the country during the summers (as he did himself) "with a half purpose of retiring from crowded ways and feverish pursuits to the calm and wholesome joys of husbandry":[14]

> Commend me to the wisdom of those notable and excellent people who cool the fever of city life under the great elms that spread their patriarchal arms about solitary farm-houses; who exchange the street for mountain streams, make bargains with the brooks, and cast their cheats for trout rather than for men![15]

The great danger of city life was that it clogged the moral sympathies; getting and spending, men laid waste their powers. "Care and trouble in ordinary life and especially in cities disturb the fountain of feeling, as rubbish fallen into the fountains of ruined cities in the East chokes them, or splits and scatters their streams through all secret channels."[16] Hence it is necessary for men to return periodically to Nature to renew their communion with God. And it is also important for men who make their living sitting all day at a desk to renew their strength through physical labor: "Every year men high in professional places—artists, judges, clergymen, senators, teachers—go back in vacation to the old homestead and feel the old inspiration of Work. They swing the flail, they follow the plough, they swing the scythe, or axe, with enthusiasm, and often with secret wishes that they had never forsaken them."[17] It is not surprising that the 1850's saw the beginning of that great American institution, the two-week summer vacation at the house in the country or the cottage by the seashore (the country club and city athletic club did not appear until later as facilities offering substitutes for physical labor).

Nonetheless, stimulating as it was to spend a few weeks in the country communing with God in Nature under the patriarchal elms, Beecher also recognized the aridity of rural life years before American writers of fiction began to attack it. He knew that people in small towns were out of touch with new ideas and often opposed them; they were bound by old customs and superstitions to their own detriment; they were afraid to act (or let anyone else act) differently from the ways their parents, grandparents, and neighbors had always acted. "Common people are restrained by law, by moral teachings, by public sentiment, by interest, by fear. . . . They become so used to caution and social conformity that they cease at length to know how much each man is the echo of each other."[18] In some respects, as we shall see, Beecher considered it important for the common people to be so controlled by traditions, training, and institutions. But to a man of original tastes and finer sensibilities it was oppressive to live in such a rigid atmosphere of prejudice and conformity.

Likewise, the city, for all its evils, at least had the virtue of providing stimuli and opportunities for training the young to face the problems of life in new ways: "The very way to train our children for heaven is to surround them by such conditions of human society as will have a powerful, though indirect, influence upon their moral amelioration and upbuilding. I would rather undertake to bring up my child to virtue and morality and piety in the city, bad as it is, than on the desert of the Sahara, or on a flat rock where there was nothing but him and me on the rock. . . . A man must have something to feed on, something to think about, something to wake him up, something to inspire him."[19] These challenges were seldom available in the small rural town.

Beecher also recognized, as did many other writers in America at mid-century, that even the rural countryside was no longer safe from the invasion of modern technology. The most notable of all the machines invading the garden of American life was the railroad, and Beecher wrote a fine sketch in 1854 which epitomizes this problem as Leo Marx has described it in his illuminating book *The Machine in the Garden*. Beecher called the sketch "A Rough Picture from Life," and in it he offered his sympathy to those who lived in fine old country mansions surrounded by broad acres and suddenly found themselves required to yield a slice of their land for the laying of a railroad track into the town. The owner awakes one day to find "his own grounds are wanted. Through that exquisite dell which skirts along the northern side of his estates, where he has wandered, book in hand, a thousand times, monarch of squirrels, bluejays and partridges, his only companions and subjects—are seen peering and spying those execrable men that turn the world upside down, civil engineers and most uncivil speculators. Alas! the plague has broken out. His ground is wanted—is taken—is defiled—is daily smoked by the passage of the modern thunder-dragon, dragging its long tail of cars. . . . They have spoiled one of God's grandest pictures by slashing it with a railroad. . . ."[20]

This was a commonplace topic in American literature of the time, and has about it much of that pastoral nostalgia with which Leo Marx's book is concerned. But there are two significant points to be noted in Beecher's little sketch. In the first place, he is not very upset about the incident: "There is something very natural in the whole process; and the appeal is rather to our pity than our censure."

Beecher was never one to stand in the way of progress, even for an old mansion or an exquisite dell. Equally interesting is his sly insinuation that the rural townsfolk are also infected by the plague of speculation and technological progress. They comfort the owner of the house that "his property is increased in value at least twenty thousand." And, of course, for them it means new business and trade for the town. There was no place to go to escape the Machine Age.

Beecher was far from opposed to modern technology. He wrote a delightful essay describing his moving into his new brownstone house in Brooklyn Heights in 1855. It is entitled "Modern Conveniences and First-class Houses," and it offers an anticipation of George F. Babbitt's reactions to his new suburban house on the outskirts of Zenith some seventy years later. Beecher was enamored of every gadget which modern technology had contrived to make the labor of housekeeping easier, and he devoted himself in this essay to describing the marvels of his new central heating system with the zeal of Babbitt describing his new automobile and its cigarette lighter. He noted jokingly that the new furnace did not always work as well as it was supposed to, but there was no question of his pleasure over this modern convenience.[21]

As a supplement to this essay, Beecher wrote another entitled "Our First Experience with a Sewing Machine."[22] In the early 1850's, when sewing machines were still a novelty, women with portable machines went from house to house hiring themselves out by the hour to do sewing and mending. Beecher's wife hired such a girl, and the family was so astonished at the efficiency of the "Wheeler and Wilson" machine that they promptly bought one. The essay is a paean to such inventions, which were lightening the load of American housewives.

Yet another essay by Beecher in 1855, "Mowing Machines and Steam-Ploughs," predicted the beneficial changes which would come with the mechanization of the farm:

> Great as is the saving of labor achieved by reapers, mowers, threshers, etc. [drawn by horses] they are all as nothing in comparison with that which must come before long—THE STEAM PLOUGH! What a revolution would take place when a gang of five or six ploughs, cutting from fifteen to twenty-four inches deep, shall plow from thirteen to fifteen acres a day! A farm of twenty acres will then be equivalent to a hundred acres now. . . . It will be better for small farmers than it would be to make every man a present of four times as much land as he had before. . . . We have never fairly harnessed mechanics or made a farmer of science. The man who invents a steam-plough that will turn twelve or fifteen acres a day, two feet deep, will be an emancipator and civilizer.[23]

For all his eulogizing of work, Beecher had done enough farming as a boy to know how hard it was. The great benefit of mechanized farming was that "Then labor shall have leisure for culture. Thus working and studying shall go hand in hand. Then the farmer shall no longer be a drudge. . . . Then men will receive a collegiate education to fit them for the farm, as now they do for the pulpit and the forum, and in the intervals of labor, gratefully frequent, they may pursue their studies."[24]

We shall return to Beecher's concept of culture and civilization, but the point to be noted here is that his nostalgia for the country, his praise of rural life, his love of Nature, were heavily larded with an equal love for modern conveniences, modern technology, modern mechanics and gadgets in every sphere of life. Likewise his ethic of hard work was tempered by a desire for leisure. With his usual verbal dexterity Beecher first made the important distinction between labor and drudgery. His next step was to make the distinction between leisure and idleness. Then he had only to indicate that leisure was a means for self-cultivation, education, and ever-increasing progress in order to clinch his argument. The gradual evolution of the human race was not based upon the sweat of the brow, which never enabled a man to lift his eyes from the grindstone. Men could only progress when science gave them the knowledge, and technology the leisure, to pursue new studies which would lead to yet better means of advancing and perfecting the world and its inhabitants.

Beecher was, as usual, treading on thin ground with many in his evangelical audience. It all seemed somehow too easy, too contrary to the Protestant ethic. There was nothing here about saving the souls of sinners, nothing about men's duty to help the poor by charity and almsgiving. Beecher had to address himself more directly to the problem of stewardship if he wished to overcome the suspicions of those who thought he was advocating not only naturalism but materialism and self-indulgence. But Beecher was as inconsistent here as everywhere else. At the same time that he was praising modern technology for increasing leisure, he was praising those who kept their noses to the grindstone:

> When you look at the globe, society, men's occupations, and the like, in the large view, the world is admirable. Its very rudeness, its hardness, its sufferings, are also a part of the primitive design, and are beneficial instrumentally. Men that love leisure never can understand what God means, who loves occupation. Men who put their supreme idea of life in self-indulgence, cannot understand what God means, who makes self-exertion, in Himself, in angelic powers, in all His creatures, the test of real being.

. . . It is a man dying with his harness on that angels love to take.[25]

On the whole, however, Beecher believed that there should and could be a proper balance between work and leisure—like the two months of summer vacation which he took each year. "You can afford, when you have done your best, to take things easy and enjoy yourself. Think, if you want to think, as long as it is pleasant to think; plan, where you ought to plan; labor where you ought to labor."[26]

The question of well-deserved leisure went hand in hand with the question of well-deserved comfort, self-indulgence, and charity (i.e., giving to others instead of indulging one's self). Beecher struggled mightily with these issues in the 1850's as he grew richer along with his parishioners. In suburban Brooklyn the new wealth of America had found a place halfway between the city and the country where it could create its own environment, its own modern houses with all the modern conveniences, its own lawns and gardens with stately elms and secluded dells. The little essays which he wrote in the newspapers were not idle speculations. They were directly related to the day-to-day problems of his wealthy parishioners, who had more money, leisure, and conveniences at their beck than they had ever seen before. Beecher became perforce the philosopher of a new leisure class.

In 1855 he wrote an essay entitled "Building a House," in which he tried to come to grips with some of these problems. It was a faulty work, a false start. In it he lamented the fact that "until men are educated and good taste is far more common than it is, this method of building houses by the architect's plans and not by the owner's disposition must prevail."[27] Apparently he was reacting against the cult of Andrew Jackson Downing, the immensely popular architect for middle-class America in this decade. In the article Beecher said he preferred the kinds of houses he had known in New England, where over the years rooms and wings, porches and sheds, entries and passageways were added piecemeal: "In this way . . . one may secure that mazy diversity, that most unlooked-for intricacy in a dwelling, and the utter variation of lines in the exterior which pleases the eye. . . ." He deplored what he called "conventional" houses, made to order from architects' plans, which had nothing of the personality of the owner and his family in them. "How many persons from out of their two-story frame dwellings, have sighed across the way for the log cabin. How many persons have moved from a home into a *house*; from low ceilings, narrow halls, rooms of multifarious uses, into splendid apartments, whose chief effect was to make them homesick. But this is because pride or vanity was the new architect."

Obviously Beecher was himself somewhat homesick for the old family homestead in Litchfield as he sat in his big new brownstone mansion. Yet very soon thereafter he had a vision of the way in which a splendid new large house might be a benefit both to the owner and to his fellow men: "Every mansion that enlarges men's conceptions of convenience, of comfort, of substantialness and permanence, or of beauty, is an *institution*."[28] Here, at last, was the right track. Institutions are a benefit to the community. "It is upon this great principle that men may become the benefactors of their race by the indulgence of beauty, and embellishments, if they be employed generously and public-spiritedly." A stately mansion "stands through generations a form of beauty uplifted." Here was the answer to the whole problem of the newly affluent middle class. "The question is not what proportion of his wealth a Christian man may divert from benevolent channels for personal enjoyment through the elements of the beautiful. For, if rightly viewed and rightly used, his very elegances and luxuries will be a contribution to the public good . . . a contribution to the education of society. . . . And the question becomes only this: How much of my wealth given to the public good shall be employed *directly* for the elevation of the ignorant and how much *indirectly*?"[29] To divide all charitable giving into direct and indirect was a master stroke. It made luxury and extravagance not only respectable but pious.

Not only were beautiful mansions educational and elevating to the poor, but so of course were beautiful landscaping and beautiful gardens. But, as he pointed out a few years later in an article entitled "Be Generous of Beauty," it was axiomatic that such gardens should not be completely hidden from public view:

> In planting one's grounds it is fair, by hedge or thicket to shut out too much gazing—all unsightly objects, noise, and dust by thick trees or fences. But a system of seclusion, that yields no part of a man's grounds to the sight of passers-by, cannot be justified. It is wanton selfishness. A lawn and garden lying upon the street, but separated from it by a high, close fence or impervious wall, so that little children, the poor, laborers, common people of all kinds, cannot see the treasures within, ought to be made an offence against good manners. . . . Can anything be more charming than to see a child's face set between two pickets like a sweet picture in a frame, wistfully looking at beds of flowers, vines, and trees?[30]

Beecher gave this quaint rationalization for conspicuous consumption and conspicuous ostentation its fullest development in the form of a dialogue between "an eccentric merchant and manufacturer" named Mr. Brett, a summer visitor to Norwood, and three of the novel's principal characters—Judge Bacon, Parson Buell, and Dr. Wentworth. Brett's conscience, it seems, "was always flaying at him and teasing him for not being more benevolent" with his wealth. He is obviously like many of Beecher's congregation, a suburbanite who has just built a large mansion for himself and his family. His wife wants him to spend more money beautifying their new home. In the course of this four-sided discussion, Beecher managed to bring out almost every aspect of the moral difficulties of new wealth. The result was a subtle transformation of the Protestant ethic from one of stewardship in the interest of saving souls to one of cultural elitism in the interest of uplifting (and controlling) society.

The conversation opens as Brett reveals that his wife and he are at odds over her desire to add a greenhouse or conservatory to their new home (it is significant that Beecher poses the problem in terms of Nature). Brett thinks this is an unnecessary extravagance; his wife believes it is essential to any respectable home. Beecher does not quite pose the question in terms of respectability and status, but clearly the situation anticipates *The Rise of Silas Lapham* in this respect.

Brett states his case simply: "I do not dare spend on myself while there is so much to be done with money—so many poor, so many ignorant, so many tenements to be built and families to be regarded and factory children to be educated and besides so much to be done for the world abroad." Parson Buell applauds this philanthropic attitude; Judge Bacon, however, defends Brett's wife's desire for a little more luxury: "I wonder you do not add one to your house. I am sure you spend too much money on benevolence. You owe a little now and then to selfishness." Brett looks "woefully puzzled" at the Judge's lack of appreciation for his sense of Christian duty. Bacon persists in needling him: "Do you really think Brett that you could cheat a single heathen out of a fair chance if you were to put up a green-house, hire a gardener, and live in a little more luxury?"[31]

Brett answers like a good New England Calvinist that he is fearful of luxury and self-indulgence: "I'm sure that it is my duty to provide my family with the necessaries of life; but luxuries I am not so clear about. . . . I have my scruples whether a Christian may, in the present state of the world, indulge in luxuries." Parson Buell, hopelessly at sea on the practical aspects of modern Christianity and totally incapable of winning an argument with the shrewd Judge, turns to the doctor for help. How far, he asks, may a Christian businessman "use his wealth for his own household?" Wentworth, like Beecher a thoroughly modern curate, has little difficulty in resolving the problem in favor of Mrs. Brett. The important point is to show the irrelevance of the old approach which poses the issue in terms of benevolence versus selfishness or soul-saving versus self-indulgence and to put the matter simply in terms of direct versus indirect philanthropy:

> No mistake can be greater than for one to speak of his family as of something separate from the community in which he lives. A family bears to the community the relation which limbs and organs do to the human body. What if a man should have serious scruples whether he should bestow food upon the whole body. The family is the digesting organ of the body politic. The very way to feed the community is to feed the family. This is the point of contact for each man with the society in which he

> lives. Through the family chiefly we are to act upon society. Money contributed there is contributed to the whole.

In Lyman Beecher's day the doctrine of Christian stewardship held that all the money a man earned should, after modest provision was made for his family, be donated to Christian charity and soul-saving. Henry Ward himself had preached such views in the 1840's, when he had spoken of the "miserly" maxim that charity begins at home. Many an agent for the benevolent and missionary societies had preached on the text of the widow's mite, implying that in many respects charity began abroad. But this outlook had, ironic as it may seem, been better received when Americans lived in an economy of scarcity. Now that they were beginning to enjoy an economy of abundance, sharing with one's neighbors and those less fortunate could take new forms:

> Nothing is more remote from selfishness than generous expenditure in building up a home and enriching it with all that shall make it beautiful without and lovely within. A man who builds a noble house does it for the whole neighborhood, not for himself alone. He who surrounds his children with books, refines their thoughts by early familiarity with art, is training them for the State. In no other way could he spend so much money so usefully for the State. He that actually rears good citizens presents the State better properties, far nobler, than ample funds or costly buildings.[32]

It is a strange argument for charity which ends by supporting aristocratic elitism on one hand and statism on the other. In one sense, Beecher was simply returning to an older concept of *noblesse oblige*. In another, he was implying that since God has rewarded the pious and industrious by making them rich, it is only sensible that they should confer that wealth upon their children rather than upon the children of those who through sin and idleness have reaped the poverty they richly deserve.

But Beecher did not really look at the matter in these terms. Rather he looked at it in terms of God's universal laws of development. God certainly wanted the human race to be uplifted. He had obviously chosen the United States and the rising middle class as the prime movers in His plan for human betterment. Ergo, what helped the middle class to produce a better generation of citizens to carry on humanity's march toward the millennium must be God's will. And, since Beecher held that society was an organic unity rather than an atomistic aggregate of individuals, whatever helped one organ of the body politic must, of course, add to the health of whole.

Beecher lived before the process of urban industrialism had progressed to the point where the massive exploitation of workingmen was generally recognized, and he firmly believed that the doors of opportunity were open to all in America. After 1900 it was tantamount to willful moral blindness for the Reverend Russell Conwell to lecture around the country about "acres of diamonds" in everyone's backyard; but in Beecher's day it did not seem at all impossible for everyone to get rich. Shortly after the panic of 1857–8, Beecher wrote a newspaper column in which he described the kind of influence in the community that a successful church should have. It should be an active, preaching church whose members were ready on all occasions to demonstrate what God had done for them. And in a time of panic it should be a voice of reassurance testifying to the goodness of God: "Such preaching by the voice of the whole church would have a power with the community" which would be enormously uplifting:

> Let a hundred merchants and eminent mechanics—known and trusted men—gather in some vast hall in New York, and testify in regard to some new method of gaining wealth. Let them, one by one, declare the reality of the riches, exhibit his own winnings, declare the facility with which thousands more could acquire, and that joint testimony of a hundred honest men would strike a fever through a city in a day, and the veins and arteries of every occupation would throb with impatient desire. Such is the power given to a truth when many men, corroborating it, give it a blessed panic-power.[33]

Beecher meant this to be an analogy for witnessing to the power of Christianity in a spiritual, not a materialistic way—though the analogy was typical of his approach to spiritual questions. The point is that he was as confident of the growing affluence of America as of the approaching onset of the millenium.

It is not, in the end, Beecher's supposed endorsement of the amoral doctrine of the survival of the fittest that marks him as a conservative in his social theory, but rather his insistence that Christian success, philanthropy, patriotism, and cultural elitism are all part of one and the same divine process. To cultivate one's self, in an organic social order, is the best way to civilize the race. This becomes more apparent when one examines more closely Beecher's endorsement of art and culture. He was not only a herald of Liberal Protestantism but also of what George Santayana called "the Genteel Tradition"—a form of social control masquerading as moral uplift for the masses.

CHAPTER SIX

Art for the People, Culture for the Masses

The nature of our institutions, the habits of the community, the very economic laws of society, compel men, in going up, to draw the common people up a little way too.

—HENRY WARD BEECHER, 1854

If Henry Ward Beecher must appear as a villain in American history, there is better evidence for this in his attitude toward art than in his attitude toward capital and labor. For Beecher believed, like so many other conservatives in his generation, that art could and should be used as an agent of reform, of education, of social control and social engineering. In previous ages, he said, art had ministered only to the needs of the state, the established religion, or the aristocracy. Now, in the nineteenth century, when republicanism was triumphing everywhere, art had a mission to perform with and for the common man. In some respects Beecher regarded this mission as providing an opiate for the masses—teaching them to bear their burdens meekly and offering them spiritual pie-in-the-sky. At other times he treated art as the means by which the upper classes would elevate and refine the poor, or perhaps keep them in a proper moral frame of mind. But most of the time Beecher maintained that in a democracy art was the servant of the people and should aim to please, enlighten, ennoble, and educate them.

The Mid-Victorian Era saw a great increase of interest in art of all kinds in America. This interest was stimulated by the increasing affluence of the American middle class and its desire to emulate the upper classes, particularly those of England. Smarting under the gibes of foreign visitors, who invariably commented on the lack of culture, the rudeness and crudity of American life, the rising middle class exhibited its chauvinism by doing its best to ape the manners and tastes of those who criticized them. This raging thirst for culture was aided and abetted by new industrial processes which made it possible to make cheap engravings, to mold inexpensive casts of classical statues, and to mass-produce imitations of expensive vases, china, and silverware. The market met the demand.

Several historians have argued that fear of the rising tide of democracy led many of the upper class in England and America deliberately to utilize art as a civilizer of the masses. Considering the lower classes vulgar, rough, and barbarous, the upper classes sought to tame and soften them by educating them to the finer things in life, just as in the Dark Ages the Christian Church had tamed the barbarian hordes who conquered the Roman Empire by the grandeur, wisdom, and authority of religion. The authority of religion having dwindled in the nineteenth century, the arbiters of taste stepped forward to maintain order and civilization. Men like Ruskin and Arnold, rejecting the ritual, dogma, and miracles of the Church, asserted that spiritual values could be found in Art and Nature, while Truth was to be sought in culture and self-cultivation. In an age of religious doubt Arnold and Ruskin taught that culture could fix absolute standards and that truth could be derived "from the use of right reason, meaning intuitive judgment, by a man of wide learning and flexible intelligence."[1] However, while Americans yearning for respectability read and admired and emulated these British authorities on culture, they did not necessarily accept the elitist and antidemocratic implications of such thinkers' views. Henry Ward Beecher's warm endorsement of the quest for culture, taste, and refinement was always equivocal on this point. He vacillated indecisively for years between his faith in democracy and the common people and his belief that a natural *aristoi* existed who must lead the nation.

By far the most incisive analysis of America's great culture quest in the pre-Civil War years has been made by Neil Harris in *The Artist in American Society: The Formative Years, 1790–1860*. It will help to put Beecher's position into context if we cite here the paragraph in which Harris notes the similarity between the cult of art and the cult of religion in Mid-Victorian America. After giving some examples of "the brooding fears of barbarism" which motivated so many of the artists, architects, landscape gardeners, and art publicists of all kinds, Harris observes:

> Words like 'communion,' 'mission,' and 'divine,' set the tone of artistic discussions; for its devotees art developed many of the characteristics of a surrogate religion, fulfilling the needs and seeking the goals of many other sects. Like them, this ideology sought to inculcate a state of mind, produce a new relationship with God, intimate immortality, and generally assist governors in their administration of the earthly world. Like other Christians, these art believers beheld a corrupt but not irredeemable man, surrounded by an uncorrupted nature. Valuable as a symbol for divine perfection, nature hinted at the glories

> of immortality; properly interpreted it was a vast allegory. By performing certain ritual activities, by spreading the gospel of love and reverence for creative achievements, the Church of Art did God's work. Like other Christians, also, art lovers debated the substance and form of their rites, and the meaning of the symbols by which men could be saved. But they agreed—even with the Transcendentalists—about the artist's divine mission. 'Unquestionably he is sent of God, to lead the people forward and to unfold to them visions of beauty. . . . He comes often as the old prophet of God came in bewildered ages . . . to lead them out of bondage.'[2]

These were all views that Beecher shared—though he, of course, saw the artist as an auxiliary of Christianity and not as the priest of a separate cult.

But while men like Arnold and Ruskin in England might preach art from an elitist point of view, thinly veiling their contempt and distrust of the masses they sought to save and enlighten, Beecher, on the whole, did not. After all, the movement of democracy in America was not about to topple any nobility from its hereditary position in the social structure. The men of property who might be frightened by some of the excesses of Jacksonian mobocracy and political demagogy were themselves, very often, only a generation removed from humble origins. Moreover, "democracy" was a term of honor and respect in America, and so was "the common man."

Beecher's concept of art and its uses consequently had a decidedly democratic bent. While the artist was a man of genius to Beecher and those who truly appreciated him were particularly endowed with exquisite taste and moral sensibilities, Beecher had to maintain that all men were open, to some extent, to the appreciation of great art, just as all were open to direct encounters with God in Nature. The basis of his religious epistemology was essentially democratic: Nature spoke to all men, though in different degrees of intensity or clarity; so art, also, spoke to all men. And art, like science and Nature, being part and parcel of God, conveyed the same message.

"It is the end of art to inculcate men with the love of nature," Beecher wrote in 1855.[3] In an essay entitled "Christian Liberty in the Use of the Beautiful" written at about the same time, he added: "God hath created beauty not for a few but hath furnished it for the whole earth."[4] A few years later, in "The Office of Art," Beecher defined art as "a language" which conveys "some sentiment or truth" by means of "forms, colors, and symmetries." Great art must "touch the secret chords of feeling" in the breasts of the beholders. While "taste changes with every age . . . the original feelings of the human soul roll on from age to age, the same, unchanged and unchangeable."[5]

In former times art "was aristocratic and hierarchic. It belonged to the palace and the church. . . . It was large, noble, magnificent. . . . It served only one element [in society, the upper class; but more recently] . . . Art was called down from great ceilings and vast walls, from churches and palaces, because the citizen was building his house, and it is a higher function for Art to serve the whole citizenship than to serve their rulers. . . . Men are nearer to God than governments."[6]

Great art is, in a way, art "which belongs to the life of the masses." Hence "no man is fit to be an artist of men who does not profoundly feel how sublime common human heart-life is." An artist must "love the things which the race loves . . . because in his soul he feels that the life of the common people is the life of God."[7] The true artist is the servant of the people just as much as any parish minister. And like the minister, he brings the people closer to God. "The true artist is he who perceives in common things a meaning of beauty or sentiment which coarser natures fail to detect. The artist is not an imitator [that is, a realist] who makes common things on canvas look *just like* common things anywhere. Artist is Interpreter. He teaches men by opening through imitation the message of deeds, events, or objects, so that they rise from the sense, where before they had exclusively presented themselves, and speak to the higher feelings." It is this democratic "mission of Art" which is "much more noble and morally grand than that which it hitherto served, as mankind are more noble and grand than their accidental rulers and their harnessing institutions."[8]

Expressed in this way, Beecher's view of art is not elitist in principle. In fact, it makes the artist a commoner, a man of the people. "There was a time when Art looked for patrons and support to nobles and monarchs. . . . But now happily Art must draw its support from the favor of the common people. . . . And artists must not demand that people shall take what artists like unless artists are first willing to paint what the people like. It is all very well to rail at the want of taste and appreciation in the community. It is the artist's business to educate the community."[9]

After he had published this statement, in August 1859, Beecher received a letter of protest from an artist who said that "if the artist, like the poet, is a teacher of something, he must LEAD and not FOLLOW." At most, he "adapts the lesson to the mind and capacity of his pupils, and thus far he may consult them." But if Beecher was to claim that the artist was a prophet of God, "Who is it that shows him the vision? Is it the people? Inspiration is of Divine source, and the man who receives it is commissioned by God, though for proclaiming this message the world should let him starve."[10]

But Beecher would have none of this: "This contempt for the common people is the worst fruit of debauched pride," he replied. It is no good for the artist to say to people who won't buy his pictures, "You *ought* to like them." And the same would be "true of every preacher, if instead of applying moral truth to the ideas and manners of the age in which he lives he should . . . feed his people on the topics" which did not interest them. The hard fact about any art in a democracy was "If it will please, it must address itself, not to an imaginary taste, but to a real sentiment in the public. . . . We protest against the arrogance of those who say or think that an artist condescends when he presents by his art the subjects which belong to the life of the masses. The life of the common people is the best part of the world's life."[11]

This sounds more like a prescription for Communist art than capitalist art—though in fact the two are the same in their effort to force the artist to paint for his employer rather than for himself or for some "imaginary" ideal. It is easy to see why the most prominent poets of the Mid-Victorian Era were the schoolroom poets: Longfellow, Whittier, Lowell, Holmes. People were happy to read *Snowbound* or *Evangeline* or *Old Ironsides* because they understood the subject and they were moved by the simple language and rhythm of the poetry. Similarly in art, the Hudson River School, the painters of animal life like Bonheur and Landseer, the painters of common farm scenes and of Biblical themes—especially paintings which had a message, a story to tell, a moral to point (titles were often vitally important)—these were the paintings which the common people wanted and enjoyed. Dogs, horses, cows, children, and cottages were the staples of the middle-class engraving trade. "God has ordained a usefulness of the beautiful, as much as of knowledge, of skill, of labor and of benevolence. It was meant to be not alone a cause of enjoyment, but a positive means of education."[12]

Beecher had another way around the problem of subjecting the artist to the taste of the people. He argued that a man could be both a great artist and one who was appreciated by the masses at the same time. To prove this, he listed those great painters of the past whose works were still admired by the public: "Raffaelle, M. Angelo, Leonardo, Correggio, Titian, Paul Veronese." However, because their works were painted on a large scale and for palaces and churches, they could not be considered democratic painters and would be out of place today. Yet their paintings when seen in museums or engravings still had the power to touch common people. "While we write," he told the protesting artist who opposed art for the masses, "there hangs before us a fine engraving of Leonardo de Vinci's Madonna (*La Vierge au Bas Relief*)." This had been painted by a Roman Catholic for Roman Catholics. "And yet in Protestant America, the picture, if less reverenced, would be as much loved as at the day and in the land where it was painted. For it is still *a Mother with Children*. . . . And in like manner, a picture that touches any affection or moral sentiment, will speak in a language which men understand, without any other education than that of being born and living."[13] Given this definition, it was difficult for any artist (except perhaps an abstract painter) to say he could never paint anything which would both please the people and touch a high moral sentiment.

But there was another sense in which Beecher thought of art as part of the democratic tide of his day and not a force acting against that tide. This was the influence which mass production was having upon art reproductions. "Look at the fabrics sold for a price within the reach of the poor. The finest forms in glass, china, wedgewood, or clay, put classic models within the reach of every table. The cheapness of lithographs, mezzotints, etchings, and photographs, is bringing to every cottage-door portfolios in which the great pictures, statues, buildings and memorials of the past and triumphs of modern Art are represented. That which, twenty years ago, could be found only among the rich, today may be had by the day-laborer. This is the true leveling."[14] And before Beecher died, Edison's phonograph had created the possibility of bringing the greatest music of the world to a mass audience.

Beecher took genuine pride in these accomplishments of American democracy and business enterprise, and he honestly believed that by spreading culture more widely America was raising up its common people above those of any other country in the world. "The condition of the common people always measures the position of any nation on the scale of civilization."[15] And since more people had more *objets d'art* in their homes in America than in any other country, Beecher was convinced that God's hand was in it. Thus art and culture could be added to the law of development along with politics, science, and religion.

Even the institutions which displayed or sponsored art and culture had to be supported by the common people in America. "When it was attempted in New York to establish music for the benefit of the rich," he wrote in 1859, "the opera failed. Nor did it succeed until it came within the reach and solicited the sympathy of common people. Lectures, literary enterprises, papers, books, all are obliged to ask the common people whether they may succeed."[16] Ultimately, in the Gilded Age, when there were more millionaires around and when the desire of the very rich was to establish cultural activities for the exclusive benefit of the rich, then it proved possible to establish a very different kind of opera company, symphony orchestra, and literary society. But in the 1850's Beecher was still close to the mood of Jacksonian America as Tocqueville describes it.

Yet Beecher was not so entirely democratic as some of these statements might imply at first glance. For there always lurked within him the old Puritan notion of the elect few and the old Federalist tradition of government by the wise for the benefit of the less enlightened masses. Like his father, he was more of a Whig than a Democrat. For example, Beecher's definition of "the common man" was a very elastic one. Sometimes he seemed to mean chiefly the day-laborer, the man at the bottom of the economic pyramid. At other times he had in mind the man who owns a cottage: "It is to the intelligent and flourishing householder that we must look" for encouragement of the arts, he said in one essay.[17] For Beecher it was probably, by and large, the householders of America who constituted the common people.

Moreover, it is clear that Beecher saw the more well-to-do members of society as the principal patrons of the arts, whatever he may have said about the importance of pleasing the common man. This is especially true when he talked about art as "benevolence" or philanthropy. Beecher wanted the rich to spend their money for art galleries, beautiful mansions, public parks and statues, and monuments the way his father had wanted the rich to give money to home missions and tract societies. Henry Ward argued, in effect, that it was more benevolent to distribute lithographs and engravings of great works of art to the poor than to give them doctrinal tracts about "the five points of Calvinism."

Beecher's patronizing attitude toward the uncultured common man is evident in many statements regarding the use of art as philanthropy: "There never can be too many libraries, too many cabinets, too many galleries of art, too many literary men, too much culture. The power of mind at *the top of society* will determine the ease and rapidity of the ascent of the bottom—just as the power of the engine at the top of the inclined plane will determine the length of the train that can be drawn up and the rapidity of its ascent."[18] But will the caboose ever catch up to the powerful engine at the top? Will not the men at the top always be doling out culture as a sop to the mob at the bottom? Beecher begged the question:

> There is a Divine hand in this thing. It is not meant that men should separate themselves from their fellows as fast as they are prospered, and leave the poor, the ignorant, the rude, to herd together at the bottom. The nature of our institutions, the habits of the community, the very economic laws of society, compel men, in going up, to draw the common people up a little way too.[19]

For him the issue was one of social responsibility, stemming from an organic view of society. His fear was not that the masses would topple the upper classes but that the rich would lose touch with the poor and the nation become "two nations." Still, the tone is obviously one of *noblesse oblige* toward the common herd; it is hardly democratic or egalitarian to talk of lifting the common people up a little bit.

It is, therefore, a moot point just how much of an elitist Beecher was in regard to culture. So far as his own congregation went, he probably felt that they were the equal of himself and the backbone of American society. But there seems little doubt that he believed many people, perhaps the majority, to be so deficient in innate taste and moral sensibility that they would never rise very high in the scale of refinement. There also seems little doubt that he thought culture did have a softening and civilizing effect upon the more barbarous and cruder elements in society. That he was actually afraid that America would fall prey to barbarism seems dubious—he was too optimistic for this. It is more likely that he merely endorsed the desires of his well-to-do parishioners to be benevolent in a different way from the businessmen of the previous era (who were certainly no more democratic). Like Beecher, the Brooklyn suburbanites were no longer enamored of soul-saving by benevolent societies. But like him also, they believed that America was a land of opportunity and the path was open for any man of talent and ambition to work his way to the top.

Because his novel, *Norwood*, is set in a rural town where there were few wealthy businessmen, he does not deal there at any great length with the question of cultural patronage. But in his portrait of the artist Frank Esel he does provide his view of the role of the artist in society, as well as some insights into his aesthetic theory.

The cultural form of social uplift is described by Dr. Wentworth in prescribing for the shattered Esel after he has recuperated from his fever following Rose's rejection of him. "As his health returned, Frank Esel betook himself to his profession with even a deeper feeling than ever before. He had become a man. For he had become a disciple of Suffering, the only schoolmaster who can bring men to their true manhood."[20] Having suffered, Esel burns all of his earlier works of art, which were mere superficial copies of Nature, lacking any perception of Nature's moral quality. "He seriously questioned whether he should not enter upon the services of the church"; but when he asks

Wentworth, the doctor discourages him: "You were born to be an artist," he writes to Esel. "Why should you change?"[21]

Apparently the ministry was no longer the best way to serve God even when one felt he had a call. Esel could better serve God and man by developing his talent as an artist:

> You can seek the moral benefit of society by your art, as readily as by sermons and probably with far greater success. Have you considered how many ways your peculiar genius can be applied to the refinement and happiness of your fellow-man. . . . A sweet landscape, painted by one who saw a soul in nature, and not merely forms, hanging in a sickroom for long months, cheers the declining invalid and becomes a minister of consolation. . . . Why should there not be drawing classes among the poor as well as sewing classes, reading classes, singing classes, etc.? Men collect funds to put books gratuitously in the dwellings of the poor, why should not some Christian artist spend a portion of his time ministering beauty to households of worthy poor?

(Notice that only the "worthy poor" would appreciate this kind of spiritual assistance.)

"The ministry of beauty," therefore, is as important, or even more important, than tracts, Bible reading, and prayer meetings. "What if one were to visit the poorhouse in each town and minister—not alone to the social feelings, to the physical wants—but to the taste and sympathy of its inmates, with gifts of beauty." Many a settlement-house worker in the Gilded Age took this lesson to heart, without realizing (and perhaps without practicing) the social snobbery inherent in Beecher's approach: To help the poor, especially the foreigner, one must patiently help him to adapt himself to the high standards of the American Genteel

Tradition. *Norwood* is in many respects a textbook on that tradition.

Beecher posed as a liberator of American taste from the narrow asceticism of the Puritans. He thought novel-reading could be uplifting, and even wrote one himself. He attended the theater, he drank wine, he approved of luxury, he praised art and music. Certainly most evangelicals up to Beecher's time and after, especially in New England, were puritanical in outlook. And for having loosened the hold of these antiaesthetes upon the American mind, Beecher does have some legitimate claim to the title of liberator in this field.

However, by making art subservient to morality and social uplift, he merely replaced one yoke with another, both upon the public and upon the artist. At best, he made it respectable for affluent businessmen to become patrons of the arts. He not only reduced art to moral didacticism, to being useful, but he insisted that only moral art was true art, that only moral men, men elevated through suffering, could be true artists, that art itself was only an instrument for moralizing and had no other value whatever.

Beecher was an admirer of Ruskin (to whom Wentworth refers Frank Esel for instruction in the true meaning of art) and had high praise in *Norwood* for both Raphael and the Pre-Raphaelites.[22] He also praised the music of Handel and Beethoven, particularly the *Messiah* and the *Fifth Symphony*. He admired the plays of Shakespeare, the novels of Scott and Cooper, the poetry of Wordsworth. He had undeniably come a long way from his *Lectures to Young Men* by the time he wrote *Norwood*.

But for the transcendental conception of "art for art's sake," and the kind of "artist of the beautiful" whom Hawthorne described in his short story by that title, Beecher had only contempt. It was undoubtedly this kind of aestheticism he had in mind when he denounced in *Norwood* "that vicious school of self-contemplatists, whose victims revolve around themselves all their lives, watching the development of their own genius and by self-culture, attaining to self-consciousness." (So much for Thoreau and Whitman!) "The scales were falling from Frank's eyes . . . his art fell down into its true place and became a mere instrument; no longer was it an end."[23]

The most insidious aspect of this aesthetic theory was not so much the banal art it produced and the severe limitations it placed upon the artist, but the same social determinism which marks Beecher's approach to philanthropy and the success myth. Most persons, he stated, are born with only limited artistic capacities both as artists and in those faculties which produce refinement and taste. While the artist can adapt his art to simpler tastes, those who lack sensibility can never truly appreciate the highest art any more than they can discern the more subtle moral qualities of God in Nature. Art is thus primarily the preserve of that gifted upper class who, out of a sense of social responsibility, should share it with the poor. Perhaps art classes for the poor may discover a genius in the rubble heap of life, but the chances are slim. It was easy, once one accepted Beecher's aesthetic view of life—for all its democratic claims—to change art "for the masses" to art "for them asses."

CHAPTER SEVEN

Transcendental and Darwinian Elitism

Cultivated people are always more or less alike the world over.

—*Norwood* (Chap. XXIII, p. 286)

It would be easy to blame Beecher's social conservatism and elitism upon Herbert Spencer and to see *Norwood* as an early manifestation of Social Darwinism. One could begin by noting how close Beecher's "law of growth" in Nature is to Spencer's theory of evolution in *Social Statics*—the alteration of all forms of life from simple, homogeneous forms to ever more complex and heterogeneous forms, stretching from the simple one-celled amoeba in the primordial ooze to the intricate mind and heart of man.[1] Beecher seems almost to paraphrase Spencer at one point in *Norwood* when he describes "the long gradations of creation" in which "matter grew to finer and finer organization and subtler uses."[2]

But Beecher was neither an agnostic nor a materialist. And he concluded this statement with the assurance that in the law of development "there came a point at which it touched something higher than itself, spiritual existence, not to be known by the senses . . . but to be discerned by the soul." This was the starting point for Christian evolutionism—which, it should be pointed out, owes a lot to certain aspects of transcendentalism. Beecher might well have adopted as the epigraph to *Norwood* the poem that Emerson prefixed to *Nature* in the 1849 edition:

A subtle chain of countless rings
The next unto the farthest brings;
The eye reads omens where it goes
And speaks all languages the rose.
And striving to be man, the worm
Mounts through all the spires of form.

Not only is man the highest point in the spiral of life, but of all living things he touches divinity most directly and most frequently. Yet even within the human species Beecher found "gradations." In fact, the spire of form seems in his philosophy to incline more sharply at its peak. As we have noted, some are born with more sensitive or highly endowed natures, capable of higher refinement and cultivation, while others are born so low on the spiral as to be virtually indistinguishable from the animals. They may have souls, but in "the scale of being" they are stunted. As one of the Yankee characters says of the Negro handyman in *Norwood*: " 'Pete hain't growed away from natur' so far but what he knows what's goin' on in beasts and birds.' "[3]

One of Beecher's specific criticisms of the New England theology which developed from Jonathan Edwards was that it was too democratic; it assumed that all men—or at least all Christians—were equally capable of living up to very high and exacting standards of true virtue: "That conception of holiness which was easy to Jonathan Edwards because he was a poet and an ethical genius, was impossible to men of slender intellect, of no imagination, and of a penurious moral sense."[4] Beecher found in the world far too many persons, even too many Christians, of "slender intellect" and "penurious moral sense." But instead of berating them, he posed as their champion, the man who would free them from the impossible burdens which Edwardsian theology placed upon their limited capabilities. It was wrong for men like Parson Buell to demand Edwardsian perfection from his congregation:

> In this unconscious way, great natures [like Edwards, like Lyman Beecher?] oppress the weak. It is putting children to the stride of a giant. It is like teaching conic sections and calculus in primary schools. Men are taught to feel guilt for not possessing religious experiences which they are no more capable of than Mrs. Heamon was of Milton's poetry or Tupper of Homer's epics.

Calvinistic pietism did in fact have such a democratic strain as Beecher rejected.[5] The Separates and Baptists, the more radical New Lights of the First Great Awakening—though not Edwards himself—argued repeatedly that God often uses the weak and foolish men of this world to confound the great and wise. (So did the Quakers.) Hence their attacks upon a learned but unconverted ministry and an established church which denied the right of unlearned but Spirit-filled men to preach the Gospel. Lyman Beecher had joined the followers of Edwards in rejecting such views, in defending the established system of New England Congregationalism, and in denouncing the "hordes" of "illiterate" Baptists and Methodist "exhorters" who were supporting Jefferson and attacking "the Standing Order." Henry Ward Beecher did not want to return to an establishment in the old sense of a tax-supported, favored denomination. But it is significant that in the town of Norwood there is only one church—Congregational—and one minister, and that when someone starts to debate the question of freedom of the will, it is immediately assumed that "the pesky Methodists" have been invading the fringes of the town.[6]

In opposing the impossibly high demands that Edwards and the neo-Edwardsians placed upon Christian believers spiritually and morally, Henry Ward Beecher was by no means advocating either sectarian pietism (which in its perfectionist form made equally high, if not higher, spiritual demands) or democratic leveling. Quite the opposite—he was expressing the pre-Edwardsian Puritan view of John Cotton and Cotton Mather that there are really upper and lower orders in society and the spiritual duties of each must be allocated in proportion to their abilities. Pietistic leveling, like Jacksonian egalitarianism, was harmful, dangerous, and wrong because it ran counter to the fundamental law of development, which postulated an upward-spiraling state of society, not a flat, homogeneous, undifferentiated plane. Just as the opposite of an ascetic life was a luxurious one and the opposite of a simple log cabin was a richly embellished brownstone mansion, so the opposite of an indeterminate, diffused social barbarism (the earliest stage of human society) was a highly institutionalized, elaborately structured, and carefully regulated "social order." As Spencer had said: "Everywhere the change [is] from a confused simplicity to a distinct complexity . . . from a relatively diffused, uniform and indeterminate arrangement, to a relatively concentrated, multiform, and determinate arrangement." Hence, to Beecher, Spencer did not so much speak for a new age of scientific agnosticism and materialism as reaffirm important aspects of the outlook of the bygone age of New England Puritanism and Federalism.

It is significant, therefore, that when Dr. Wentworth in *Norwood* expresses his criticism of Edwards for setting impossibly high standards for men of slender intellect and moral capacities, he is answered by a Quaker who places the matter in a different context:

> The things which men cannot perform teach them far more than the things which they can easily do. The whole world pulls at the body and will have it animal. Therefore the heavens must draw upon the spirit. What if Jacob could not climb the ladder whose top was in heaven? It taught him a lesson. It connected the very stones under his head with the clouds above him, and taught him that there was a way unseen by mortal eyes from the lowest thing to the highest.[7]

At last it is Wentworth's turn to be abashed, the doctor has finally "found his man." He now realizes that the Edwardsians had been right, after all, to set for the poor and weak higher tasks and standards than they could handle, because it forced them to stretch themselves upward. Did Beecher recognize the irony of having a Quaker espouse Edwards to put down Beecher? Was he influenced, perhaps unconsciously, by George Bancroft's history? Or was he merely pointing out how far up the scale of respectability and good order the Quakers had come since the days of George Fox and Mary Dyer?

Beecher's social philosophy, then, may be seen as an odd, though very American, amalgam of Calvinist elitism, Federalist class-consciousness, transcendental hero worship, and Spencerian Social Darwinism. All these elements were subsumed under the rubric of Liberal Protestantism and substantiated in terms of mystic yet natural laws of growth and love, laws of development and civilization, laws of elevation and perfection for the human race in its upward march toward union with God. Any contradictions were resolved by the assumption that God is in control of it all, that He is ever present and working out His will in Nature and in history, that He is beneficent and seeks man's welfare, redemption, and reunion with Him.

To spell this out in a somewhat more orderly fashion, we may say that Beecher's social philosophy rested upon six general assumptions: *first*, that there exist certain elemental moral and natural laws (Spencer called them laws of sociology), and that all social and religious institutions must be organized in harmony with them; *second*, that the most basic of all natural laws is "the law of growth," which requires that social institutions be organized hierarchically, or at least acknowledge a hierarchical set of values and leaders; *third*, that because of certain providential aspects of human birth (heredity) and of development (environment) some persons have far greater gifts (or faculties) and advantages than others and, being better equipped and trained, they are the natural leaders of society and in a well-ordered republic will rise to the positions of authority; *fourth*, that the presence of a God dwelling in Nature and in history reconciles religion and science and means that truth is available (in varying degrees) to all men through progressive revelation; *fifth*, that the progress of the human race, guided by God through His evolutionary laws, has produced a higher and higher form of civilization as it has of human beings and that in this scale of civilization the Anglo-Saxon race (that is, England and America) has developed the most perfect economic, social, and religious systems (laissez-faire capitalism, constitutional democracy, equal opportunity, and Liberal Protestantism) and consequently these peoples are destined by God, Providence, and the laws of Nature to seize the helm and guide the ship of mankind to the millennial harbor; *sixth*, that in America the highest form of social organization up to that time had been achieved in New England (though it had fallen upon bad times and needed some refurbishing), and hence the nation would do well to adopt its institutions, beliefs, customs, and leadership—"For the brain of this nation is New England. There is not a part that does not derive its stimulus from that fountain of laws and ideas . . . that part of this nation which has been the throne of God."[8]

It was, then, because Beecher saw New England as representing in microcosm America as it should be that he set Norwood there rather than, say, in the Midwest or Brooklyn Heights. Acting here in the role of literary artist, Beecher used his novel to instruct America in the way it should go.

It is significant, therefore, that the book's opening pages are devoted to explaining that the town is divided into three classes, "an upper, middle and lower class," and that there was "a wholesome jealousy of their rights"—by which he means a kind of pecking order rather than natural or civil rights. He points out, also, how a "foreign element" (Irish Celts) has "greatly modified [read "spoiled"] society" in the seacoast towns of New England by constituting a new racial (and probably unassimilable as well as inferior) group disruptive of the old Anglo-Saxon homogeneity.[9] It turns out, however, that the lower classes in Norwood (though Anglo-Saxon) are as genetically frozen into their social rank as the Celtic foreigners on the seacoast, for while racially homogeneous with their betters, they are morally and intellectually "penurious" (or unfit) members of the race, "chiefly composed of the hangers-on—those who are ignorant and imbecile, especially those who, for want of moral health, have sunk like sediment to the bottom." Though Beecher blames intemperance and laziness for the plight of these irredeemable poor, they are in fact "sedimentary" by birth, because they are deficient in their faculties, moral and mental. Since such persons are beyond hope, Beecher devotes little time to them. His main concern is in distinguishing between the upper class and the various layers of the middle class.

The latter, it appears, is divided into an upper middle and a lower middle. The upper middle is represented by men like Abiah Cathcart, the hero's father, and a prosperous farmer; Jonah Chandler, a successful businessman; and Mr. Brett, the manufacturer and merchant—all men who by soundness of judgment, hard work, and respectable piety have made their way up in the world to positions of well-to-do propriety and respect. Beecher's alter ego, Dr. Wentworth, is pleasantly surprised to discover that many businessmen, as exemplified by Mr. Chandler, have developed into rather genteel and refined persons who love good books and the fine arts. As for the lower-middle class in Norwood, it is composed of typically eccentric but honest New England characters like Deacon Marble and his wife, Hiram Beers the hostler, Tommy Taft the cooper, Mrs. Taft the midwife, Turfmould the sexton and coffin-maker—all of whom have rough exteriors but hearts of gold. Beecher displays a certain respect for the shrewdness and honesty of the lower-middle class: "There are many fine natures hidden under coarse forms."[10] But, essentially, they too are frozen into their social rank by the innate limitations of their sensibilities. They are good and valuable members of the community, essential for its ordinary daily tasks, but they have little comprehension of the finer things in life and little to contribute to the task of uplifting the race.

One of the minor tragedies in the novel is that Tommy Taft, the lovable cooper, had as a youth been denied an education by his uncle. He had gone to sea and lost a leg before retiring to Norwood to spend his last days. As he lies dying, Rose Wentworth comes to nurse him: "She knew the rugged strength of his mind and the unusual sagacity of his perceptions. Why was he lying useless at the bottom of society? His power should have ranked him among the first."[11] But unfortunately he had not been given proper training. After his death Judge Bacon remarks: "I have always been of opinion that Taft would have been a man of great power in society if he had been subject to early training and fortunate circumstances. The rough material was in him and education might have shaped it to the proportions of an uncommon manhood."[12] As it was, Taft's life was more or less wasted, and even his salvation is in doubt. Parson Buell, while willing to entertain the bare possibility that he may have gone to Heaven as a result of his last-minute conversion, notes that "there are infinite degrees of excellence and happiness in heaven"; some enter in glory and sit close to God, others barely exist on the outer fringes. Even in Heaven, "one is a pauper and the other well-advanced in society."

Beecher probably did not carry his own view of social gradations as far as does the old Calvinist parson whom he criticizes so often in *Norwood*; but he clearly had this view of life on earth.

Beecher is fundamentally concerned in *Norwood* with describing the members of the upper class. These are the only people capable of growth or change. The others remain static throughout; they are "good folk," amusing, but not "interesting." Upper class people are distinguished on the surface chiefly by having a higher education; but what is more important, they possess an inborn "largeness of nature" and of moral sense which education has refined and enhanced. These natural aristocrats, whom he elsewhere calls "the nobility" of America, possess "the sensibility of exquisite taste"—"tastes refined by literature and good society."[13] By and large, the upper class consists of the professional people of the town—the minister, the doctor, the lawyer. It is significant that while Beecher says specifically that the minister is "the most important man in Norwood," the story makes it perfectly evident that it is in fact the doctor who is intellectually, spiritually, and culturally the leader of the community. Beecher's conservatism was not of that reactionary type which hoped for a revival of clerical domination of the nation—a point which distinguishes him from Horace Bushnell.[14] He wore his profession as loosely as his orthodoxy and was more at home with lawyers, doctors, businessmen, and editors than with his colleagues in the ministry.

The way in which Beecher adapted transcendentalism to his social philosophy can be seen in the idealized portrait of his central character, Dr. Wentworth. In the description of Wentworth and in the social views he expresses, it is possible to see just how Emerson's philosophy—which seemed so nonconformist and anti-elitist in the 1830's—eventually was adopted by the robber barons of the Gilded Age to defend their privileged position in society. For transcendentalism did have its elitist aspect, an aspect brilliantly described by George Frederickson in *The Inner Civil War*[15]—and it was this (apart from its idealistic epistemology) that Beecher chiefly took from it. This important side of transcendental thought, as Frederickson indicates, was its glorification of the specially gifted intellectual or artist. Although this side was more apparent in the works of Carlyle, Wordsworth, and Coleridge than in the American exponents of the movement, the latter did share it. Dr.

Wentworth epitomizes this aspect in his celebration of his own private life, his own self-cultivation, and the education he gives his family. Beecher demonstrates how the world beats a path to Wentworth's door, even though he is a modest, introspective man who loves privacy, because he has something they want and need—not a better mouse-trap but a better way of life, a higher sense of truth, a greater self-assurance.

Wentworth is an Emersonian individualist, a sublimely confident inner-directed man. He does not follow the mob or tradition; he does not accept the old theology or the old church or its old minister any more than he accepts the conventional wisdom of the common man or the traditional New England architecture or way of life. Such self-reliance, as Frederickson says, is the most effective possible repudiation of Jacksonian democracy and of its philosophy of the omnicompetence of the average man. Wentworth does not seek office by pandering to the mob, but has social leadership thrust upon him by the deference of the people. His disciple, Barton Cathcart, is likewise chosen as a leader during the Civil War. First, he becomes commander of his regiment and then a general in the Union Army, not because he has sought these posts, but because he has followed first and always the promptings of his own super-heart.

Beecher lavishes a great deal of attention upon every aspect of Dr. Wentworth's self-cultivation—upon his house and its furnishings, upon his library and choice engravings, upon his garden and grounds, and of course upon his philosophy of life. (Beecher was partly a utopian and partly a practical model-builder for the *nouveaux riches* seeking respectability and self-assurance as they rose in society.) For all his modesty, Wentworth clearly emerges as a radical egoist of the first rank. If Barton becomes the hero in action, Wentworth is the hero as scholar, poet, and philosopher. Beecher clearly worshipped both kinds of heroes and wanted his reader to do so as well. Hence this pastoral idyll was not a retreat into nostalgia, a longing for the good old days of Puritan New England, or a retreat from the present. It was a very practical handbook for his congregation, and others like it across the nation.

In abandoning the busy world with its strife, its materialism, its madness for reform and for self-aggrandizement, Dr. Wentworth upholds a new philosophy of elitism, a new theory of social order, a new approach to progress. It may be summarized as patrician leadership and Christian nurture within the context of a consumer-oriented, laissez-faire economy. It places a high valuation upon culture, as defined by the patricians, for culture is, like religious experience, one of the means of reaching ultimate truth. The patricians also rely heavily upon institutions (notably the home, the Church, the Sabbath, the class system) as a means of inculcating order and virtue; and finally, as we have already noted, they are concerned especially about inculcating refinement or taste as a means of social uplift and inspiration.

How closely Wentworth's transcendental elitism borders upon the elitism of social Darwinian thought can be seen in the concluding dialogue between him and the wealthy manufacturer Mr. Brett. Having explained to Brett his duty to build a greenhouse and otherwise embellish his home and grounds in order to elevate the community (indirectly) and be "useful to the State," Wentworth goes on to tell a little parable which might be described as the moral accountability of hollyhocks and elm trees applied to American businessmen. One day, Wentworth begins, I was sitting in my garden, when I heard the great elm tree "creaking and groaning" in moral anxiety like a newly awakened sinner. I asked the tree what was the matter:

> It seems the tree had fallen into a moral difficulty. 'Here I am with my huge bulk, occupying space that might serve for scores of trees; and when the sun shines, I take its whole glory on my head and nothing below can get a fair share and my roots are drinking out of the ground an enormous supply of food and moisture, and I am under condemnation [in my soul] for this great selfishness of my life.'
>
> I comforted the arborescent penitent the best way I could. 'Everything, my great heart,' said I, 'that makes you large and healthy, makes this village happy. Hundreds sit down in your shadow; this house, of which you are a dendral guardian-angel, is blessed in your prosperity; weary laborers stop and rest under you; all the village is proud of your beauty; sick people look at you out of their windows and are comforted. Besides, how many myriads of insects and how many thousands of birds are kept by you, and in turn disport themselves for our happiness. It is true that it takes a great deal to keep you, but you pay it all back a hundred-fold in use and beauty.[16]

If the family is the stomach of the body politic, the successful businessman is the great elm tree in the social garden. How many of his well-to-do evangelical parishioners, one wonders, did Beecher counsel in this fashion, reassuring them that they were the guardian angels and Mr. Great Heart's of modern America?

Parson Buell helps bring the parable down to brass tacks by asking for its "application." Wentworth explains it in terms of "the leader in material things" as "an example to the community," or what Thorstein Veblen was later to call the instinct of emulation and the duty of conspicuous consumption:

> Whatever expenditure refines the family and lifts it into a larger sphere of living is really spent upon the whole community as well. If no man lives better than the poorest man, there will be no leader in material things.

Beecher is thinking, as usual, more in terms of *noblesse oblige* than of status-seeking, though it was easy to confuse the two.

> A community needs examples to excite its ambition. A noble dwelling is, in part, the property of all who dwell near it. Fine grounds not only confer pleasure directly on all who visit or pass by, but they excite every man of any spirit to improve his own grounds.

The reference to "every man of spirit" is the key to the social message at the heart of this parable of the elm. Here is the tie between the old Protestant ethic and the Horatio Alger success myth. It is also the link between laissez-faire enterprise and survival of the fittest. What seems like a plea for beautifying the home as the center of society is really a statement of Lamarckian determinism: The environment shapes the species.

> A family of children upon whom wealth has been employed judiciously, if they are at all worthy, represent in the community a higher type of life than can be found in poverty. Fine dress may be looked upon either as a matter of display or worthy example. In the latter aspect it is a duty as well as a pleasure.

Having transformed Mr. Brett's anxieties about the evangelical sins of luxury, fashion, and vanity into the Liberal Protestant duty of setting an example for our inferiors by the pleasure of "judicious" or tasteful self-indulgence, Beecher goes on to transfer the religious functions of the plain, white, clapboard New England church to the ornate brownstone Victorian mansion. Man's chief obligation is not to worship God and serve his fellow man, but to serve the State and improve his children:

> You teach us, Dr. Buell, that everything which makes the church noble and beautiful is an honor to God. The same principle applies to the domestic household. Every element that adds to the pleasure and refinement of the family puts honor and dignity upon the family state. Whoever makes home seem to the young dearer and more happy is a public benefactor.

This "little talk about money" ends with Beecher's returning again to the environmental aspects of social and individual progress, a factor of basic importance for social control and social engineering:

> Not all dissipated young men, of course, are children brought up in a meagre economy. But it is very certain that children whose homes are not interesting to them by affection or by attractive objects are more easily tempted into places and company fraught with danger.

Which may be more crassly stated as, Not all those who grow up in the slums will become paupers, criminals, or alcoholics, but most of them will. If their fathers spent less on drink and tobacco (and gave less to their grasping Catholic priests), they would have more to spend enriching their children's environment with fine music, paintings, and gardens, and the latter would not be tempted, in later life, into pool halls, gambling dens, and brothels. Conversely, not every man will try to work harder and rise in affluence because on his way to the factory or mill he passes the elegant home of his boss, *but every man of spirit will*! And, of course, only the mean-spirited will question how the manufacturer made his profits or complain about the uneven distribution of national wealth.

Beecher had touched upon this subject of "public spirited

embellishment" of middle-class homes and gardens in an article published in 1854 entitled "Christian Liberty and the Use of the Beautiful" and another in 1859 entitled "Be Generous of Beauty."[17] In the former he specifically praised that principle or instinct of emulation which Veblen later found so baneful:

> Society grows, as trees do, by rings. There are innumerable circles formed with mutual attractions. The lowest section feels and emulates that which is next above; *that* circle is aspiring to the level next above *it*; this one, in its turn, is attracted by one yet higher; and that by another . . . there are certain organic conditions of life founded upon gradations of mind-power or development.
>
> The ditcher aspires to the position of a husbandman; the apprentice emulates the prosperous master-mechanic; the mechanic looks up to those whose wealth is allied to education; the plainly-bred citizen aspires to the mental activity of professional men and scholars. . . . When a man has no longer any conception of excellence above his own, his voyage is done, he is dead. . . .[18]

The step from Emerson's "Circles" or spirals to Spencer's "change from a confused simplicity to a distinct complexity" was not difficult for a man of Beecher's eloquent rhetoric and verbal dexterity. Nor is it difficult to see how the honest ambition of the Protestant ethic shifts to the aspirations of status-seeking.

Nonetheless, it is a mistake to charge Beecher with simply being an apologist for capitalist exploitation. Beecher lived in a simpler era than that of the muckrakers and Socialists, simpler even than that of the Social Gospelers and certainly than that of William Graham Sumner and Thorstein Veblen. He seemed unaware of the distances which were separating the suburban rich from the urban slum dweller. Or rather, he recognized an intellectual distance but not a social one. He utilized the democratic faith in equal opportunity and individual initiative to cover up these problems. He made no mention of the factory workers in company towns and mill towns who never even came close to the suburbs where the rich lived. He ignored the slum dwellers who lived "on the wrong side of the tracks" and whom policemen drove back "downtown" if they came loitering around "uptown" homes, where it was assumed they could only be up to no good.

Somehow Beecher felt in these Mid-Victorian years, before the strife of industrial warfare began, that the poor would be uplifted, or uplift themselves with sufficient ease and rapidity to keep them from any thought of class antagonism. There might be innate intellectual and moral gradations in society, but he saw no fixed class barriers. His most famous statement on the subject of poverty was made in 1875: "There may be reasons of poverty which do not involve wrong; but looking comprehensively through city and town and village and country, the general truth will stand, that no man in this land suffers from poverty unless it be more than his fault—unless it be his sin."[19] In this respect there was no alteration in his application of the Protestant ethic.

Beecher generally associated the urban slum, where the sediment of the social system sifted down, with the "foreign element" in the coastal cities, people who had not been brought up in the wholesome environment of a country town and who had therefore imbibed none of the Protestant ethic and rural virtues of American life. Such persons undoubtedly grew up in urban sinkholes of Europe and were probably sedimentary material before they came to America. This was the outlook which immigration restrictionists were later to propagate so effectively with the aid of eugenicists and pseudo-scientific sociologists.

His second approach to the problem of poverty was that adopted later by Andrew Carnegie, whose famous "Gospel of Wealth" (first published in 1873) was pretty well foreshadowed in *Norwood*. Carnegie believed in helping those who helped themselves and thought charity lavished indiscriminately upon the poor was wasted money and effort. As an agnostic and admirer of Herbert Spencer, Carnegie could hardly be expected to sympathize with the work of fundamentalists, like the legions of the Salvation Army, who expected the Lord to work miracles by converting the worst bum, drunk, and thief into a hard-working Christian in the twinkling of an eye. But he sympathized with Beecher's "liberalism" in suggesting that libraries, art museums, and public parks be open to the public on Sundays for the uplift of the poor (or at least of those who had the spirit to take advantage of them). He would certainly have agreed that Mr. Brett was far better able to dispense his money himself than the do-gooders who ran the benevolent and philanthropic societies.

Society did, however, need more than the individual philanthropy of the rich, intellectual, cultured, and business elite. Beecher recognized that. A democracy based upon Lockean natural rights and Jacksonian egalitarianism was in grave danger of lacking the institutional means of training and educating its citizens and so best utilizing their energies and talents. "The way to make a man safe," he said, "is to educate him."[20]

CHAPTER EIGHT

Social Engineering in a Democracy

New England character and history are the result of a wide-spread system of influences of which the Sabbath was the type.

—*Norwood* (Chap. XVIII, p. 137)

Henry Ward Beecher would have been morally outraged had he thought anyone would ever accuse him of being an elitist, a believer in the survival of the fittest, a defender of the exploiters of the poor. Not only did he frequently proclaim his belief in democracy and consider himself a democrat—"I am not to be understood as speaking of democracy in any party sense. . . ."[1]—but he insisted that "the tendency of the Gospel of Christ is to be on the side of the masses of men. . . . It may be said that the history of the preaching of the Gospel has been a history of the development of Christian democratic ideas."[2]

The connection between Christianity and democracy was obvious, he wrote in 1862: "The root idea is this: that man is the most sacred trust of God to the world; that his value is derived from his moral relations, from his divinity. Looked at in his relations to God and the eternal world, every man is so valuable that you cannot make distinctions between one and another."[3] Democracy, particularly the form of democracy which said that government rests upon the consent of the governed, was the only system which had recognized this truth: "All governments are derived from him [the common man] and for him, not over him and upon him. All institutions are not his masters but his servants. . . . This is the American idea—for we stand in contrast with the world in holding and teaching it that men, having been once thoroughly educated, are to be absolutely trusted."[4]

But the crucial phrase in this statement was "thoroughly educated"; for Beecher did not trust men just because they had a spark of the divine in them. That spark had to be carefully nurtured, developed, and sometimes—when it flared up too high, as in the case of that noble but fanatical prophet, John Brown—dampened. So after his paean to democracy Beecher noted, almost as an afterthought, that "The education of the common people follows then as a necessity. They are to be fitted to govern. Since all things are from them and for them, they must be educated to their function, to their destiny." It is in the process of describing how they are to be "fitted" and educated to their "function" that Beecher's elitism becomes most apparent. For someone must educate the masses; someone must teach them how to govern. He said, almost as anxiously as Alexis de Tocqueville, in this same sermon, entitled "The Success of American Democracy," that "In America there is not one single element of civilization that is not made to depend in the end upon public opinion."[5] Obviously, then, where so much depended upon the people, it would be the greatest foolishness to leave the people uneducated, unfit to govern, uncontrolled at least by a carefully nurtured self-discipline.

Consider, for example, the rude, rough, and undisciplined frontier people of the West; it was essential to smooth "the rude edges of violent men who form the pioneer advance of a great people."[6] And then there were the benighted poor in the cities: Who can be "ignorant of the vices and the moral loathsomeness of the masses of men" and who does not "see the mischiefs that belong to uninstructed poverty"?[7] And there were those worthy poor who needed only the opportunity to improve themselves; those in the higher ranks of society must remember that "They too are our brethren who are undeveloped, unpolished, who perform the menial offices of life; who live narrowly upon slender means."[8]

Sometimes Beecher seemed to be worried about the enormity of this task: "It is not easy to lift up society from the very foundation. That is the work of centuries."[9] Sometimes he seemed to be trying to reassure himself and his congregation in the face of criticisms by European travelers who were shocked at the apparent anarchy and tumult of American politics: "A foreigner would think, pending a presidential election, that the end of the world had come. The people roar and dash like an ocean. 'No government,' he would say, 'was ever strong enough to hold such wild and tumultuous enthusiasm and zeal and rage.' "[10] But Beecher insisted that he himself had full faith in "true Christian democracy" and in the "power of self-government among an intelligent and religious common people."[11] Just "educate men to take care of themselves individually and in masses, and then let the winds blow." Most Americans have "come to ridicule the idea of danger from excitements."[12]

Yet Beecher seemed at times to be trying to placate the

mob by praising them: "We have an order of nobility in this country. We call it *the common people.* We believe it to be the most sublime order of nobility that the world has ever seen."[13] But while he doggedly upheld the ideal of republicanism, he sometimes worried about its immediate success. Perhaps mankind was not yet sufficiently civilized to sustain it:

> The republican form of government is the noblest and the best, as it is the latest. It is the latest because it demands the highest conditions for its existence. Self-government by the whole people is the teleologic idea. It is to be the final government of the world. As to whether the world is ripe enough to develop such a government, which shall be able to maintain itself through any considerable number of generations, it is useless to speculate. . . . It is not a settled fact at all that because we have come into a republican government this nation is going to live and be perfected in it.[14]

This was as close to pessimism as Beecher ever got; but it was written during the course of the Civil War, in November 1862, when matters were not going very well for the Union. However, the difficulty was a moral one, not a political one: "If men are ignorant or morally low, even under republics, they will cease to be self-governing. They will be led by cunning men, who will gain power over them by courting their passions and lead them not according to the decisions and judgments of the masses but according to the schemes and plans of those who acquire a surreptitious influence over them."[15] The problem, then, was how to educate the masses so that in their decisions and judgments they could not be misled by flattering demagogues catering to their passions.

Education had many facets. We have noted the educational uses of philanthropy and culture to be undertaken by the wealthy, and the educational function of art to be undertaken by the artist. Every man should use his talents to help his brothers. Beecher propounded to his congregation a stewardship of talent as well as of money, and tried to urge upon them a sense of community as part of their Christian duty.[16] Sometimes he even tried to frighten them into helping the poor from whom they were being separated by wealth and suburban living. In 1859 he wrote:

> This variety of climate and diversity of interests is one great cause of danger;—as ships built too long and not strong enough, are in danger of breaking in the middle, so we, with conflicting interest upon one side and upon the other, our citizens so separated by distance as to lack personal sympathy and frequent intercourse, are in like danger of parting somewhere.[17]

The most important way to train the populace to govern themselves and the country was by means of institutions:

> The family—the school—the church—regulated and virtuous civil society—wholesome and normal occupation, which increases physical comforts—all these make the number of children reared to high moral character greater, and the training of such children easier. Therefore, the very way to train our children for heaven [and democracy] is to surround them by such conditions of human society as will have a powerful, though indirect influence upon their moral amelioration and upbuilding.[18]

Schools inculcated the moral virtues and social loyalties embedded in McGuffey's Readers; they disciplined the mind by requiring rote memorization and recitation; most important of all, they taught men how to understand and to obey the natural laws by which God governed the world:

> The difference between a stupid and ignorant man and a wise and intelligent man is simply the difference of the

> control that they bring to bear upon natural laws and the use to which they put them. And the difference between civilization and barbarism is the difference between knowing how to use natural laws and not knowing how to use them.[19]

The greatest virtue of the American school system (an inheritance, he always noted, from the Puritans) was its public nature, its availability to all, its support by the taxes and interest of all. It is significant that when he was asked to deliver an address at the laying of the cornerstone for the Brooklyn Armory in 1858, he chose to list the school as one of the armories of democracy: "They teach all alike, the children of all religious faiths, nationalities, ranks and conditions; they teach them all the common ideas and duties of American citizens. These are our truest armories and the cities which have these are inexpugnable [sic]."[20] American schools were based upon the notion that ideas are weapons and that the best defense against the "diversity of interest" and races which might break the Ship of State into pieces was to Americanize or assimilate all the nationalities and all the faiths that were pouring into the country.

Only a few years earlier, New York City had been torn by a bitter fight over its public school system when Bishop John Hughes declared that the school system was forcing a Protestant education upon Roman Catholic children. Hughes went so far in his effort to obtain public funds to support parochial schools that he tried to form a third political party in the state, a Roman Catholic party in politics. This was precisely the kind of threat to social unity that Beecher feared most. This was why he and so many other Mid-Victorians who saw the public schools as the armory of American democracy passed laws in these years prohibiting the granting of public funds to private and religious schools and even tried to amend the Constitution to this effect.

In the same Brooklyn Armory speech Beecher explained how the family, as an institution of social control, was also a bastion of democracy: "Wherever you shall find a father and mother, and a houseful of children, there is the best commander, the best drill-sergeant, the best soldiers. The free and well-conducted families—these are our armories." He even spoke of the laboring class as industrial armies: "Wherever you shall find an intelligent laboring population . . . and at every point where you can congregate a band of these laborers, men who sing while they work, and come from town wiping the sundown sweat from their brows, to be cheered with the comforts of home and wife and children—these are our armories." He concluded this Fourth of July oration with a few words on the churches, "whence, as from a fount, we draw our truest notions of personal manhood, of personal liberty, of municipal privileges and municipal rights. These are some of the institutions which supervise our domestic armories and make them efficient."

This address was entitled "Patriotism and Liberty," and had it been preached during the Civil War instead of in 1858, it would be easy to say that Beecher had been influenced in writing it by the heated patriotism and the necessities of centralization and efficiency in fighting a war. But the fact is that his social philosophy was inclined in this direction long before the war came. It was the heritage of his Puritan, Federalist, New England, Whig past. It was his inborn fear that man was innately loathsome, wicked, depraved—whatever the new theology of Liberal Protestantism might say about the doctrine of love—which made him long for that strict institutional indoctrination that would mold society's members into an obedient, hard-working, moral, efficient, patriotic people. Only by inculcating self-discipline, respect for others, respect for property, respect for God, and loyalty to the nation could America possibly hold together such a vast number and variety of people spread over such a wide territory and governed by so weak a federal government and so few regulatory laws.

Being a New Englander, Beecher was convinced that the most important institutions were religious institutions—"the Sabbath-day, the Bible, prayer, religious reading, religious conversation and religious institutions are indispensable to the present condition of the race and the world. . . . They are the means of educating men in religion. They are instruments merely for the production of a certain result. . . ."[21] "These are the machinery . . . the schoolmasters" of social order.[22] In another sermon, in 1859, entitled "Congregational Liturgy" he argued that "any well-instructed and rightly-trained church" should be devoted to social action. And "the legitimate end of the ordained ministry" was to develop "a social religious ministering power to the congregation."[23] The minister's duty was "to drill a body of Christian men so that they shall individually and collectively be a witnessing and ministering body" to the community. The minister should "strengthen, comfort, inspire and warn his people; but all these things should be but part of a system of drill, by which the whole church shall become in like manner a teaching body."

It may be unfair to stress this military language—Beecher was merely arguing for a more committed sense of Christian responsibility in the Church. But, taken together with his general insistence upon the importance of order, discipline, "regulated Christian liberty," it is certainly in keeping with his concept of institutional training to compare it to military life. It does not come as a complete surprise to learn that Beecher once said: "If I were not a preacher, I would choose to be a general."[24] As it was, he spoke of the ministry as a quasi-military profession, drilling order and discipline into an unruly and motley band of recruits for God's army—"Onward, Christian soldiers, marching as to war."

An even more unpleasant aspect of Beecher's preoccupation with social engineering is revealed in a statement of the view that most men are quite limited in their innate or hereditary capabilities: "If a man was not born eloquent, he cannot be bred to eloquence; if a man was not born to a sense of color, he cannot be educated to a sense of color . . . if a man was not born to a quick creative genius, he cannot be trained to it."[25] While this may have been phrenology, it was hardly good Jacksonian democracy—and certainly far removed from the behaviorist psychology of John B. Watson in the twentieth century. Nonetheless, this view was very much in line with the uses to which behaviorism was put by Frederick W. Taylor, the great efficiency expert for American industry in the early twentieth century. Beecher inclined to the view that some people were square pegs, some round, and some triangular, and that the job of education was to fit every individual into his proper slot in society. Whatever gifts a man has, "Education makes them better and more usable." Beecher's analogy was horticultural, not mechanical. He compared education to the process of cultivating a better breed of potato:

> We know that the gifts which men have do not come from the schools. If a man is a plain, literal, factual man, you can make a great deal more of him in his own line by education than without education, just as you can make a great deal more of a potato if you cultivate it than if you

> do not cultivate it; but no cultivation in this world will ever make an apple out of a potato.[26]

This line of thought, if not the image, is very similar to that of the elite scientists in control of Aldous Huxley's *Brave New World*. They carried Taylor's scientific management of society to its ultimate by breeding special classes of test-tube babies and training them from birth to perform only one social task—and to love it. Beecher left the breeding of talent up to God and only the training of it to man. Beecher's horticultural eugenics and Huxley's behaviorist human society are both based upon the assumption that some men must rule and some must obey, some make good garbage collectors and some good magistrates. But it is a very static system, for all Beecher's claims about social mobility and all his faith in the success myth. The best any man can do is to rise to his predetermined niche in the social organism—some are the hands and some are the feet and some the brains of the body politic. The good society simply helps each peg to find its proper slot, each biological cell to fulfill its function.

There is an amusing side to this. Louisa May Alcott, in describing her father's utopian transcendental community called Fruitlands, noted that the farmers planted only the "aspiring" vegetables like peas and string beans but not the downward-growing ones, like carrots and beets. Beecher had something of the same attitude when he described how God's spirit infuses itself into those more nobly endowed men who aspire to higher things:

> Turnips and other crops that have long roots, and depend mostly for their nourishment on the soil, exhaust the soil; while these crops that have broad leaves and take the greater portion of their nourishment from the air, organizing it, and turning it into the soil, enrich the soil . . .

> that which makes this life rich is that broadleaved experience which derives its support from the air of the future world.[27]

It is funny, that is, until one recalls the story of the great elm tree in Dr. Wentworth's garden, or until one ponders this leafy metaphor of society which Beecher struck off in 1854:

> Yet we know that it is in society as it is in vegetation. It is not the sun upon the *root* that begins growth in a tree, but the sun upon its *top*. The outermost wood awakes and draws upon that below it, and sends progressing activity down to its root. Then begins a double circulation. The root sends up its crude sap, the leaf prepares it with all vegetative treasures, and back it goes on a mission of distribution to every part, to the outmost root. And thus, with striking analogy, is it in society. The great mass are producing gross material that rises up to refinement and power, that, in turn, send back the influence of refinement and power upon all the successive degrees, to the bottom.[28]

Or, to put the analogy more baldly, God sends his gracious rays of enlightenment to the men of noble nature, the leaves at the top of the social ladder of aspiration toward Him, and it is indirectly, through these noblemen at the top (and not through any direct enlightenment by God of the roots at the base of society) that the common people are lifted up a bit—some of them may even become leaves. The "gross material" among the laboring class, the worthy poor, can be refined and lifted up by the "treasures" (the noble mansions, the gardens, the art and culture) of those at the top. And thus society grows ever upward in a mutual give-and-take, organic relationship. Sometimes it seems as though Beecher's real gift as a poet of the pulpit was his ability to transpose into botanical analogies what Herbert

Spencer and the Social Darwinians expressed in the more complex, abstract metaphors of biology and physics. Biological analogies led to eugenical metaphors and were, in terms of the Victorian attitude toward sex and breeding, a bit too crude. Botanical analogies in terms of aspiring, leafy vegetables and patriarchal elm trees seemed somehow more palatable, wholesome, "natural."

We return, in the end, to the view that the world has a few talented leaders and a great many ordinary minds who do the heavy labor: "A high order of intellect is required for the discovery and defence of truth; . . . Those who enlarge the bounds of knowledge must push out with bold adventure beyond the common walks of men. But only few pioneers are needed for the largest armies, and a few profound men in each occupation may herald the advance of all the business of society. The vast bulk of men are required to discharge the homely duties of life; and they have less need of genius than of intellectual industry and patient enterprise."[29]

Beecher was never quite candid enough to say so directly, but obviously his view of the different levels of human endowment and innate ability led him to favor a different system of education for the elite than for the common people. To some extent this problem could be got around by asserting, as Jefferson did, that the gifted members of society would be admitted to seminaries, academies, colleges, and professional schools while the common people would have sufficient education when they had completed eighth grade. By the conclusion of grammar school the average man had acquired a basic knowledge of reading, writing, and arithmetic, and that was all the intellectual furnishing he needed or was capable of. The native geniuses "raked from the rubbish heap" (to use Jefferson's aristocratic phrase) by the public school system would then go on to preparatory school and college. As Beecher put it: "The nearest approach to a line drawn between the common people and an aristocratic class in New England is that which education furnishes. And there is almost a superstitious reverence for a 'college education.' "[30]

Hence in *Norwood* all of the significant upper-class characters are college graduates, and one of the crucial events in the story is the decision of Barton Cathcart, a farmer's son, to attend Amherst—contrary to the expectation that he would follow in his father's footsteps and take over the family homestead as his father grew older. But because he is obviously a person of superior mental and moral endowments, he is persuaded by his friend, Dr. Wentworth, to go to college. It is a great break with his past, and his mother worries terribly over it. As she sits with him before the hearth, pondering the fearful decision, she says to him: "on the one side is the home and purity and security; on the other, the great wide world, full of all manner of life and danger."[31] But in the end she concludes that it is God's will, and "When God stirs in us deep thoughts for things that are right, they are prophecies and we must heed them."

Barton, of course, succeeds magnificently at Amherst; he is valedictorian of his class and goes on to rise in importance, becoming principal of the academy in Norwood, then training for the law; and finally, when the crisis of Civil War comes, God's prophecy is fulfilled: As a general, he helps to save the nation. That, it seems, had been his mission all along.

But because Beecher was a liberator—that is, because he had found so much of the old Calvinism and moral philosophy of his day so dry, dull, and lifeless—he also had to raise serious questions about the system of education founded on their assumptions. If Lockean moral and mental science was inadequate for religious purposes, it was also inadequate for educational purposes. Beecher's whole family was concerned with educational reform in that era, particularly his sister Catharine and his brother Edward, and consequently he may have purposely steered clear of making any direct pronouncement in this area. But his works are riddled with observations about education, and it would not be difficult to assemble all his remarks if one wanted to describe his educational philosophy. Fortunately we have in *Norwood* a fairly clear, though indirect, presentation of what it entailed.

One of the most direct statements about the failings of the teaching profession itself is made by Dr. Wentworth's uncle, a salty New England bachelor of means who answers this way to young Wentworth's question about whether he should use his talents to become a schoolmaster:

> No sir; a man should never be a schoolmaster. That's a woman's business. Be a professor or nothin'. Even then it's a poor business. Who ever heard of a college professor that was not poor? They dry up in a pocket like springs after the wood is cut off from the hills. They are apt to get very dry in other ways too. A man that teaches cannot afford to know too much. A teacher is like a needle. He should be small and sharp. If large, he cannot run easily through the garments to be made. The College President ought to be a great man—a sort of specimen—something for the boys to remember as a pattern of men.[32]

But college presidents were chosen men, and they were seldom chosen from the ranks of professors. They were the intellectual generals of Mid-Victorian America.

Early in the novel Beecher describes Wentworth's undergraduate career at Harvard. Wentworth, a man of great gifts, "a juicy man," not a dry one, finds the rigid classical curriculum too narrow for his wide-ranging mind: "A respectable student in the regular course, he had the reputation of being very busy with studies outside of the course. He early manifested a strong taste for Natural Science but was never satisfied with the part which the books contained."[33] Harvard, which was Unitarian and more liberal in its education than most colleges of its day, nevertheless had little to offer a man of versatility and scope interested in science (as Henry Adams and John Fiske both discovered in the 1850's), and Beecher's criticism of the dry college curriculum was widely echoed in his day. Even when young Wentworth decides to pursue a career in medicine, he finds that he has to go to Vienna and Paris to truly learn his profession.

Beecher makes another interesting statement about education for the elite in discussing Barton Cathcart's career at Amherst. This is the advice Wentworth gives the young man as he departs: ". . . much of knowledge is growth not accumulation. . . . Don't fall into the vulgar idea that the mind is a warehouse and education a process of stuffing it full of goods. . . . If you must have a figure, call it [the mind] a sensitive plate on which nature forms pictures [as on a daguerreotype]. The more fine the surface and sensitive the quality, the truer and better will be the knowledge."[34] Beecher more than once compared the human mind and nervous system to a mechanism of some kind: sometimes to a photographic plate, sometimes to a barometer or thermometer—and once to a Chickering piano. In each case, the finer the mind, the more sensitive it is at recording the emanations from God in Nature. The common mind, by analogy, was but a crude instrument, a weather vane, a one-stringed banjo, a Jew's harp capable of only a very limited range of melody and no harmony.

Beecher also stressed the importance of physical and emotional health for education: "Quantity and quality of nerve mark the distinction between animals and between men from the bottom of creation to the top." Wentworth tells Barton that it is more important to keep mentally healthy and alert than to memorize dry classifications, Latin grammar, and Greek syntax all night. True education comes from being alive to Nature, not to books.

All of this is spelled out more precisely in the description of Dr. Wentworth's training of his own daughter, Rose, "the child of nature," who is to become Barton's savior when he unfortunately gets carried away by his scientific investigation of Nature. Beecher was always an admirer of women and long a champion of women's rights, perhaps out of respect for his sisters' great abilities. In Rose Wentworth we have the ideal Victorian personality in its transcendental, romantic, Liberal Protestant form. Rose is a person born with the fullest range of human faculties, a Chickering grand piano, with a large and noble spirit capable of infinite refinement and cultivation, someone who can fully respond to all the delicate harmonies of Nature. For such a high nature a suitably refined and noble educational program was necessary. "In estimating the causes of character, men ascribe much to circumstance, much to training and much to the fullness and force of one's original endowments."[35] In describing Rose's education, Beecher provides us with his theory of Christian nurture, a theory perfectly in harmony with his concepts of heredity and environment.

Though he never mentions them, Beecher sympathized with many of the educational concepts of Froebel, Pestalozzi, and Bronson Alcott. But he was not willing to flout respectable public opinion by attacking the prevailing system openly. Rose thus receives in this novel a double education: the conventional one provided by her mother, Agate Bissell, Parson Buell, and the public school system, and the modern one at the hands of her father and a Negro servant who is (in his way) close to Nature. She must memorize the shorter and longer Westminster Catechism; she must read and memorize Biblical texts, she must pray regularly, attend church and school; she must practice charity (becoming her rank) among the town's poor. But she masters this conventional training very easily, and these lessons are portrayed as of little importance compared to the esoteric moral and spiritual training offered by her father. Rose finds the deepest knowledge and truth, as Dr. Wentworth does, through her sensitivity to the moral language of Nature.

Beecher even allows himself to poke fun at catechetical instruction, as he does at Parson Buell's New Haven theology. To the shocked indignation of Mrs. Wentworth (virtually the only scene in which she appears in the novel), the doctor follows Rose's catechism lesson with a parody of it in terms of Nature: "Rose, what do the apple trees principally teach?" her father asks wrily. Rose, of course, knows the game and answers that apple trees "make me think how beautiful God is."[36]

What Beecher was driving home here was the Romantic and Liberal Protestant belief that children (at least refined children) are not born inherently wicked and depraved but are in fact closer to God and Nature than adults. Not in entire forgetfulness, and not in utter nakedness, but trailing clouds of glory do they come from God, who is their home. Since "heaven lies about us in our infancy," it is possible to see God in and through children as clearly as we can through Nature. "God speaks to the young," said Beecher; "Children are unconscious philosophers"—"always trust the children."[37]

Beecher had publicly denounced the doctrine of total depravity eight years before he wrote *Norwood*. He implicitly reiterated this in the novel by making Parson Buell look ridiculous for believing that "until Rose was converted there were no right affections in her . . . natural excellences, amiable dispositions, in unregenerate people, have no moral excellence and do not diminish that perpetual danger which overhangs every child of Adam until he becomes a Christian."[38] To give this view the lie, Beecher, as Orestes Brownson noted, fails to portray any conventional conversion experience for Rose (though he does for many lesser characters in the book). Rose grows up being a Christian without ever knowing the time when she was not one. Horace Bushnell could not have asked for a better presentation of his theory.

Probably, however, there is more transcendentalism in Beecher's approach to Rose's education than Bushnell would have liked. Basically her education is a gradual refinement of her taste, a gradual extension or development of her faculties, a continual exercising of her sensibilities through direct contact with Nature on sunny days and indirect contact with it on rainy ones—by means of poetry, art, music, painting, and all the cultural advantages of an affluent Victorian home. She is an apt pupil because she was born with such a large measure of "ideality," imagination, moral intuition. Rose is "double child. Her outward nature was sensible, practical, worldly; her inward nature was deep in feeling, solemn, and mystical, but veined and traced throughout with the richest flow of imagination."[39]

Like her father, she feels a moral sympathy with spiders, worms, frogs, and toads, which she carries in her pockets as a child. She "bugs" her mother by dropping insects in her lap from time to time.[40] Even as a child—especially as a child—"she had learned of her father the secret things which flowers tell to all who have their sense exercised to understand the secret lore of Nature."[41] And of course "her sensitiveness to truth, which was particularly displayed toward Nature," was "as real, though less manifest, toward society" and "gave Rose an almost unerring insight of people's disposition."[42]

Rose is such an unusual girl that, having finished her grammar school education in Norwood, "She spent three years [in Boston] partly at Professor Agassiz's school and partly in the study of music and art."[43] Thus does she become a fit mate for the noble hero.

Formal education, however, is not enough to sustain democracy; religious guidance and moral suasion are also essential.

As might be expected, among those whose natures must contain great genius and who are called to lead the world in defense of truth, are the ministers of the nation. In a sermon entitled "The Day and the Desk," in 1859, Beecher eulogized the Sabbath and the Pulpit as the two prime social institutions for molding, upbuilding, and training the people of a democracy: "We see nothing in the ordinary influences of society which tends to rectify" men's selfishness and lead them toward benevolence. "Nothing in secular institutions; nothing in the course of business. Schools and seminaries cannot frame the man's habits nor train the moral nature. It is in this view that we regard the Sabbath and the Pulpit as indispensable to society." The Sabbath is "the day for religious education" and "The Pulpit is the popular religious educator. . . . Week by week men should hear their daily life discussed, not from selfish principles, not from a ground of expediency, nor from popular points of view, but from the highest religious grounds." Men should learn "habitually to look at all things from the religious standpoint." It is the duty of the preacher to see that men are

> taken out of their low and selfish attitudes and lifted up into the light of God's countenance, and then measured, judged, repressed, or developed, and wholly bathed or inspired by the spirit of conscience and of love, then they are receiving a moral education. . . . And we regard the Day and the Desk to be as needful to the refined and philosophic as to the rude and unlettered.[44]

If Beecher could not be a general, at least he could be a prophet—a prophet in the voluntary service of the state, refining and educating its citizens and training them to be honest and moral "habitually," instinctively, without having to think about it.

Beecher was not entirely antidemocratic. At least he had faith that the solid middle class could be trusted to choose the right leaders, and he thought many average citizens possessed sound moral judgment: "Think it not strange that a farmer's wife should deeply ponder questions which have tasked the deepest thinkers," he said in *Norwood* of Barton Cathcart's mother.[45] But his faith in the average citizen was, like Jefferson's, a limited one. They do very well on simple moral questions if properly trained and bred, but they are not capable of governing or of reasoning on the highest philosophical problems. What made the middle class of New England so admirable was the institutional environment which nurtured them, forced them to live up to their best nature, developed what talents they had:

> Now and then, and in New England often, are to be found plain and uncultured persons whose unconscious thoughts deal habitually with the profoundest questions which man can ponder. The very intensity of religious convictions—at once the cause of so much that is good and the occasion of so much ill repute—tends at length

> to breed among the common people an aptitude for deep moral problems.[46]

Hence even the strict New England Sabbath, considered old-fashioned in Brooklyn in 1867, merited Beecher's defense. When Judge Bacon states in *Norwood*: "I think our Sundays in New England are . . . days of restriction rather than of joyousness," Dr. Wentworth answers:

> I am hardly of your opinion. I should be unwilling to see our New England Sunday changed except perhaps . . . to make it attractive to children and relieve older persons from *ennui*. But after all we must judge things by their fruits. . . . New England character and history are the result of a wide-spread system of influences of which the Sabbath was the type.[47]

Some years later, Beecher was to advocate a relaxation of the Sabbath blue laws in the suburbs and to suggest that the opening of museums, libraries, and art galleries on Sunday might provide wholesome moral enlightenment and relieve ennui. But in *Norwood* he contended that "The sturdy, unsophisticated laboring class in New England [i.e., the farmers] are all in favor of the Sabbath because they know its restrictions are for their own good." And for those who did not know it, Wentworth explained:

> Men do not yet perceive that the base of the brain is full of despotism, and the coronal brain is radiant with liberty. I mean that the laws and relations which grow out of men's relations in physical things are the sternest and hardest and at every step in the ascent toward reason and spirituality, the relations grow more kindly and free.

The terminology is that of the new science of phrenology, but the essence is an old-fashioned belief in moral depravity. In his discussion of the Sabbath in *Norwood* Wentworth justifies all kinds of social controls and institutional restraints in terms of the ultimate good of the race.

> Now it is natural for men to prefer an animal life. By-and-by they will learn that such a life necessitates force, absolutism. It is natural for unreflecting men to complain when custom or institutions hold them up to some higher degree. But that higher degree has in it an element of emancipation from the necessary despotisms of physical life. If it were possible to bring the whole community up to a plane of spirituality, it would be found that there and there only could be the highest measure of liberty. And this is my answer to those who grumble at the restrictions of Sunday liberty. It is only the liberty of the senses that suffers. A higher and nobler civil liberty, moral liberty, social liberty, will work out of it. Sunday is the common people's Magna Charta.[48]

There was a tendency in Victorian elitist thought, which Beecher exemplifies perfectly here, to be terribly distrustful of the common man and, "for his own good," to impose all kinds of restrictions upon him so as to forcefully "hold [him] up to some higher degree." The elite were capable of self-discipline, they could develop their own "inner check"; but the common people had to have discipline either externally imposed upon them or bred into them by institutional means. Who knew what the base of the brain might compel a man to do who had spent sixty hours of the week laboring in a textile mill and then was allowed to have all of Sunday free to do as he pleased with it?

There was always the pious hope, as here, that these restrictions would be only temporary—"for the present," or "for the foreseeable future." The promise was held out that ultimately they might be done away with, when the masses had reached a sufficiently high moral plane. But New England had endured the Sabbath for 250 years when Beecher wrote, and still the common man seemed insufficiently elevated to relax its rigor. It would seem that its virtue in New England was really that the people did not *want* to relax it—it had become so habitual that now they liked it. If only, Beecher must have thought, *Norwood* could become the *Uncle Tom's Cabin* for the era of Reconstruction. Otherwise might not the alien influences of foreigners and the barbarism of the South and West destroy the newly reunited nation and thwart God's destiny for it?

"Liberty," Wentworth concludes his lecture on the Sabbath, "is not an outward condition. It is an inward attribute, or rather, a name for the quality of life produced by the highest moral attributes." The Puritans were not given to poetry, but "The one great poem of New England is her Sunday. Through that she has escaped materialism. . . . New England's imagination is to be found—not in art, or literature—but in her inventions, her social organism, and above all her religious life." Then comes the warning: "When she ceases to have a Sunday, she will be as this landscape is now [with night approaching], growing dark, all its lines blurred, its distances and gradations merging into sheeted darkness and night." Beecher feared a society without gradations and carefully delimited boundaries. As far as he was concerned, mankind would never be able to live without institutions like the Sabbath, for the result would be chaos. *Norwood* is not simply a novel of theological liberation, but of missionary zeal for a well-ordered society.

Another important New England institution that Beecher considered basic for the moral education of the young and the strengthening of the national fiber was the custom of family prayer. Now long since a dead tradition, it was still powerful in middle-class homes both in England and America when Beecher wrote; twice a day, at sunrise and sunset, the paterfamilias gathered his family and servants together to conduct the old matin and vesper services, reading the Bible and offering a prayer (services which the boarding schools and colleges of the day, acting *in loco parentis*, also made mandatory). Beecher made a great deal of this practice in *Norwood*. But what strikes the reader is that he chose to make particular reference to it in connection with the beginning of the Civil War. As the nation faced the crisis of disunion, family prayer took on new meaning in Norwood—though, since the book was written after the event, it may be more accurate to see this passage as an indication of how prayer and Providence preserved the Union. The war lent a new aura of sanctity to patriotism in America and produced a new insistence on national loyalty as a religious duty. The key passage occurs in a description of the day the people of Norwood learn that Lincoln has called for troops to put down the Southern rebellion:

> The sun had gone down. Every household in Norwood and wide about was a scene of excitement. That night prayer was a reality! Never before had the children heard from their father's lips such supplications for the country. Never before had the children's hearts been open to join so fervently in prayer themselves. Men seemed to be conscious that they were helpless in the presence of an immeasurable danger. By Faith they laid their hearts upon the bosom of God, till they felt the beatings of that great Heart whose courses give life and law to the Universe.[49]

This was a very different mood from the "God's in his heaven, all's right with the world" of early Victorianism. It is the solemn mood which made Millet's *Angelus* (painted in 1859) one of the most popular engravings in American homes after the war.

It would be interesting to know more about American family prayer in these Mid-Victorian years. Obviously as an institution it was already dying out. Yet Beecher thought and hoped that it might revive; for in the home, in the love of father and mother, reciprocated by faithful children, a new institution might rise to support the faith of the nation. The home as a religious institution comes up in another context in *Norwood*, when Dr. Wentworth, himself the archetype of a godly paterfamilias, remarks: "I have always esteemed the family table to be a kind of altar, a place sacred and so to be made as complete in its furnishings as may be."[50] In the decay of the Church and the loss of faith in its doctrines and ministrations which Beecher saw no way of stemming, a more real sense of communal strength and spiritual harmony seemed to flow across the Sunday or evening dinner table than from most church altars. The father cutting the roast was the priest offering the sacraments. The mother, beaming at the other end of the table, was like Jesus, God, and the Virgin Mary in exuding spiritual comfort and love over the libations—(what T. S. Eliot later called "mactations, immolations, oblations, impetrations"). The Victorian Mother, madonna of the dinner table—if one wishes to find her portrait, he need only look at the advertisements in the ladies' books of the day.

But the most interesting aspect of Dr. Wentworth's casual remark is his notion that the furnishings of the family table should be as complete and, presumably, as richly finished, as the sacred plate of the communion table. Here is a crucial turning point in American social history. Not only is this another reversal of the plainness and simplicity of the Puritan church and its furnishings (to which the elaborate Gothic brownstone churches of the city and suburbs already afforded an ample contrast), but it represents again the subtle intrusion of material comfort, luxury, and affluence into the home. As God's altar, the Victorian dinner table could freely indulge in the most extravagant display of heavy silverware, fine china plates, ornate condiment servers, rich cut-glass bowls, magnificent crystal goblets, double-damask table clothes and napkins, curiously worked salt cellars, and all the other expensive accessories of dining that were to make Tiffany's famous. Somehow the affluence that we find portrayed so voluptuously in paintings of seventeenth-century Dutch Protestant bourgeois had invaded austere Puritan New England.

One other institution of a religious, and hence quasi-educational, nature with which Beecher was greatly concerned was revivalism. Religious revivals had been a basic aspect of American religious life since the First Great Awakening in the 1740's. America had seen a new outburst of revivalism in the early years of the nineteenth century which has since been called the Second Great Awakening. The First was associated with the revival preaching of Jonathan Edwards, George Whitefield, and Gilbert Tennent; the Second, with the Methodist and Baptist circuit riders on the frontier who preached to thousands in pastures and forest clearings at what were called camp meetings. In both periods, the conversion of thousands of souls in a few days was considered a miraculous outpouring of the spirit of God, a divine "shower of blessing" from Heaven.

By the 1820's, however, revival preachers had learned that there were certain techniques by which these showers could be induced to come more regularly—techniques of seeding the divine clouds, as it were. The feeling gradually developed that these outbursts of religious feeling were neither so spontaneous nor so miraculous as they had at first seemed. There were, in fact, certain definite measures or means by which a skillful revivalist could produce a revival. It merely required that he follow certain procedures which had been observed to work in previous revivals.

Finally, in the 1830's, the greatest revivalist of the nineteenth century, Charles Grandison Finney, concluded that revivals were not miracles at all but simply the "philosophical result of the right use of the constituted means." Finney published a handbook on revivalism in which he said that "God has connected means with ends through all the departments of his government—in nature and in grace."[51] Or, in simpler terms: "The connection between the right use of means for a revival and a revival is as philosophically sure as between the right use of means to raise grain and a crop of wheat." The use of Finney's how-to-do-it handbook created a new breed of minister—the professional revivalist, specially endowed and specially trained in the mechanics of working up revivals. Throughout the nineteenth century, churches, towns, and eventually whole cities employed these specialists to do a job the local ministers were often unable to do themselves—that is, save souls in great quantities in order to keep the churches full.

Lyman Beecher, as we have noted, was no friend of Finney's, and most New England ministers considered him crude and heterodox—partly because he had no college education, partly because he attacked Calvinism, and partly because he advocated perfectionism and abolitionism. But Henry Ward Beecher had no such feelings toward him and the theories he advanced about revivals. Beecher was as convinced as Finney that God always worked according to natural laws and if there were laws of human behavior governing the religious affections or emotions, God must have created them in order to draw men to him. Professional mass revivalism was too crude for most New England ministers prior to the Civil War; but in *Norwood* Beecher notes that Parson Buell, consciously or not, has employed its means to produce a revival in the town. Judge Bacon, the scoffer, sarcastically indicates that he sees through this mechanistic technique for filling the church, and he outlines the process scornfully to Dr. Wentworth:

> I know how it will end. By and by there will come a break down; then, like frightened sheep, a crowd will make a rush toward the church-doors, pell-mell. After a while a count will be made and the results published. The upshot of it will be that while before one hundred selfish, bustling, disagreeable people lived outside of the church, afterwards they will live inside the church—that's all.[52]

To the Judge, revivalism is simply emotional hysteria, an appeal to the animal affections, and he is too pietistic a scoffer to want to belong to a church that allows within its fold hypocrites who mistake aroused emotions for spiritual regeneration.

But Dr. Wentworth cannot accept this naturalistic or psychological critique. He tells the Judge that he believes in revivals. Bacon is astonished, having supposed that the doctor was "too firm and intelligent a believer in Natural Law" to accept the concept of a miraculous shower of blessings. But Wentworth answers sententiously: "It is on that ground that I believe in Revivals." He then proceeds to explain the natural theology of these phenomena: "In every department of life men are moved in masses, and, as it were, with social contagions." These mass movements are the result of social affections which God has implanted in us for the advancement of the race: "Social enthusiasms have characterized the progress of the race in every department of society."

Beecher is not specific, but obviously he has in mind

moral reform movements, patriotic actions, and philanthropy, all of which are based upon mass emotional responses to human needs and feelings. What Judge Bacon sees as mere animal affection, the doctor insists is precisely what differentiates men *from* animals: "Men are susceptible of such excitement in proportion as they recede from animal conditions." Animals do not have national pride, charity drives, reform movements. "In art, in amusements, in social improvement, in patriotism, men tend to act in masses, to be kindled by each other to enthusiasm" for worthy causes. Again Beecher applauds that enthusiasm which the Edwardsians feared: "Social excitement is favorable to taste, affection, judgment and reason. I do not know why moral emotions should be exempt from this same law." That is to say, just as patriotism unites the masses to make sacrifices for the love of their country, so revivalism unites masses of people for their moral improvement.

For some reason Beecher never managed to confront the evil aspects of human nature and mass emotionalism in his novel, even when he came to discuss the Civil War. The euphoric quality of American Victorianism after the North's victory in 1865 may have been in part responsible for this. So too may the didactic, hortatory nature of all that Beecher wrote; a believer in uplift does not dwell on the sordid but on "the more smiling aspects of life," as Howells put it. The charge against him here is similar to that often made against Emerson's writings. Emerson's doctrines of Circles, Compensation, the Oversoul, Self-reliance all somehow managed to encompass and mask what the Calvinists had considered the work of the Devil. If God and His love directed the universe, as the Mid-Victorians yearned to believe, there was no room in it for the Devil or for Hell. Human violence, destruction, bloodshed were only transitory adjustments in man's progressive adaptation; at worst, they were temporary evils, at best, inevitable necessities for the good of the race. Besides, as Spencer said, these were early stages of barbarism, and the civilized Anglo-Saxons were all but past them on the road to the millennium.

Judge Bacon makes one final protest against the mass enthusiasm of revival meetings in the course of his perennial debate with Wentworth. Revivals are no longer spontaneous; they are purposely "got up": "I can give you a prescription for a revival."

"Why not?" Wentworth calmly replies. "Is not education 'got up'? Is not art, culture 'got up'? Is not your own profession and mine 'got up'? Why should men be afraid to speak of moral states as the result of deliberate and intentional effort?" In short, revivalism was now a profession; it had become institutionalized like law, medicine, the ministry, because men had progressed to the point where they understood the basic natural laws underlying the religious and social affections governing human action in groups. "Why should not men apply the term education to moral faculties as well as to others and study for moral results as they do for social or aesthetic? Are not the moral sentiments subject to laws as much as any other parts of the mind?" And could anyone deny that revivals improved the morals of any community in which they occurred?

But did not institutionalization and professionalism take the supernatural quality out of revivals and reduce them to mundane affairs, man-made rather than God-made? Only if one insisted on maintaining the old dualistic view of the natural vis-à-vis the supernatural; only if one denied that the act of spiritual rebirth itself was accompanied by the divine infusion of grace. "I do not the less believe that a divine influence is experienced," says Wentworth, "because it pursues the channels of established law. Men account for phenomena by natural laws as far as their knowledge goes and then they ascribe whatever is left over, beyond their knowledge of causation, to superior beings. The higher ranges of human experience are the most complex and subtle, and seem mysterious because the lines of causation are finer and more spiritual. But the profoundest mysteries of human experience will one day be found to furnish the most admirable illustration of the universality of natural laws." A better illustration of the fundamental assumption of Liberal Protestantism (and ultimately of the social engineering of John Dewey and the Progressive Instrumentalists) could hardly be found, or a more naturalistic approach to religion.

But Beecher did not conceive of this approach as in any sense naturalistic or secularistic. For the doctrine of progress implied the gradual perfection of the human mind and spirit to the point where (when mankind had at last plumbed all the mysteries of the universe) human beings would in fact become semidivine and the millennium would arrive. Revivals are thus part of God's social engineering, not man's:

> All nations pretending to moral life have been subject to these outbursts of feeling. It is all very well to declare that a gradual and constant progress in goodness would be better. Such is not the law of development. Nations advance by paroxysms. The race has gone up not by steady improvement but by leaps, with long rests between.[53]

One can guess what Beecher had in mind as those "paroxysms" in goodness which had brought man up from barbarism: the Reformation, the Puritan movement, the Glorious Revolution, the First Great Awakening, the American Revolution, the Second Great Awakening, the

Civil War—and had he lived long enough, the Spanish-American War, World War I, and World War II. Beecher's language is not far removed from Spencer's in his summary of the importance of revivalism: "At a later period, when society has reached a higher plane than at present, progress may become even, uniform, and constant. At present that seems impossible. And we are to regard these moral freshets [no matter how induced] as admirable, relatively to the wants of the whole community."

Under this canopy of spasmodic moral progress Dwight L. Moody, Billy Sunday, Billy Graham, and their cohorts have had little difficulty since Beecher's day in persuading Liberal Protestant ministers—who disagree with their fundamentalist theology—that their urban mass revival campaigns are really civic reform crusades for the moral improvement of the community and the uplift of mankind.

Thus did Beecher's philosophy and the Liberal Protestant movement for the liberation of American life and thought become trapped within its own concept of progress as achieved through an institutionalized social order directed by men of superior moral talents and sensibilities. If man, or the human race, advances in paroxysms of excitement, if certain gifted leaders are entrusted by God to promote these excitements, and if society needs to institutionalize them for its own self-discipline, then we are well along the way to the political philosophy of Progressivism as it was espoused and practiced in politics first by the Mugwumps, then by Theodore Roosevelt and Woodrow Wilson, and finally, at the apex of Liberal Protestantism, by Franklin D. Roosevelt. The social philosophy of Liberal Protestantism, and of the Progressive elitist political ideology which it sponsored, went hand in hand with the social engineering of John Dewey's instrumental philosophy. It has received its final assessment in Aldous Huxley's *Brave New World*.

After reading *Norwood*, it is not difficult to visualize General Barton Cathcart, called again from his civil pursuits, battling up San Juan Hill in 1898 and then accepting the new call to leadership of the nation as its President; nor is it difficult, on the other hand, to visualize Dr. Wentworth chosen as a college president, becoming a writer on American and British constitutional democracy, thrust into the governorship of his state almost against his inclination, and finally taking up the cause of "the New Freedom" to make the world safe for democracy. What a pity that Henry Ward Beecher lived in the era of Grant, Blaine, Conkling, and Chester Alan Arthur. How he would have loved Theodore Roosevelt and Woodrow Wilson—cultured, moralistic, anointed!

CHAPTER NINE

The North, the South, and the Civil War

The population is in the North and West. The wealth is there. The popular intelligence of the country is there. THERE only *is there an educated* common people. *The right doctrines of civil government are with the North. . . . The institutions of America were shaped by the North!*

—HENRY WARD BEECHER,
October 9, 1863

If the South had won the Civil War, or even managed a negotiated peace, what a false prophet Henry Ward Beecher would have been! And what a triumph for fundamentalism! Liberal Protestantism might never have emerged from the womb, or if it did, would have been maimed from birth. American politics might have seen the triumph of rural Populism over white-collar Progressivism, and William Jennings Bryan would have been our first four-term President. But the North won, and Beecher's faith was vindicated.

When Beecher said that "The lips that taught me to say 'Father' taught me to say 'Fatherland,' "[1] he meant that New England institutions and education had bred patriotism and love of God into his heart at the same time. He conveniently forgot that two years after he was born, New

England's Federalist leaders at the Hartford Convention had tried to lead their section out of the country in a secessionist movement. New England did not become part of the Union again in its feelings or institutions until after Daniel Webster's famous debate with Robert Y. Hayne in 1830. Thereafter every New England schoolboy (and those in most other public schools in the North and West) had to memorize at some time in his life the famous peroration to that speech which concluded: "Liberty and Union, now and forever, one and inseparable." Unfortunately Webster neglected to add "under God"; but Beecher did that.

Beecher was an ardent advocate of "Christian democracy" long before the Civil War: "I am a citizen; a Christian citizen. Is anything higher than that?" he asked in 1858.[2] And when he dedicated the Brooklyn Armory that same year, he compared George Washington to Jesus Christ. Noting that "the ladies of America" were at that moment "engaged in the work of purchasing the grounds and tomb of Washington at Mount Vernon" as a national monument, he concluded his oration on "Patriotism and Liberty" with this comment: "Now the women of America go to the tomb of Washington, and who will roll away the stone? God grant that they may find the stone rolled away and the living spirit of Washington, which is the spirit of liberty sitting upon it, to hail, to cheer, and to bless them."[3]

However, as George Frederickson has pointed out in *The Inner Civil War*, a conservative revolution took place in the minds of many Americans during the years 1860 to 1865, and especially among New Englanders. The latent social conservatism of the Puritan–Calvinist–Unitarian–Federalist outlook hardened during the war into the belief that if the nation was to survive and prosper, it must abandon its old anti-institutional, humanitarian, perfectionist, natural-rights approach and concentrate upon a highly centralized, carefully controlled, strongly institutionalized system based upon order, efficiency, duty, and sternness. Along with this new conservatism went the conviction that to be a good Christian one must be a good (Northern) patriot, and vice versa.

Beecher was at first very fearful that the war and its harsh demands might have adverse spiritual consequences. After all, he had been preaching a very sentimental and romantic view of Christianity which offered scant preparation for the horrors of war. In a sermon delivered in May 1861 on "The Camp, Its Dangers and Duties," he warned of the shock that violence and bloodshed might give to the minds of Christians sensitized by the gospel of love and benevolence:

> We must remember that the aim and end of war is physical violence. Now men cannot be associated with objects of violence and not receive collateral moral impressions from them. . . . Some are cured of cruelty at the sight of blood. They revolt from it with the whole force of being. Some have a natural tendency to it; and when they come into the exercise of it, they speedily sink into degeneracy and drag others down with them. . . . This living for an end of violence must affect the whole moral nature. A life supremely devoted to resistance, to contention, to destruction, must be full of dangers [to the soul].

On the other hand, he noted hopefully that a firm Christian faith would see those of sterner will through these dangers: "If men are educated, and if they bear with them a stern will, and look upon war as a terrible but necessary evil, they may go through it and escape unharmed . . . but raw, unenlightened, untrained natures cannot but be hardened and depraved by [it]."[4]

By 1863, however, he had so far overcome his view that war was a necessary evil as to decide that it was a positive good—at least when it was fought in a righteous cause:

> Now war is good for nothing if it is not intense and cruel. It means organized force; and it is nonsense to go into the field with anything except guns in your hands and swords at your side. The attempt so to fight, as in the earlier periods of our struggle, as not to hurt anybody, is most disastrous whether in prudence or in civil successes.[5]

Beecher's hesitancy about urging "war to the knife" in the early phases of the Civil War may seem odd, considering the fact that during the days of "Bleeding Kansas" he had urged not only war to the knife but "the knife to the hilt." He had told the New England emigrants to Kansas that "Sharpe's rifles are a greater moral agency than the Bible." (His church pledged twenty-five rifles to the Kansas Emigrant Aid Society, which occasioned an indignant rebuke from the pacifistic Garrison.) But this remark, which led to the renaming of the Sharpe's rifle as "Beecher's Bible" and the renaming of Plymouth Church as "the Church of the Holy Rifles," was not so bloodthirsty and warlike as it seemed. Beecher insisted that the defense of Kansas by armed emigrants from the North was a defensive and not an offensive measure; "border ruffians" from Missouri were coming into Kansas to support a proslavery constitution against the will of the predominantly antislavery Yankee settlers. These proslavery ruffians were the aggressors, and against such renegades a well-armed citizens' army was the best possibility for peace. "A battle is to be fought," he said, but "If we are wise it will be bloodless. If we are firm and prompt to obvious duty, if we stand by the men of Kansas and give them all the help they need, the flames of war will be quenched before it bursts forth."[6]

The hope proved vain. But it is not possible to understand Beecher's whole approach to slavery and to the Civil War without understanding how desperately he tried to avoid it—an effort shared by most churchgoers in the North as well as by Abraham Lincoln.

As we have noted, Beecher came late to the antislavery cause. Not until 1846 did he first preach against slavery. His stand before that time is neatly summarized in two sentences from his *Lectures to Young Men* in 1844:

> The poor man with Industry is happier than the rich man in Idleness, for labor makes the one more manly, and riches unmans the other. The slave is often happier than the master who is nearer undone by license than his vassal by toil.[7]

When Beecher did finally join the antislavery ranks, he frequently thundered his own hatred of slavery: "it is a great sin . . . it is a national curse"; "if I could have my way, every man on the globe should be a freeman, and at once."

> The American doctrine of slavery is no analogue or derivative of the Hebrew or any mild form of slavery. It is the extremest and worst form of the Roman doctrine of slavery; the harshest that the world has ever seen. It is a dehumanizing of men. It is the deliberate taking of men and putting them in the place of cattle or chattels, and violating every one of their natural rights.[8]

And if God is just, "it is not possible for a nation systematically to violate every natural right of four millions of people and go unpunished."

But when one analyzes the solutions Beecher offered for this horrendous crime against man and God, it becomes clear that most of his rhetoric on the score of human rights was mere bombast, the cheapest form of hypocrisy. For in the same breath in which he said that if he could have his way he would free every slave at once, he added: "But as they cannot be, will not be [free] for ages, is it best that bitter discontent should be inspired in them, or Christian quietness and patient waiting?"[9] For a prudent, cautious man like Beecher the answer was obvious, and he was always at great pains to dissociate himself from those fanatical, irresponsible, immoral abolitionists who heedlessly cursed the South and encouraged the slave to think freedom was their immediate right.

In a famous speech entitled "The Nation's Duty to Slavery," delivered while John Brown was in prison awaiting trial, he made it quite clear that Brown was a madman whose actions would hurt more than help the slaves. True, "his soul was noble," but "his work" was "miserable." "I disapprove of his mad and feeble schemes. I shrink from the folly of the bloody foray."[10] He admitted that Brown had been driven to his madness by the border ruffians who had killed his son, and he honored Brown for his refusal to try to palliate his offense; but the best he could say for his action on behalf of the antislavery cause was: "What is average citizenship when a lunatic is a hero?"[11]

As for William Lloyd Garrison, "we regard him as one of the most unfortunate of all leaders for the best development of anti-slavery feeling." True, he was "a man of no mean ability, of indefatigable industry . . . enterprise . . . perseverance . . . courage"; but his approach to the delicate and complex problem of slavery "amounts to recklessness." Garrison lacked "a balance," a sense of "conciliation, good-natured benevolence," and "a certain popular mirthfulness"; he had none of "the moderation and urbanity" necessary for such a task.[12] It is significant that Beecher ascribed the qualities he saw Garrison as lacking to William Wilberforce, the leader of the British antislavery movement earlier in the century. For when Garrison was just starting his career in Boston, the man he admired most and whose help he wanted most was Lyman Beecher. And Lyman, having sized Garrison up precisely the same way his son did later, told him: "Your zeal is commendable, but you are misguided. If you will give up your fanatical notions and be guided by us [of the clergy], we will make you the Wilberforce of America." Somehow Garrison managed to achieve that goal without the aid of either the father or the son.

Garrison was a pacifist, and Beecher could accuse him only indirectly of stirring up the slaves to insurrection. But there were many abolitionists who had argued that the slave had the same natural right to revolution as the American colonists had to rise up against their oppressors in 1776. Beecher struggled with this problem, but the outcome of his struggle was foreseeable. "The right of a race or nation to seize their freedom is not to be disputed," he began. "But the use of this right must conform to reason and not to mere impulse." And what did reason dictate in the case of the slaves? It indicated that they had "not the slightest hope that their rebellion will rise to the dignity of a successful revolution."[13] Since only revolutions with good prospects of success were reasonable or justifiable, the slave had no right to rebel nor had anyone the right to suggest that he should try. "Does any man believe that this vast horde of undisciplined Africans, if set free, would have cohesive power to organize themselves into a government, and maintain their independence?" he asked. And the answer being obvious, that put an end to the right of revolution for the slaves.

When the South seceded, and came very close to having the power to effect a successful revolution, Beecher had to advance to the next position and to argue that "if we will legalize and establish the right of any discontented community to rebel and to set up intestine governments within the government of the United States," we would have no government at all. That would be "the right of disintegration."[14] For Americans the right of revolution had ceased to exist.

Beecher had essentially four different ways of dealing with the slavery question, though he usually mixed them up judiciously so as to reach the widest possible rapport with his audiences. His first line of argument was that slavery was a dying institution and so long as it could not extend its boundaries, it would ultimately wither away. It was accursed of God, and if abolitionists would stop agitating the question, and the North in general would firmly oppose all compromises allowing for its expansion, He would bring about its end in His own good time. "It is because statesmen [like Calhoun and Douglas] propose stepping in between slavery and the appointed bourne to which she goes, scourged by God and Nature, that we resent these statesmen."[15]

Beecher used a great variety of images to portray slavery as dying: It was a wounded beast, a dying weed, a dragon perishing in its own "slime," a paralyzed, stricken monster. "All the natural laws of God are warring upon slavery. We have only to let the process go on. Let slavery alone. Let it go to seed."[16] Of course, if its branches and roots began to creep over or under the wall into free-soil territory, they should be cut off: "Cut off every branch that hangs beyond the wall, every root that spreads. Shut it up to itself and let it alone." Slavery was a blight on the Southern economy: "Every slave state that has had exacted and enforced labor has itself felt the blight and curse of slavery in its agriculture. What is the land in Virginia worth today? It is worn out and abandoned. . . . the agriculture of slavery is an exhausting agriculture and . . . it wears out every part of the country that it touches." This was God's way of cursing the Southern whites: "The master takes away his [the slave's] right to his labor and the slave turns round and says, 'I curse the soil.' The soil is cursed, and it is a witness of God."[17] (This was, of course, the reverse of God's blessing upon the free labor of the North.) The economic argument thus supplemented the argument of God's moral law, and many Northern churchgoers were perfectly willing to let the matter rest in God's lap.

The same argument for keeping slavery carefully enclosed within its present boundaries so that it would gradually die out, justified Beecher in what seemed to be a position almost as radical as his support of armed emigration to Kansas: his defiance of the Fugitive Slave Act. For him this act was one of aggression against the freedom, the states' rights, the free air, of the North, and not by any stretch of the imagination a defense of the Southern slaveholder's right to his property:

> When the Congress goes beyond the Constitution and demands, on penalty, that citizens of free States shall help and render back the flying slave, we give a blunt and unequivocal refusal. We are determined to break any law that commands us to enslave or re-enslave a man, and we are willing to take the penalty.[18]

Christian duty compelled a man to help any slave who had the courage and determination to seize his liberty. Beecher believed that only "the more enlightened and liberty-loving among the Southern slaves" would take this risk, and these he felt obliged to help. But it is revealing that in explaining which slaves would be so enlightened and courageous, he casually remarked that it would be those who bore "their master's blood."[19] Pure-blooded Africans would not have such enlightened notions of freedom; but slaves born of a black mother and a white father inherited some of the freedom-loving Anglo-Saxon spirit and thus came up a step in the spiral of civilization. As we shall note later, Beecher was not one of those who feared the mongrelization of the races (though he opposed racial intermarriage). With his perennial optimism, he always assumed that the superior raised up the inferior, not vice versa. It was not a view shared by all racists.

Beecher's second line of argument was that the slave should be lifted up so that he would be less like an animal and more like a man and thereby compel his master to free him. "The Pauline treatment is the most direct road to liberty"—a reference to the Apostle Paul, who, having converted Philemon's escaped slave, Onesimus, and instructed him on how to be a good Christian, made him return to his master but urged in a letter that Philemon treat him as befitted a Christian brother. Beecher argued similarly: "If you wish to work for the enfranchisement of the African, seek to make him a better man. Teach him to be an obedient servant and an honest, true, Christian man. These virtues are God's step-stones to liberty. . . . Truth, honor, fidelity, manhood—these things in the slave will prepare him for freedom. It is the low animal condition of the African that enslaves him. It is moral enfranchisement that will break his bonds."

And the way this moral enfranchisement worked was upon the conscience of the master. For "the higher a man is raised in the scale of being, the harder it will be to hold him in bondage and to sell him; while the more he is like an animal, the easier it will be to hold him in thrall and harness. The more you make slaveholders feel that when they oppress and sell a man they are oppressing and selling

God's image, the harder it will be for them to continue to enslave and traffic in human beings. Therefore whatever you do to inspire in the slave high and noble and godlike feelings tends to loosen his chains. . . ."[20]

But how was the slave to be inspired to "noble and godlike feelings"? After the war Beecher castigated the missionary and Bible and tract societies for having refused to push their way and their views into the South: "The great publishing societies that were sustained by the contributions of the churches were absolutely dumb. Great controversies raged round the doors of the Bible Society, of the Tract Society and of the American Board of Commissioners for Foreign Missions. The managers of these societies resorted to every shift except that of sending the Gospel to the slaves. They would not send the Bible to the South for, they said, 'it is a punishable offence in most of the Southern States to teach a slave to read, and are we to go in the face of this State legislation . . . ?' The Tract Society said, 'We are set up to preach the Gospel, not to meddle with political and industrial institutions.' "[21]

All of which was true enough. Neither tracts nor missionaries were allowed in the South if they sought to change the status of the slave. But Beecher had another explanation of how the slave might be freed despite this iron curtain across the Mason–Dixon line. Somehow freedom in the North would silently drift into the South, like the scent of flowers over a garden wall, and there it would germinate and inspire the notion of freedom:

> The good influence of national freedom will gradually reach the enslaved, it will surely inspire the restlessness which precedes development. Germination is the most silent, but most disturbing, of all natural processes. Slaves cannot but feel the universal summer of civilization.[22]

Somehow this germinating power of freedom would produce restlessness without insurrection. The "yearnings" of the slave for freedom and manhood are "a very different thing from surly discontent, stirred up from without, and left to rankle in their unenlightened natures." But just how all this would come about and how long it would take, Beecher could not say. Perhaps eons, certainly "ages."

His third line of argument involved the use of moral suasion upon the consciences of the slaveholders. "We must work upon his master. Make him discontented with slavery and he will speedily take care of the rest." (Significantly, if matters were left to the white man, they would be done "speedily," but if left to the black, they would take ages.) But in stirring up the master, we must remember to do it in all kindness and Christian love; we must always keep in mind that the Southern slaveholders are "our brethren." Even in 1859 Beecher was insisting that "we must maintain sympathy and kindness toward the South. We are brethren and I pray that no fratricidal influence be permitted to sunder the Union."[23]

> I am for holding the heart of the North right up to the heart of the South. Every heart-beat will be ere long, not a blow riveting oppression, but a throb, carrying new health. . . . They are a lawful prey to love. . . . 'We love you, and hate your slavery. We shall leave no fraternal effort untried to deliver you, and ourselves with you, from the degradation, danger, and wickedness of this system.'[24]

It was a nice sentiment, and those who still think (with Beecher) that the invective, harshness, and fanaticism of abolitionist rhetoric were a cause of the Civil War, should applaud Beecher's position. But how was the goal to be achieved? Southerners simply had to be told, persuaded, cajoled, and loved into doing four things, performing four simple acts which would demonstrate their Christianity and their adherence to the "Pauline" approach to slavery: They must grant Christianity to the slave—giving him the Bible, churches, ministers to preach to him; they must give the slave the right of marriage and the sanctity of the home; they must send him to school to learn to read; and they must grant him the right to seek redress for his wrongs in civil courts and to have his word accepted in law. That was all:

> The things which shall lead to emancipation are not so complicated or numerous as people blindly think. A few virtues established, a few usages maintained, a few rights guaranteed to the slaves, and the system is vitally wounded. The right of chastity in the woman, the unblemished household of love, the right of parents in their children—on these three elements stands the whole weight of society. . . . Withhold these rights from savage people and they can never be carried up. . . . We demand and have a right to demand of the Christian men of the South, that they shall revolutionize the moral condition of the slaves.[25]

As for the civil rights of the slave, Beecher said in a speech on "American Slavery" in 1851: "Ah, if you will only bring American slavery on the platform of Hebrew slavery—if you will give the slave the Bible, and send him to the school, and open the doors of the courts to him, then we will let it alone—it will take care of itself." "There is not a court from Mason and Dixon's line, through to Texas where a slave can open his mouth as a witness and be believed" even in petitioning against his abuse.[26] It turned out that Beecher merely wanted the whole basis of American slavery altered so as to allow the slave to raise himself up: "if any one will enter into a calculation, he will find that the Hebrew slave had about one-half of his time to himself. Moreover, the Hebrew slave had every motive held out to him to rise. He could under certain circumstances, hold property—he could better his condition, advance, establish himself independently." It was the veriest pipe dream. Why would Southern legislatures pass laws that would "vitally wound" their system? Beecher may have espoused this position out of his unquenchable faith in the power of love and its ability to move the human conscience. Or he may have been simply naïve. The best that can be said for this approach is that just because it was so mild, so conservative, so noncontroversial, its continual rejection by the South—even to the point of refusing to let slaves read the Bible—made it increasingly difficult for any honest Northerner to remain hopeful that the South might someday change its mind about slavery.

Beecher's fourth line of argument was more plausible and more worthy: "If we would benefit the African at the South, we must begin at the North. This is to some men the most disagreeable part of the doctrine of emancipation. It is very easy to labor for the emancipation of beings a thousand miles off; but the practical application of justice and humanity to those about us is not so agreeable."[27] Until the North could show that it was willing to clean its own house, it ill-behooved it to cast stones at the South.

> How are the free colored people treated at the North? They are almost without education, and with but little sympathy for their ignorance. They are refused the common rights of citizenship which the whites enjoy. They cannot even ride in the cars of our city railroads. They are snuffed at in the house of God or tolerated with ill-concealed disgust. Can the black man be a mason in New York? . . . Can the black man be a carpenter? . . . Can the black man engage in the common industries of life?

> There is scarcely one from which he is not excluded. He is crowded down, down, down through the most menial callings to the bottom of society. We tax them and then refuse to allow their children to go to the public schools. . . . The African owned may dwell in America, but unowned he must be expatriated.[28]

At least this was not hypocritical, and Beecher himself refused to ride upon a streetcar line in Brooklyn that would not allow Negroes as passengers. But the next point in his argument hardly followed; every step, he said, that is taken to help the Negro in the North "is a step toward emancipation in the South." The North had taken a good many steps against slavery since 1776, but they had had no effect upon the South. So once again the end result of Beecher's position was to deflect attention from the real problem of slavery in the South, to push it to the back of the Northern mind, to put to rest all uneasiness about it. For all his eloquence—and after the war he constantly preened himself upon how radical he had been about slavery and how many enemies he had made in standing up for the rights of the slave—Beecher was the most valuable soporific to Northern consciences that Southern apologists for slavery could have asked for. They doubtless did not see it that way, but so it was.

Beecher was consequently of little direct help to the antislavery cause even though he became increasingly vocal on the issue after 1854. Perhaps it could be argued that simply by talking about the issue so much, he may have helped to keep the Northern mind agitated. For Beecher could not resist being part of any general public excitement.

Probably the most spectacular of all his actions on behalf of black people were the auctions he held in his pulpit in Brooklyn to purchase the freedom of slaves. It is hard to believe that people did not see through these performances, did not feel some guilt at their crass exhibitionism and the pitiful spectacle they made of the slaves concerned. But there is no evidence that they did. The most sensational of the auctions involved female slaves and children.

It is not clear exactly how many times Beecher put on these auctions and how many slaves were thus freed by weeping men and women heaping rings, watches, and jewelry upon the collection plates as the objects of their generosity sat pathetically on the platform. We have accounts of at least three instances. Beecher's son, in a eulogistic biography published after his death, noted that in one case in 1848 the slaves set free were "two respectable young women of light complexion." In another case Beecher reputedly declared that "a young woman had been sold by her own father to go South—for what purpose you can imagine when you see her." A newspaper account describes this slave as "of medium size and neatly dressed. The white blood of her father might be traced in her regular features and high, thoughtful brow, while her complexion and wavy hair betrayed her slave mother." She came up to the pulpit platform, wrote the reporter, and "sank down, embarrassed and apparently overcome by her feelings." Beecher's son wrote: "A handful of photographs of children, white and beautiful, who had been set free, have come to my hand . . . white-faced, flaxen-haired children, born under the curse of slavery."[29] There seems some cause to wonder why Beecher and his congregation took such particular interest in fair-skinned girls and children.

Beecher often made a point of remarking that "It is well known that slavery is maintained for reasons of profit, of politics, of indolence in the whites and of motives of passion even worse than these."[30] Perhaps in the long run these titillating aspects of slavery had as much effect as anything else Beecher said or did to keep his congregation far and wide agitated over the issue. If he ever auctioned off a slave girl who was very black and very homely, it has not been recorded by biographers friendly or critical.

What makes it difficult to find anything admirable in Beecher's stand on slavery is that everything he did and said brought him great notoriety, applause, and pleasure. But when he had to consider any action that might cause him inconvenience or make him look eccentric, he found excuses not to do it. His attitude toward Garrison and other abolitionists is the most obvious instance. But consider also his statement on the possibilities of boycotting slave-made products, incorporated into a sermon for a fast day declared by President Buchanan on January 11, 1861. Beecher devoted many pages of this address—which was entitled "Our Blameworthiness"—to discussing how guilty the North had been and how the imminence of civil war was a divine retribution for "the spread of avarice among our people," for "the intense eagerness to amass wealth," for "luxury, extravagance, ostentation and corruption of morals," for "vice and crime in our great cities," for "the growth of corrupt passions in connection with the increase of commercial prosperity." Much of the wealth of the North, he said, was the result of a "gigantic bargain" between it and the South: "It is for us just as much as for them that the slave works; and we acquiesce":[31]

> We clothe ourselves with the cotton which the slave tills. Is he scorched? Is he lashed? . . . It is you and I that wear the shirt and consume the luxury. Our looms and our factories are largely built on the slave's bones. We live on his labor.[32]

It is a fine and accurate indictment of Northern guilt. But then comes the lame conclusion:

> I confess I see no way to escape a part of the responsibility for slavery. I feel guilty in part for this system. If the relinquishment of the articles which come from slave labor would tend even remotely to abridge our end of the evil, I would without hesitation forego every one; but I do not see that it would help the matter.

Suddenly all the guilt evaporates. A boycott of Southern cotton would be unthinkable. The partial sense of responsibility admitted is quickly withdrawn. "I confess it before God and pray for some way to be opened by which I may be freed from what I hate bitterly." It is all back in God's hands. The sermon ends on the usual lullaby of love: "Love God, love men, love your dear fatherland."[33]

When the war came, Beecher was delighted to find that the love of fatherland overcame all of the greed, corruption, materialism, and self-indulgence that had blighted the North. Suddenly everyone became very patriotic, self-sacrificing, hard-working, and deeply committed to the higher good of saving the Union. While Beecher delivered many sermons and speeches during the four years of the war which attempted to explain it, he was so caught up in the onward rush of events that his views changed from day to day. Fortunately *Norwood* gives a general summary of his thinking about the conflict seen from beginning to end. It deserves attention because it probably reflected the views of most evangelical churchgoers in the North.

One major aspect of the novel is Beecher's deliberate contrast of the Northern and Southern temperaments in terms of two of his leading characters—Barton Cathcart and Thomas Heywood. In his letter to Robert Bonner describing the kind of novel he planned to write, he explains his intention as follows:

> I propose introducing a full company of various New England characters, to give a real view of the inside of a

> New England town, its brewing thought, its inventiveness, its industry and enterprise, its education and shrewdness and tact. I purpose to introduce a Southerner of a rather noble type and show him off, faults and virtues, on this background of New England, and I may transfer the story in its close to the seat of war and introduce one of its campaigns.[34]

Heywood, the dashing young Virginian, is introduced midway in the novel, and it is through his eyes that we see the capture of Fort Sumter. But Heywood, though he ends up a colonel in Lee's Army of Virginia, has been so won over to Northern views by his summer visits to Norwood that he is at the start of the war opposed to secession, and he weeps when he sees Colonel Beauregard commence hostilities by firing on the Stars and Stripes.

Beecher's contrasting portraits of Southerner and Yankee are not particularly original. They fit well into the categories which William R. Taylor has described in his excellent study of these conventions, *Cavalier and Yankee*. Heywood, a member of one of the finest families in Virginia, is "elegant," "charming," socially *galant*, with winning manners and a lofty air, and full of high moral sensitivity and nobility. He expects to find New Englanders smug, long-faced, overly serious, sharp, inflexible, and stingy. In order to make a good impression, he tries to "look as earnest and as anxious" as he possibly can. He soon discovers, however, the warm hearts that beat under his hosts' gruff exteriors, and he quickly becomes friends with the Wentworths, Cathcarts, and other first families of Norwood. After all, Beecher notes, "cultivated people are always more or less alike the world over."[35]

However, there are real sectional differences. Heywood writes to his family that "here people take quarrels to law where we thrash it out. In the South there is more liberty of action and in the North of thought." In New England there is a continual "repression of impulse in favor of principle." Beecher himself, being torn between his admiration for New England and his rebellion against it, is able to take the same ambivalent attitude toward it as Heywood. (Beecher's father once wrote of him: "Tho' I have good hope of his piety yet his temperament & spirit is of a kind which would make him susceptible of Southern influence assailing him on the side of honour & spirit. . . ."[36])

The contrast is made specific in comparing Heywood and Cathcart, the paragons of their respective regions:

> Heywood's face was genial and when excited, radiant. Excitement shot fire through every feature of Cathcart's face; but everyone felt that more lay behind than was expressed. There was a sense of repressed feeling and reserved enthusiasm. Heywood would flame soonest, Cathcart would burn the longest.[37]

Differing in emotional nature, they are also different in intellect; Heywood seems the embodiment of the Understanding, Cathcart of Coleridgean Reason:

> Barton Cathcart's mind was reflective, Tom Heywood's perceptive. Both were reasoners; but Heywood loved physical facts and reasoned upon them. Cathcart reasoned more deeply upon relations of facts and upon more subtle philosophies. As was natural, Heywood loved to reason upon the actions of men, the events of society. Cathcart inclined to the study of the causes of events, the nature of the mind and the structure of society. . . . Heywood's conscience developed in the form of Honor. Cathcart's moral sense had been trained as a deep, reflective, religious feeling rather than as a social element.

And of course it followed that their religious natures and their attitudes toward the Protestant ethic were very different:

> Heywood did right as in the sight of men; Cathcart as in the sight of God. . . . Heywood had been reared in affluence and had never learned to work nor to have sympathy with those who did. Barton Cathcart had been inured from childhood to toil and was drawn by vital sympathy to all who labored. The Virginian was born to command. He had looked down upon men from the necessity of his social position. . . . The New Englander had been reared in a true democracy, in which classes represented the relative forces of the actors, into which and out of which men passed at their pleasure and in which there were few leaders and no aristocracy except that which was conferred by the consent of all.

Beecher held to John Adams's view of the contrast between a natural and an artificial aristocracy: The true, natural aristocrat is a man who can command one vote besides his own. Yet strangely enough, the aristocrats of North and South have more in common than their sectional differences and personality conflicts might imply. While they end up on opposite sides of the war, Heywood and Cathcart become close friends in Norwood. Beecher was clearly well along the road to reunion by 1867.

Nevertheless, Beecher, throughout his comparison of the two men, obviously gives the Northerner the advantage. The Southerner appears superficial and flighty compared to the deep-natured, persevering Northerner. Yet if Heywood is a Jeffersonian aristocrat, his Episcopalianism is not quite so deistic as Jefferson's, just as Cathcart's Congregationalism is less Unitarian than Adams's:

> Reared an Episcopalian, Heywood regarded religious truths as something settled beyond all questioning—worked out and fixed as definitely as are the elements of mathematics. He had never searched the grounds of truth. The [Episcopal] church he believed to have been shaped

> and patterned by God as much as the natural world was. He would as soon have thought of discussing the authenticity of heat or the propriety of frost as of the services of the church.[38]

Cathcart, as we have seen, has been taught to reason religion through for himself. Yet since the two men argue only over the institutional aspects of religion, they see no significant differences that Christian love and brotherhood cannot overcome.

Where the two men really differ is in those temperamental qualities so central for the Victorian mind—earnestness and levity. Nothing "seemed half so strange" to Cathcart as "Heywood's utter levity regarding human life and society. From his childhood Barton had looked with the deepest solemnity upon man's duty to his fellows. Society did not seem to him, as it nearly did to Heywood, a contrivance for his pleasure and aggrandizement. On the contrary, he was oppressed with a sense of duty to society which tasked him and after his utmost industry still chastized him for negligence." In short, Cathcart knew the importance of being earnest and Heywood did not. If Heywood preferred the easy life to the morally responsible life in times of peace, however, there was no doubt of his earnestness and sense of duty when the war came.

On the issue of slavery, which Beecher fails to discuss at all in the novel, he notes only that the two men disagreed so strongly about it that out of mutual respect and considerations of hospitality they agreed not to discuss it. On this score social courtesy overcomes Northern earnestness—an important omen for Reconstruction.

Heywood's failure to win the hand of Rose Wentworth, like the South's failure to win the war, is intended as proof that the Southern character, institutions, and values were somehow inferior to those of the North. The reader never shares Barton's fear (though he is supposed to) that Rose might choose Heywood, even when Beecher tries to make the Southerner seem to be winning the war of love. Yet though Rose is too deep and noble to accept Heywood's offer of marriage, she never loses her respect for him, and she deeply sympathizes with Barton's sister Alice, who does love Heywood, only to lose him in the war. There may be hidden symbolism in the fact that Rose, Alice, and Agate Bissell all try in an army hospital to nurse Heywood's wounded brother, also in the Confederate Army, back to life and health.

Concerning the war itself, Beecher made a stab at trying to explain the conflicting attitudes within the South by giving the reader an inside view in a conversation between Heywood and Governor Pickens of South Carolina on the eve of the firing on Sumter. Pickens divides Southern opinion into three groups: "First are the old politicians who do not want secession and threaten it only to secure for the South further concessions which shall prolong its political ascendency." Pickens has no use for such pretense. "Next is the great middle class, containing the active young men and most of the families of wealth," who not only threaten but "welcome" secession, "but with a distinct understanding among themselves that it is the shortest road to a reconstructed Union." Pickens considers these people old-fashioned, because they hold to "the antiquated superstition of a single Nation." He admits that the reconstructed Union would be dominated by the South and would never be able to include New England: "New England which has been the firebrand of the continent may smoulder and go to ashes among her rocks. We will have none of her. . . ." But even so, such a nation would never succeed in maintaining itself. So Pickens sides with the third group, "the only one that has a clear and distinct plan and principle"—a separate Southern nation: "We mean to establish a Southern Confederacy confined if possible to latitudes in which Slavery can profitably exist." It is this group which takes the lead in forcing the war by firing upon Fort Sumter.[39]

Hidden in here is Beecher's own view in 1860 that the Southern states should have been allowed to secede in peace.[40] There is a strange statement by Dr. Wentworth on the eve of the war in which he seems to accept the view that the United States cannot increase its size indefinitely—that it must someday allow certain sections of the country to separate from it peacefully because they cannot be governed from Washington.

It is worth quoting this passage in order to indicate Beecher's, and perhaps the nation's, bad conscience in 1867 over the punishment inflicted upon the South. It may also be indicative of the recognition that the victory on the battlefield had not solved the problem of sectionalism but merely created more complex problems—even though, on its face, the statement tries to lay all the blame upon rash and hasty Southern leaders like Governor Pickens and Colonel Beauregard for forcing a confrontation and war instead of letting their section drop off the branch of nationhood like a ripe fruit in due time. Musing on the firing upon Fort Sumter, Wentworth reflects that

> My judgment has long told me that a conflict of arms must grow out of such radical conflict of principles. But my feelings of hopefulness constantly set aside my political logic and like others I did not expect bloodshed. For thirty years, it is now apparent that the two great halves of this nation were deepening into radically antagonistic convictions—not about politics, in its common sense, but upon the whole question of humanity which underlies and finally controls states, churches, philosophy and religion itself.

> The only hope was in localizing these influences and keeping them apart. That could have been done had there not been a central government which both parts strove to appreciate and control. We now see that the Federal Government had little power to control, and much to divide, the nation. That will always be the weak place in our nation. The prodigious power which is generated in wide-lying States, absolutely independent and sovereign except in a few arbitrary and artificial arrangements, cannot be controlled by the Federal Government except by such an increase of its power as would prove fatal to local liberty.[41]

This part of Wentworth's statement almost seems a throwback to the mood of New England in the early years of the century, when the Federalist Party opposed the Louisiana Purchase out of fear that the nation was expanding too rapidly to maintain order and civilization. But at the same time Wentworth's views also reflect a perennial American fear of a large, bureaucratic, overwhelmingly powerful central government in Washington which would be necessary to hold such a large nation together. Beecher's concept of good government, like that of New England since its beginning, had been one of town-meeting democracy, a nation run by the common people from the grass roots.

The Civil War had posed the dilemma in new and startling terms. It was one thing to rally 'round the flag, to make sacrifices and choose leaders to defend the Union from attack; it was quite a different matter, when peace had returned, to unite upon a policy of reconstruction administered by an army of occupation and by a central bureaucracy in Washington that might, in the long run, accrue so much power and be so oppressive of states' rights and local self-government as to undermine completely democracy as Beecher conceived it. In addition, peace brought with it the awareness that the nation now extended from coast to coast and contained far more factions and diverse interests than were represented in North and South, New England and Virginia, Cathcart and Heywood. And, as Wentworth notes, the South had set a frightening precedent:

> It is slavery today. The next time it may be a commercial influence. But whatever it is, it must be some unifying influence which, like slavery, has educated the community to diverse strange and unnational customs, morals, political principles and civic feelings that can secretly organize such a body of States together as to frame a formidable rebellion.

The conspiratorial view of history so deeply embedded in the American psyche (Richard Hofstadter has called it "the paranoid style in American politics") could not help projecting future possibilities of the same kind: the secret organization of states and interest groups to subvert the nation. Beecher, looking at the problem in pre-Civil War terms of establishing national institutions to keep the country from disintegrating, now recognized how easy it might be for "diverse strange and unnational customs, morals, political principles and civil feelings" to arise in other parts of the country—the new Southwest, the mountain states, the Great Salt Lake basin (where the Mormons had set up a semi-independent government), the middle border, California, the Northwest, the prairie region. Perhaps the task of holding all these sections together and still maintaining town-meeting, grass-roots democracy controlled by the common people was impossible, and the Federalist Party had been right after all:

> Because men now are seeking to pluck the unripe fruit of separation and new nationality, it does not follow that

> in coming times the ripe fruit may not drop of itself without opposition and be gathered up cheerfully and willingly. States will hardly be allowed to draw off because they differ. That will make them enemies. But if they are agreed and divide in some future day simply because the vast bulk of such an Empire of states is too great to be conveniently grouped in one Federal Government, there might be less resistance. Now the tendency is toward unity. That may expend itself. The next tide may be to variety.

Was Beecher hinting in these remarks of Dr. Wentworth's that what the South had lost by force of arms it might yet obtain by national goodwill? Did he foresee that the course of empire might soon advance beyond the West Coast and out into the reaches of the Pacific? Was he suggesting the possibility of an American Commonwealth of Nations? Or was this merely a momentary loss of nerve caused by his own and the nation's inability to unite upon a plan for the re-entry of the seceded states?

However doubtful Beecher may have been about these prospects, he left no doubt in *Norwood* that the war itself was "a Divine decree" and the defeat of the South ordained by God. Beecher was convinced that the Civil War was an irrepressible conflict. "The differences were radical" between the two sections and had to be "brought into conflict," even a conflict where "one must destroy the other." The North and South were "brought into conflict by a course of events which moved with such breadth and power as to give all the signs that it was impelled by a Divine decree."[42] "Uncontrollable events that were working out their own career and would not suffer men to restrain them" were to blame. It was a Providential event in the progress of the nation and of mankind.

As might be expected, when matters at last came to a

head, the staying power of the Northern Cathcarts eventually won out over the flashy but short-winded Southern Heywoods. Beecher occasionally remarked in the novel that while the war was fought for the principle of freedom, its primary cause was "national honor"—to save the Union, not to free the slave. Like so many of the Northern intellectuals George Frederickson has described, Beecher was caught up during the war in the strident nationalism and statism it evoked. In *Norwood* the leaders of the Union are men of high moral character and nobility, the patricians of old New England ancestry like Arthur Wentworth, Rose's brother and high-minded farmers' sons like Barton Cathcart. And, like Francis Parkman, Beecher saw the war as purging America of its materialism and selfishness.[43] "Before men had seemed swallowed up in material interest and dead to heroic sentiments." But then "the trumpet sounded the resurrection" of national honor and morality, and "in an instant they came forth into a life of heroic sentiment and placing honor, duty, and patriotism high above all sordid interest they offered up to their country their ease, their wealth, and life itself." The war spirit "was kindled not by the young but by the old and sage as well. It was fed not by the ignorant and violent but by women, scholars, Christians." It was as pure and holy as motherhood and the Church. "The recruiting ground was not in low and dark corners, among the ignorant and roving," as in the conscript armies of Europe. This was a citizen's army fighting for its own rights and ideals. Beecher even notes, indirectly, the unwillingness of the Irish workingmen to fight, for he states that the most ardent soldiers were volunteers not "chiefly among laboring men, but preeminently in academies and colleges, in Sabbath schools and churches"—the Union Army was a Protestant, evangelical host. And its cause was not a desire for conquest or gain but "an enthusiasm for an abstract sentiment, an invisible quality of patriotism—for law, for liberty, for government."[44]

Yet these high principles, even patriotism, have a decidedly sectional quality for Beecher. The war is a battle between the sections which Heywood and Cathcart respectively symbolize:

> This was a battle between the men of the tropics and the men of the temperate zones. It was to be decided whether the gods of the valleys or the gods of the hills were mightier. The far Southern soils, tilled by enforced labor, made war on the rocks of the North, where men by hard labor had learned patience and skill. Two battles there were waged in one. Principles were contending in the air while men were fighting on the ground.[45]

The Battle of Gettysburg "was not only the defeat of the army [of Virginia] but far more of the political economy, the genius of government, and the evil spirit of a perverted religion that had inspired the conflict and given moral significance to the Rebellion."[46]

In short, there were two ways of life at stake; but whether the issue of forced labor was more important for Beecher than that of patriotism or of "perverted religion" may be doubted. Sometimes the Protestant ethic of hard work seems to become the most fundamental concern. Beecher does say in the novel that he respects the South's attempt to build a new nation, but he disagrees with its methods:

> Pity it is that admiration for the uprising of millions of men to found a new State should be stripped of its sublimity by the debasing conceptions of the new civilization which blinded its leaders. Yet our moral disapprobation of the secret and potential causes which were at work need not withhold from the common people the credit

> of the most earnest sincerity, witnessed by offering up all that man holds dear for the cause which they had been misled to believe was the cause of liberty and honor.[47]

Here is the typical American attitude toward all those defeated in our wars: sympathy for the "misled" common people and hatred for those who misled them. True, the theory of a misled people hardly squares with Beecher's claim that the whole basis of Southern civilization and religion was perverted. But, in any event, God had decreed the war, and out of its horrors He brought forth a new and more perfect union. Those who entered the war did not see, could not see, "the new heavens and the new earth that followed the convulsions of the old, a nobler liberty, a purer justice, a better friendship, a more lasting brotherhood."[48]

The "more lasting brotherhood" between North and South was naturally the brotherhood of the whites on both sides. Beecher did not trouble himself in this novel with the fate of the freedmen. The important question in 1867 was to bind up the wounds between white brothers. As Beecher put it, when peace came,

> In every generous [Northern] bosom rose the thought, 'These are not of another nation but our citizens.' Their mistakes, their evil cause [rebellion, not slavery] belonged to the system under which they were reared [not to the leaders who misled them?], but their military skill and heroic bravery belong to the nation that will never cease to mourn that such valor had not been expended in a better cause. . . .[49]

There is one final statement by Beecher regarding the war which deserves mention. I have said that Beecher's novel was essentially a forward-looking one: It looks to that new day when the age of Victorian doubt and anxiety will give birth to a new faith and assurance of truth, a new unity of national purpose, a new sense of God's mission for the Anglo-Saxon race. As Walter Houghton has said, the Mid-Victorians were basically optimistic, they believed in progress, they assumed that eventually a new era of peace and utopian happiness would dawn.[50] The American Mid-Victorians for and to whom Beecher spoke had more than their share of that "will to believe." But in *Norwood* the millennial faith which emerges is not based upon science and scientific inventions. Rather it consisted, as Houghton says it consisted in England, of "a faith in progress as a law of the universe, a world-process which must occur regardless of human affairs." Beecher, like many other Victorians, derived this faith from Herbert Spencer, and it was later confirmed by Darwin—though what is surprising is that Beecher, the Christian evolutionist, should so often sound almost as naturalistic about progress as these agnostics.

The problem of progress, however, became more stark for Americans during the war. How could they square their conceptions of God's benevolence and America's pursuit of happiness with the horrors of violence, carnage, and death which the war heaped up? Science and the efficiency of the Sanitary Commission offered at least some alleviation of the difficulty. In praising the volunteer war work of those who aided the commission, Beecher displayed his usual elitism: "They came from every position in society, yet to the honor of true culture be it said, that women from circles of wealth and refinement led in this merciful crusade."[51] Beecher demonstrates how the dedication of nurses like Agate Bissell, Rose Wentworth, and Alice Cathcart brought order, efficiency, skill, and love to those whom the war had shattered in mind, body, and spirit.

While he is vivid in rendering the horrors of battle, he is equally concerned to demonstrate the skill with which these wounds were bound up.

For example, Rose Wentworth, who has been given some medical instruction by her father, is described as finishing off the amputation of a soldier's leg when the surgeon she is assisting on the field during the Battle of Antietam is killed: "The patient was left bleeding. Seized with inspiration, Rose without an instant's hesitation, put her hand to the saw, completed the severing, tied the arteries, joined the flaps, and bound up the wound. The man recovered."[52] There was nothing namby-pamby about Beecher's heroines.

But what of those who did not recover—those left to die on the battlefield or remain crippled through life? George Frederickson has noted the varied rationalizations Americans made to solve this problem.[53] Beecher was too much a Christian to adopt the survival-of-the-fittest theory accepted by some. Nor could he adopt the pantheistic answer that the horrors were unreal and death was simply a reunion with the Oversoul and immortality. Neither did he agree entirely with the view that Divine Providence had willed it and we must accept the doings of that mysterious will on faith, without questioning. His ultimate explanation lies much closer to what Frederickson calls the Hegelian viewpoint epitomized in Walt Whitman's *Chanting the Square Deific*. "Hegelianism," says Frederickson, "represented one avenue of consent to the pain and death of the moment on the theory that it contributed to a cosmic whole." This contrasts with the Providential-consent doctrine epitomized in Julia Ward Howe's *Battle Hymn of the Republic*—that God was executing judgment on America with "His terrible swift sword" so that His truth could go marching on. Beecher relied less upon the beauty of the lilies in which Christ transfigured wrath into love than upon romantic naturalism, a cosmic force or "life force" of goodness implicit in Nature itself.

His view bears comparison to that of Frank Norris in his trilogy on wheat—as witness the closing lines to *The Octopus*:

> Greed, cruelty, selfishness, and inhumanity are short-lived; the individual suffers, but the race goes on. Annixter dies, but in a far-distant corner of the world a thousand lives are saved. The larger view always and through all shams, all wickednesses, discovers the Truth that will in the end prevail, and all things surely, inevitably, resistlessly work together for good.

One might see this as pure naturalism or, given the earlier reference by Norris to the "Nirvanic calm" of the wheat, as pantheistic or even as Emerson's transcendental conception of "Compensation," if he did not recall that the text embedded in this final paragraph is from the Bible: "The Truth is great and will prevail." It is this mixture of romantic naturalism and Christian transcendentalism that Beecher adopts in his peroration on the Battle of Gettysburg in *Norwood*. It might properly be called the Gettysburg Address of Liberal Protestantism, and despite its length it must be quoted in full in order to comprehend the mood Beecher is trying to convey:

> There are no contrasts more striking than those between human feelings and the moods of the atmosphere. On this fourth day of July [the morning after the battle] a joyous sun arose over the most sorrowful scene it could well look upon. Three days had converted a peaceful valley into a Golgotha. No form of injury which the human body can receive was wanting. The ingenuity of nature in the production of life is not greater than the ingenuity of death in the destruction of life. Leaves and flowers are not more varied in form than were the wounds.

> From the crown of the head to the sole of the feet, there was not a point of the human body which had not been pierced. The wildest caprice had revelled in singularities of effects. Men received a mere scratch of a glancing ball, and the shock overthrew their nervous system. Another, with wounds on every limb, the lung pierced, bones broken, the head torn, trampled on by men, run over by artillery, stabbed, shot, hacked, bruised, given up by surgeons, still clung to life and climbed back again to health.
>
> The fields bore ghastly harvests of suffering men. The sun came up and shined upon them as if they were but heads of wheat. Their tremblings and shrinkings were to nature only as the quivering of leaves in the frolicsome wind; their groans and sighs passed for no more than the singing of the birds or the low moaning of the pines. . . . What mockery of grief was it, as the mother sat down by the corpse of her only son, that the heavens cared not, that it spread its brilliant arch without sympathy for aught below, and that the heartless sun marched on over anguish, desolation and despair, as if this had been not a battle but a banquet.[54]

Had Beecher stopped here, his argument would have seemed to embody more the amoral naturalism of Zola than the romantic naturalism of Norris. But he went on to evoke a God above Nature:

> Could a pitiful God look down through the air on such a scene and not fill it with his sympathy, and change it to a somber hue? Alas! This great field of war was but a point, a mere punctuation mark of blood in the history of the world which groans and travails in pain until now. As the mid-wife in the throes and groans of the Mother, heeds not the pain but waits for the child that shall bring joy out of woe, so we must needs think the Merciful [God] heeds not the forms of suffering but looks beyond

> at the blessing wrought by them. When, at last, account shall be taken of all the blood that has been shed and of all the tears that have fallen, then the most wonderful name of God will be, THE LONG SUFFERING. And God has taught the Sun to see beyond and through the beginnings of things to their ends.

This moves us from naturalism to the Providential view. But Beecher is not yet done. What is it that God and the Sun "see beyond" to justify this long suffering? Beecher had no intention of leaving that mystery unplumbed:

> For the sun forever sees life and not death. It beholds in the revolution of the sod, not the roots that die but the harvests which shall spring from their death. Death is but the prophet of life. The evil is but for a moment. The benefit runs through the whole season. What if twenty thousand wounded men lie groaning here? It is the price of the nation's life. The instruments of their conflict were carnal, but its fruits spiritual.

The argument has now been pushed forward to embrace the doctrine of Hegelian nationalism: The individual is nothing; the development of the state is all. Yet Beecher continues:

> War ploughed the fields of Gettysburg and planted its furrows with men. But though the seed was blood, the harvest shall be peace, concord, and universal intelligence.

Here at last is the key: "Universal intelligence" is more than the good of one nation—it is the good of all mankind:

> For every groan here, a hundred elsewhere ceased. For every death now, a thousand lives shall be happier. Individuals suffered; the nation revived.
>
> Shine on, O, Sun, that beholdest evermore the future. Thou wilt not, glorious Eye of Hope—ever looking at the

> ends—be veiled or mourn because the ways are rough through which God sends universal blessings!

The Truth shall prevail throughout the universe. Those who gave their lives at Gettysburg did not die in vain. Not only will the nation survive and spread the blessing of liberty to the world, but also the resurrection of the torn Union is the beginning of the climactic phase of the spiritual redemption of mankind. God is not only looking down from on high, He is working out His will in human history.

CHAPTER TEN

White Supremacy and Anglo-Saxon Destiny

I regard the African race as destined to a future—if not such a one as belongs to the European races, yet one that shall be signal for its own light and its own glory.
—HENRY WARD BEECHER, 1863

The key to Henry Ward Beecher's and Mid-Victorian America's whole approach to slavery and the meaning of emancipation lies in the pervasive and unquestioned belief in white supremacy: Every nation and race, of course, had its own destiny, accordingly as God had endowed it, and all men in brotherhood should help each other to develop their talents to the fullest; but the white, Anglo-Saxon race as it had developed in England and America was by nature, experience, and innate capacity destined to lead them all. Beecher spoke for the majority of Northern white Americans who were willing to grant a minimum of political freedom to the slaves because they felt that such a backward, childish, irresponsible race would never be serious competitors to the Anglo-Saxons. He also spoke for that same body of whites who were willing to be generous in their treatment of the South after the war because they believed that Southern whites were merely misguided or misled. The sooner they were readmitted to the Union, the better off the Union would be and the better off the freedmen would be.

At first, there was some controversy over the issue of readmitting the Southern states and their people to full citizenship; but Beecher, and subsequently his friendly biographers, claimed that the speedy reunion he advocated in 1865 was afterward generally acknowledged to have been the best solution, though it was not heeded then. Beecher explained his ideas on reconstruction in a sermon on October 29, 1865, before President Andrew Johnson had yet made his own views clear—and thereby antagonized a large segment of the Northern public who were not so generous as he and Beecher wished to be. Entitled "Conditions of a Restored Union," Beecher's address flatly argued for the speedy readmission of the Southern states as best for them, best for the freedmen, best for the Union. He denied that the South was especially reprehensible and the North especially praiseworthy:

> It was not because we were by nature more virtuous than the people of the South; but we were under the influence of great organic laws that were inciting us to conduct which was wiser and better than we individually knew or purposed. . . . And they of the South, on the other hand, were unconsciously under the influence of great organic laws which sprang from radically vicious institutions.[1]

The war had been a battle between two ways of life, one good and one bad, but both greater as forces than the people who lived under them. Yet it is important to note that neither here nor anywhere else did Beecher express the Manichean view that the "radically vicious institutions" of the South had been designed and led by the Devil. The South had been, instead, in the grip of "great organic laws" growing out of its own moral blindness and weakness. Consequently the victory had not been due to the valor or moral virtue of the Northern armies so much as to the immanent wisdom of God, who guided the operation of the organic laws of the universe so as to educate and uplift mankind.

Beecher took this semideterministic line toward the war (now that it was over) partly because he had always argued that the world operated under divinely directed natural laws and partly to deflate those self-righteous Northerners who believed that the South must be humbled for its sins:

> It is said that there should be a spirit of humility on the part of the South, that there should be the appearance of their having been convinced of the error of their ways, before we receive them back. It is said that God does not receive sinners back till they are humbled.[2]

But Beecher did not want the North to play God, and so he denied it the credit for its victory. It was part of his own personality to want everyone to love him; he therefore wanted God to love everyone and he wanted to play himself that kind of loving, nurturant role as a minister of God.

In some ways his sentiments were admirable. He did not desire to see Southerners humbled any more than they already had been by death, destruction, and defeat: "I think it to be the great need of this nation to save the self-respect of the South." Anticipating the views of later generations, he assailed those who were attacking Robert E. Lee and demanding his resignation from the presidency of Washington College in Virginia on the grounds that traitors were unfit to be college presidents. Beecher did not condone

Lee's fighting against the Union, but he defended him for following his conscience; moreover, "when the war ceased and he laid down his arms, who could have been more modest, more manly, more true to his own word and honor than he was?"[3] Lee should not be removed, nor should Southerners be required to take loyalty oaths swearing that they no longer held any of the ideas they had held before 1860. Men's ideas cannot be changed that way:

> Let men say that secession *ought* to have been allowed—if they accept the fact that it *is forever disallowed* by the people of this continent. A man who believed in Calhoun's theories and still believes in them may be a good citizen. . . . These theories, if let alone, will die out. The age and the country is against them. The course of events refute them.

As usual, Beecher was too sanguine. The Lost Cause has still not died out, and the beliefs of Calhoun—those regarding Negro inferiority if not those of the concurrent majority—are as powerful today in many minds as they ever were. Beecher did, it is true, recognize that the position of the freedmen lay at the heart of the problem of reconstruction. But he took too simplistic a view when he asserted that "The only cause of antagonism was slavery; and now that slavery is destroyed there is no ground for conflict."[4] (This was not in fact what he had said during the war.) He admitted later in his sermon that there was much more to it than that when he faced up to the question of granting equality to the freedmen: The Negro should have the right to vote; he should have the right to own property, to exercise legal rights in the courts, to labor when and where he pleased. But "declaring the colored man's right to citizenship in this country does not make him your equal socially. . . . Do you suppose that the Irishman who has just landed on our shores, who becomes a citizen, but to whom our ideas are foreign, instantly becomes our equal in a social point of view?" The moment a man becomes a citizen, "do I rush into his arms and beg him to become my son-in-law . . . ?" The thought was absurd. "I have never seen the time when I desired black people and white people to intermarry."[5]

Thus, granting certain basic political rights to Negroes did not make them the social equals of whites, any more than granting these rights to Celtic Irishmen made them the equals of Anglo-Saxons. Beecher made it clear several months later why he felt Negroes were not socially equal, and in so doing, he virtually cut the ground out from under his own earlier assertion that the suffrage was an inalienable natural right:

> Civilization is a growth. None can escape that forty years in the wilderness who travel from the Egypt of ignorance to the promised land of civilization. The freedmen must take their march. I have full faith in the results. If they have the stamina to undergo hardships which every uncivilized people has undergone in its upward progress, they will, in due time, take their place among us.[6]

What their "place" was, and how long "in due time" was, he did not say. But he remained convinced that the freedmen would be far better off under their old masters—even if the latter still held to Calhoun's theories—than under the protection of an army of occupation or with any other governmental assistance. Negroes, though eons behind in the march of civilization, were going to have to rise to the level of the white race through their own efforts. (No wonder Lyman Abbott, writing an encomiastic biography of Beecher in 1903, compared his stand to that of Booker T. Washington.[7])

Beecher's exposition of his racial views also helps to explain why he supported President Johnson's veto of the

Freedmen's Bureau and why the majority of Americans reacted so apathetically to the decisions of the U.S. Supreme Court in the 1880's which invalidated the Civil Rights Acts Congress had passed to protect the freedmen's rights after the army of occupation was withdrawn:

> We are to raise them in intelligence more and more until they shall be able to prove themselves worthy of citizenship. For I tell you all the laws in the world cannot bolster a man up so as to place him any higher than his own moral worth and natural forces put him.[8]

This sermon was delivered in October 1865, ten years before the second Civil Rights Act. But while he called upon the nation "to educate the Negroes and to Christianly educate them," he was not at all specific as to how this should be done. "I do not think it would be wise for the North to pour ministers and colporteurs and school masters into the South making a too marked distinction between the black people and the white. We ought to carry the Gospel and education to the whites and blacks alike."[9] That was as close as he came to a program to help the freedmen. Nothing so practical as Booker T. Washington's program of industrial and vocational training occurred to him. A Christian education trained a man in the basics of reading, writing, and arithmetic, and the rest of his way he made up the ladder of life by piety and hard work.

> And if the colored man is industrious and accumulates property and makes wise use of that property, you cannot long withhold from him his civil rights. We ought to demand universal suffrage, which is the foundation element of our American doctrine; yet I demand many things in theory which I do not at once expect to see realized in practice. I do not expect to see universal suffrage in the South; but if the Southern people will not agree to universal

suffrage, let it be understood that there shall be a property and educational qualification.[10]

This is where Beecher stood in 1865—favoring literacy tests and poll taxes imposed by former slaveholders as qualifications for voting; and that is where the freedmen stood for the next one hundred years.

In his march through the "wilderness" to "civilization" the figurative forty years did not represent a very helpful measurement for the Negro. Nor is it clear just how far up the human spiral Beecher thought he would ever be able to climb. In considering the "dark and mysterious" continent of Africa in 1863, he declared that he refused to accept the view of those who "despise the African people as a stock incapable of civilization." He refused to believe that God had made a "whole continent of people" unsusceptible to that "development and civilization which is the common property and lot of the whole human family." Nevertheless, his estimate was not optimistic: "I regard the African race as destined to a future—if not such a one as belongs to European races, yet one that shall be signal for its own light and its own glory."[11]

The best insight into Beecher's views of the Negro may be obtained in *Norwood.* Since the story takes place in New England, it offers no opportunity for a discussion of slavery; but it does have an important Negro character named Pete Sawmill, general handyman to the town and later, during the war, body-servant to General Barton Cathcart. Pete, it would appear, embodies the Negro character for Beecher, and on the basis of his description in the novel the future prospects of the Negro race seem dim indeed.

Despite what he undoubtedly considered an affectionate, sympathetic, even eulogistic portrait of Sawmill, Beecher's prejudices are all too patent. First of all, he is always referred to as "Pete." No one ever calls him by his last name, though the Yankee characters are very discriminating about how they are addressed. In the second place, he is six feet five inches tall—a man of prodigious, brute strength. He has acquired his last name, apparently, not only because he has worked in a sawmill but because he once succeeded in holding back the rotary blade in the mill with his hands even after the water power was turned on full force. Third, he is generally regarded as a ne'er-do-well, a man without a trade, unable or unwilling to work regularly because he lacks self-discipline. And fourth, he does not have the moral self-restraint to abstain from alcohol. Even if his color were not black, all of these things would be enough to damn him, given Beecher's criteria of "manhood."

But the less conscious aspects of Beecher's racism are far more striking. Thus, Beecher cannot refrain from comparing Pete Sawmill to an animal almost every time he is mentioned. Sometimes it is a bear or an ox to which he is likened, for his strength; but far more frequently it is a dog, the faithful servant of man. Pete "sidles up like a puppy"; he points with his "muzzle . . . like a hound"; he is as "jolly as a dog," and he generally expects to be treated as a dog, that is, as a gentle, protective, faithful family pet. When he is not compared to an animal, he is referred to as like "an overgrown child"—he is irresponsible, nonintellectual, clumsy, foolish, outlandish, childish, unable to take care of himself or to reason adequately. In short, Pete Sawmill lacks all of the virtues of the Protestant ethic, all of the elements of a morally sensitive person.[12] He is the perfect foil for the hero and heroine, for they are at the top of the spiral of human life and he is at the bottom. Reviewers of the novel took Sawmill to be the village idiot or moron, but Beecher did not mean to portray him that way. He thought Sawmill represented the Negro as he was.

Sawmill is closer to the animal world than to the human; nonetheless, Beecher, with his transcendental view of Nature, does try to make something significant out of this. Sawmill seems in some passages to be portrayed as a noble savage, a child of Nature unspoiled by civilization and hence closer to the supernatural in Nature than some civilized men. He is a kind of black Natty Bumppo or Chingachgook. Dr. Wentworth trusts Sawmill to know all about the best places to find wild berries, the location of the spring's first wild flowers, the habits of birds and bees. Agate Bissell considers him a "half-witted nigger" and cannot understand why the doctor entrusts his daughter to Sawmill's care and lets him take her on walks in the woods. But Beecher specifically repudiates Agate's opinion in a statement by Hiram Beers: "The Doctor thinks Pete is a true child of Nature."[13] Pete knows how to handle an axe (though he is never given a gun); he is an expert at spear fishing; he is the best butcher in town, and an unequaled gardener: "Everything lives that he puts out" in the garden. He has a sixth sense in dealing with animals, especially horses, and this gives him a high station in Beecher's eyes. His uncanny knowledge of how to deal with animals, wild and domestic, is explained by one Yankee character: "Pete hain't growed away from natur' so far but what he knows what's goin' on in beasts and birds."[14]

Pete Sawmill is given several heroic acts to perform in the service of his employers which allow him to display his physical prowess and natural resourcefulness (he is far more at home in the woods than the higher types). It is Pete, ironically, who rescues the Southerner, Heywood, when he slips from a cliff, and it is he who finds the best way to carry the injured man through difficult terrain back to the wagon road. He helps Barton Cathcart escape from Confederate guards when he is captured, and he shows the same resourcefulness in getting the wounded Barton to safety. For all of these acts he is duly admired and loved by the hero and heroine. He never tries to rise above his place: "he don't take on airs." He is happy, like a faithful pet, simply to be near his master and mistress. And their love for him, at this level, is portrayed as deep and sincere. In one of the more unintentionally ludicrous scenes in the book, Beecher describes in all seriousness how General Cathcart requests his bride to permit his warhorse to attend the wedding (under the old elm in the garden). Of course, faithful Pete and faithful horse stand together throughout the ceremony.

However, a close reading of the passages dealing with Pete Sawmill's relationship to Nature reveals that Beecher's approach is something less than that of James Fenimore Cooper and more like that of Jack London. Pete's rapport with Nature and its creatures does not stem from any innate moral sense or sensibility but from an atavistic animalism. He is close to Nature because he has only recently emerged from Nature. Beecher calls him "an undeveloped man," meaning that he is still part animal. Like "Buck" in *The Call of the Wild*, he has a veneer of civilization and a sense of submission to his master and his master's children; but underneath he still belongs to the wild.

Beecher constantly describes Sawmill as having a "venatorial instinct," meaning that his instincts in hunting are almost as alert and sensitive as those of an animal. In one of the first descriptions of him Beecher sounds the note that London and the red-blooded school of literary naturalists were to make so famous at the turn of the century. Sawmill is walking through the woods carrying young

Rose Wentworth, a child of five or six, on his huge shoulders:

> Blindly along his nerves crept something of the atmospheric influences, stirring, it is probable, no such nascent poetic influences as thrilled the charming little nosegay of a child on his shoulder, but which in him were developed in ways of which Rose was quite unconscious. The venatorial instinct seems in undeveloped men to be the rude germ of that which in civilized men grows into scientific wisdom. Persons of fine organization, but without education, are often far more quick to discern and far more in sympathy with the instincts and habits of animals than wiser men are. There is a political economy of the woods and fields as well as of the cities and towns—an animal economy as well as a civic economy. Men utterly devoid of the knowledge of property, production, wages, rents, and values of any kind, have a clear insight of squirrels, foxes, marmots, fish, and birds in all their varieties.[15]

The key phrase is "animal economy." Sawmill is not part of the human economy of civilized men. The gap on the spiral between the highly developed Rose, with her poetic moral sensitivity to Nature's spiritual "influences," and the undeveloped Sawmill, with his "instinctive" sensitivity to Nature's animalistic influences, is far wider than the gap between Sawmill and the marmots. His "fine organization" consists in his physical health and strength. His intellect and moral sense are quite "penurious." There is no hope that he will ever be able to improve these, no suggestion that education would be anything but a waste of effort. Rose, though young, has "nascent" endowments which Christian nurture and a luxurious home environment will refine to near-perfection. She has the moral strength of will and intellect to develop self-control through self-improvement. Pete Sawmill, who both literally and figuratively spends much of his time "on all fours," will always remain a near-animal.

The contrast between Pete Sawmill and Rose Wentworth is more than that between beauty and the beast. It is a contrast embodied in Beecher's conception of racial "stock" and in his theory of education and moral training. Sawmill is given no education or moral training because he has no capacity for it. He cannot speak intelligibly; he apparently has not learned to read or write (and Rose does not try to teach him), and he is incapable of even understanding what the Civil War is all about. Yet Sawmill is by all odds the most superior black man portrayed in the novel. Beecher makes a large concession when at the conclusion of the novel he describes how Rose, with tears in her eyes, persuades Sawmill to take the total-abstinence pledge to touch no more liquor. But even this is an act of devotion, undertaken more out of love for his mistress than out of any growth of moral character or self-discipline.

The insidious aspect of Beecher's theory of education becomes evident here. The training lavished with such care upon Rose Wentworth would be useless for less gifted children, black or white. As a counterweight to the prevailing rigidity of educational theory in his day, Beecher's approach was undoubtedly a liberating force. He had himself suffered excruciatingly from the religious severity of his father and the narrow rote-learning of the Boston Latin School, Mount Pleasant Academy, and Amherst College. His own sensitive nature had, he felt, been almost crushed under the heavy tasks of dry pedantry and speculative philosophy, and he fought to free others as sensitive as himself from such torments. Nevertheless, the point is clearly made in *Norwood* that a transcendental form of Christian nurture would be profitable only for the upper class; those in the middle are perfectly well off under the prevailing system, and the lower class is more or less beyond help—though institutions which instill good habits and instinctual reflexes of obedience, loyalty, and patriotism may still be of some value and are, in any event, the only hope. But education in any other sense is for the *aristoi* only.

Obviously anyone with such deep-seated prejudice against Negroes was bound to have similar feelings toward other races and an exaggerated view of the supremacy of his own. It used to be common to see the rise of Anglo-Saxon racism as a product of the Gilded Age and the Social Darwinian views which came into prominence then. But William Stanton's *The Leopard's Spots*, Winthrop Jordan's *White Over Black*, and David B. Davis's *The Problem of Slavery in Western Culture* have disabused us of that notion. Beecher was expressing views of Anglo-Saxon superiority that went back long before the Civil War and long before he had read Herbert Spencer. The war and the crisis over emancipation merely reinforced his position on race, since they forced him to formulate more clearly the principles at stake in the war. The significant fact is that he found it as easy to reject "natural right" principles as any slaveholder when faced with the question of accepting the Negro as an equal.

He did of course insist that, as a Christian, he firmly believed in the Fatherhood of God and the brotherhood of man: "The spirit and the letter of Christianity require us habitually to regard man in his essentials and not in his accidental relations," he wrote in the 1850's. "They too are our brethren who are undeveloped, unpolished; who perform the menial offices of life; who live narrowly upon slender means."[16] The "spirit of missions" represented one example of Christian brotherhood. But how did he describe this? Only so as to exalt the white men who brought Christian culture to their inferiors: "The attempt of Christian nations, at a vast expense and with great trouble, to civilize poor, miserable barbarians, has been itself a testimony to the worth of poor miserable barbarians."[17] He even purported as a Christian not to "distinguish men one from another merely by the difference of their thought-power. . . . The point where true manhood resides is in the neighborhood of love."[18] But just what social obligations did this put upon a Christian, other than to be fair and kind to all men in their "accidental" stations? It certainly did not require social equality—and it scarcely required much humanitarianism.

Consider, for example, his comparison of the Indian to the Negro, which indicates that for white supremacists there were depths even beneath depths. He was astonished, he said in 1865, to read that some member of the President's Cabinet had seriously proposed shipping all the freedmen back to Africa:

> Now you may carry vagrant Indians from one place to another. They are venatorial in their habits. They are not agricultural. Nor have they such social connections as the colored people have in the South. It is possible to put Indian tribes on a certain territory and keep them there. But the African is entirely different. . . . They do not live in tribes or communities by themselves. They clasp the white people. They like to live in white families.[19]

When Beecher wished to make his congregation feel guilty about America's inhumanity to man, he was, to be sure, willing to put before them the case of the Indian:

> Every crime in the calendar of wrong which a strong people can commit against a weak one has been committed against them [the Indians]. We have wasted their substance; we have provoked their hostility and then chas-

> tised them for their wars; we have compelled them to peace ignominiously; we have formed treaties with them only to be broken; we have filched their possessions. . . . A heathen people have experienced at the hands of a Christian nation almost every evil which one people can commit against another.[20]

But the point, in the end, is not a plea of humanitarian concern for the Indian; it is a spiritual rebuke to the Christians for their sins:

> Admit the laws of race; admit the laws of advancing civilization as fatal to all barbarism; admit the indocility of the savage; admit the rude edges of violent men who form the pioneer advance of a great people and the intrinsic difficulties of managing a people whose notions and customs and laws are utterly different from our own, and then you have only explained how the evil has been done but you have not changed the fact or the guilt.

The concern is with guilt, and not with human justice or human rights.

Beecher has provided his congregation with all the excuses they need and asked them only to repent. (Repent, let it be noted, not so much for their own deeds as for the wickedness of rough frontier people and thoughtless Washington officials.) There is no word in this sermon about making any restitution to the Indians or taking any political action to right the many wrongs still being practiced against them. It is all turned inward. The rhetoric of Christian love and brotherhood was a fearsome thing on the lips of such a man. But Americans loved him for exposing their guilt and at the same time silently taking its weight off of them. To externalize it, to understand it, was to forgive it. Especially since the cause of the Indian was hopeless anyway—and likewise for the Mexicans, who "have felt the same rude foot."

More could be said in Beecher's favor in regard to his willingness to accept the national guilt for these crimes had he not devoted far more breath to expatiating on the glories of the Anglo-Saxon race that had committed them: "We boast of the Anglo-Saxon race; and if bone and muscle, an indomitable sense of personal liberty, and a disposition to do what we please are themes for Christian rejoicing, then the Anglo-Saxon may well rejoice."[21] And who can doubt that Beecher found liberty, bone and muscle, and the freedom to do as one pleased to be Christian and democratic virtues? Even if they were not, the fault lay in the "great organic laws," the natural laws of race, and not upon any individual: "There are sins that belong to races . . . the sins that I have enumerated are sins that belong to our stock." Well, if that were so, what could anyone do about it? It was as inevitable that the Anglo-Saxon should push the Indian, Mexican, and Negro around as it was that these races should be pushed around. So far had Beecher's Liberal Protestantism become trapped in its own doctrine of immanentism and natural law. Or rather, so far was it a product of its own cultural captivity.

That the Anglo-Saxon race was anything but an asset to the world and the nation was unthinkable. The Civil War itself could almost be blamed upon the African: "Our Constitution nourished twins. It carried Africa on its left bosom and Anglo-Saxony on its right bosom; and these two, drawing milk from the same bosom, have waxed strong and stand today federated into the one republic," he proclaimed on the eve of the war. "One side of the body politic [the North] has grown fair and healthy and strong; the other side [the South] has grown up as a wen grows and a wart, vast, but the vaster the weaker."[22] And so, naturally, the North was bound to win; but the Anglo-Saxony of the South was somehow not so much to blame as the

African race (and its concomitant, slavery) to which it was bound. (Or perhaps the blame, if any, fell on the framers of the Constitution for permitting Southern Anglo-Saxons to preserve slavery.)

It must be said for Beecher that he was so convinced that the Anglo-Saxons could, in the free climate of American democracy, compete and win against any race, that he saw no reason to exclude any group from entering the country. In opposing the exclusion of Chinese immigration in the 1880's, he showed more faith in his racial superiority than most of his fellow white supremacists, who feared that because Chinese could live on dogmeat and rats, they could live and work for less than American workingmen and thereby take their jobs away: "I am entirely opposed to collecting $100,000; $200,000; $300,000 every year and sending missionaries to China and then refusing to allow the Chinaman to come here and breathe our air."[23]

Beecher did not worry about the low subsistence level of foreign labor, because he believed that once the Chinese breathed American air, they would want to eat like Americans—they would give up dogmeat for beefsteak. What was more, any foreigner had only to be converted to Christianity and he would then be committed to the principles of the Protestant ethic. He rejoiced in the fact that "God has poured a mixed people upon this land. Races mingled together make a better population than consanguineous stocks." But he assumed, with his usual optimism, that America was not the world's dumping ground for other nations' sick, paupers, criminals, and social undesirables (which was the stock argument of immigration restrictionists). He assumed that those who left the Old World for the New were "too restless and enterprising to remain at home. . . . They whose young blood cannot walk the old paces and take the old stale customs. We take them as a tribute from every nation under the sun—the young, the earnest, the best blood, the motive power of the nation. Such blood mingled with ours, if educated and Christianized, will give stamina, variety, genius, and all the elements of national power and progress such as were never before brought together."[24] This was written sixteen years before the Statue of Liberty was dedicated in New York harbor with the poem of Emma Lazarus in its base, and it speaks with that spirit. Beecher did not preach, as the eugenicists (following Sir Francis Galton, Darwin's errant cousin) were soon to do, that mixing the blood of various races was certain to weaken or "mongrelize" the purer breed. But Beecher had his own purification process: The alien stocks must be Christianized and educated. And even then, of course, the better people would not really consider them social equals and allow their daughters to marry them.

During the war, when the Irish became extremely hostile toward Negroes and several Midwestern states were passing laws to prevent freedmen from coming north into their territories, Beecher preached against "Those in our midst who have lately fled from the oppression of crowns and sceptres—peasants of Europe who have come to this country that they might secure the rights of freemen—[who] are turning to crush those beneath them as they were crushed by their tyrannical lords. . . . The great State of Illinois has voted that no more black men shall come within her borders. . . . A party seems to be forming [against] the African."[25] Whether Beecher was sincerely concerned for the rights of the Negro or whether he feared the rise of a divisive factionalism in the nation is not clear. But it is interesting that in the next paragraph he went on to assure everyone concerned that equality for the Negro was not a significant political issue: "I do not say that the black man . . . shall walk in the same conditions that you do." What he seemed to fear was the reawakening of the spirit of "that most un-American Native-Americanism." And he found cause for rejoicing that in the war men of all nationalities had fought together in the Union Army. In his eyes that made them blood brothers in support of American democracy:

> The blood of the Yankee has met the blood of the Irishman. Right alongside of our Curtis was the noble Sigel. Right by the side of the wounded American lay the wounded German. Two tongues met when they spoke the common words, Country, Liberty, God, and Freedom. And now there is no foreign blood among us. They are ours. They have earned their birth here. . . . War with all its horrors is not without its incidental advantages.[26]

Yet at the same time, he loved to boast of his own ancestry: "I love every drop of Puritan blood that the world ever saw, because it seems to me that Puritan blood means blood touched with Christ's blood."[27] When the war came, it was "peculiarly gratifying" to him, "who [had] always believed in the essential, though latent, heroism of our Puritan stock and of the whole loyal population, to see this heroism developed, in spite of the charge which has been made against us abroad that we were a trafficking [commercial] people, without heroism, and incompetent to act for an idea."[28]

While on a visit to England during the war, Beecher constantly stressed the kinship of the English and the Americans; they were the nations destined to rule the world:

> . . . Never were mother and daughter set forth to do so queenly a thing in the kingdom of God's glory as England and America. . . .
>
> . . . the same blood is in us. We have the same mission amongst the nations of the earth. . . .

> . . . The day is coming when the foundations of the earth will be lifted out of their places and there are two nations that ought to be found shoulder to shoulder and hand in hand for the sake of Christianity and universal liberty and these nations are Great Britain and America. . . .
> . . . England and America together for religion and liberty are a match for the world. . . .[29]

Beecher seems to have fallen somewhere between the Anglo-Saxon racism of the 1890's at its worst and the genuine desire of the Jacksonians to welcome men of all nations on an equal footing. He was deeply convinced of the superiority of the Anglo-Saxon race, but he was equally convinced that the free spirit of America could assimilate any immigrant. He did insist upon the Christianization of the immigrant, but he did not seem to advocate racial purity. He opposed racial intermarriage as socially improper, but he believed in giving the basic rights of citizenship to all inhabitants. He talked a great deal about the inferior capabilities of lesser breeds, but he never spoke of the "mongrelization" of the Anglo-Saxon race.

He was saved from some of the worst aspects of racism in part by his commitment to Christian brotherhood and in part by his commitment to the American democratic faith. "My love of country," he said, "is next to my love of my God."[30] But all too often the two seemed to merge: "You are members of the great civil society," he told his congregation, "and no Christian minister that understands his duty in America can fail to indoctrinate his people in respect to their Christian duties as citizens. . . . You are bound, as a part of your fealty to Christ, to think also of national character, of national morals, and of national welfare."[31] Slavery was a national sin, and since the nation was in covenant with God, that sin was visited upon every individual, not just upon the slaveholder. Part of that covenant was America's mission to the world. Beecher and his audience were fully committed to the notion that America, with England's aid, was the big brother, the policeman, the schoolteacher to the world: "We are bound to take care of the world."[32]

However, the Civil War forced Beecher and his followers in the North to turn inward and to take a new look at what the nation meant. To the Founding Fathers, government was a rational experiment based upon certain self-evident propositions; it operated under fixed laws, was guided by reason, and bounded by a constitution. The Federalists and the Jeffersonians both saw the nation in these rationalistic terms—a nation of laws, not of men. But in the nineteenth century new conceptions of political theory produced a new kind of nationalism. Heinrich von Treitschke in Germany and John W. Burgess in America were leading theorists of the new approach. Its essence lay in the concept of a nation as the embodiment of a mystical folk spirit, of the inner being of the particular race of people who constituted it; in place of law, reason, constitutions, this new, organic nationalism placed its emphasis upon feelings, emotions, sentiments, instincts. In short, it was a romantic, irrational conception, not a rational one.

Beecher, being a romantic, fully endorsed this approach. Like most romantic nationalists, he focused upon the symbols and institutions, the myths and ideals, around which the mystique of nationhood was organized. Sometimes that symbol was the Constitution itself, spoken of in such highly rhetorical terms as Daniel Webster used; sometimes it was the concept of liberty, sometimes Anglo-Saxon destiny. But when the Confederate troops fired upon the American flag at Fort Sumter in April 1861, suddenly the flag became the paramount symbol of the nation; around it clustered national honor, national glory, national pride, national destiny. (And it was soon after the war that the pledge of allegiance to the flag became a mandatory part of all public education and formal occasions.)

During the course of the war Beecher delivered a sermon on "The National Flag" which embraced all these elements of the new nationalism. One paragraph will suffice:

> And now this banner has been put on trial! It has been condemned. For what? Has it failed of duty? Has liberty lost color by it? Has it refused to shine on freemen and given its light to despots? No! It has been true, brave, loyal. It has become too much a banner of liberty for men who mean and plot despotism. Remember, citizen! remember, Christian soldier! the American flag has been fired upon. . . .[33]

The "brave, true, loyal" flag was the personification of the corporate nation; to shoot at it was to wound the body politic. At this moment it became clear to Beecher that the institutions of New England Puritanism had been designed by God to prepare America for this great struggle as the ultimate test of whether or not the American people, and the Anglo-Saxon race as a whole, were worthy of the mission He had ordained for them. The war was "a testing time," a time of "national self-purification," and the preservation of the Union was "a mission." A Christian citizen, properly trained, responded automatically, instinctively to the call of his country, for he heard in it the call of God. His was not to reason why, his but to fight and, if need be, die. "Glory, glory, hallelujah! His Truth is marching on." And Christian soldiers marched on with the Stars and Stripes going on before.

EPILOGUE

A Popular Prophet: "Thoroughly American"

There is not a man in the United States who is doing so much to "Americanize" religion . . .

—The *Christian Examiner* (Unitarian) on Henry Ward Beecher, 1860

The meaning of Henry Ward Beecher is partly to be found in the hopes and fears he gave voice to and partly in the way he voiced them. It was not his job to be a doer; that was for politicians who were concerned with the practical problems of existence. His task was to hold up eternal and universal values, the ideals of Christianity and of American democracy, to reconcile Christ and culture. Because America was a pietistic country, no one expected the reconciliation to be perfect: Men could not be perfect until the millennium, and Beecher was only a man. But he could be reassuring; he could tell his hearers, and did, that the human race was rapidly approaching perfection; that Americans were in the forefront of human history, as they had been since the days of the Pilgrims; that the millennium was near; and that it would surely start in the United States. "The latter day is already dawning," he proclaimed in 1860. "The will of the Republic is to be the law of the world," he predicted in 1863.[1]

But these had always been central concerns of American religion. What is significant about Beecher is the way he preached them in the years 1840 to 1870. The two persistent themes which emerge from all his sermons, essays, and lectures are the constant upward progress of life and the loving superintendence of God. For Beecher the universe was in perpetual motion—not the cyclical or orbital motion of classical thought but the dynamic, striving, growing, aspiring, upward motion toward ultimate union with God which coincided with the biological concept of evolution. The recurrent image of the infant yearning for a maternal breast which recurs so often in his sermons suggests both the instinctive quality of this striving and the helplessness of the striver. The need for nutriment sometimes appears greater than the certainly of finding it; however, the yearning of the infant for the mother's sustenance predicates a reciprocal instinctive yearning of the mother to give it.

Similarly, Beecher's constant insistence that a truly Christian life involves the attainment of manhood or manliness also implies some doubts as to the possibility of self-sufficiency; for Americans both happiness and maturity are goals, not achievements; the pursuit of happiness, like the search for the New Adam, can never be truly successful on earth. Consequently, in Beecher's theology, manliness and Christian dependence upon God—Who sustains a maternal, symbiotic relationship with His children throughout their lives—are two sides of the same coin. The prevailing American notion of manliness is therefore actually overcompensation: The cocksure are unsure. God is both a father and a mother to Beecher, and he provided the same double image, represented by God the Father and Christ the Mediator, for Mid-Victorian Americans. One could infer much about America's oedipal complexes, its uneasy attitude toward sex, from this fact; it helps to explain the view of sex as part of our animal nature which Christians were sloughing off as they grew toward union with God. Beecher and the Mid-Victorians repressed their sexuality; romantic, evolutionary evangelicalism was, in essence, the sublimation of sex.

Following hard upon the theme of growth and development in Beecher's religion was that of duty: the obligations—often the burdens—of lifting up others. "We are responsible for existing evils in such a nation as ours," he declared.[2] "There is no such invective as [that] from the lips of Jesus Christ against men who were utterly devoid of sympathy toward their fellow-men."[3] No man is an island; no Christian is free to look out only for his own soul; no American can refuse to help his neighbors and brothers whether they be next door, in the slums, in the Cherokee Nation, or in the miseries of heathendom across the seas. This was the old Puritan doctrine of personal stewardship, of man's obligation to use the gifts, the wealth, the talents which God has given him to fulfill his obligations to God, the giver of all things. To be a Christian American was to be an upbuilder with and for God.

But with this notion was coupled the awareness, and the preaching, of guilt. For too many of those who had "moved up" in the world had failed in their obligations of stewardship. They had taken God's love for granted, taken their success for granted, flattered themselves that they had earned it solely by their own efforts. In addition, most of "the rising middle class" were guilty of refusing to share their wealth and talents: "There is cause for alarm and humiliation before God in the spread of avarice among our people. The intense eagerness to amass wealth."[4] Materialism was holding back man's development.

This in turn led Beecher to the theme of fear: fear that God would curse the well-to-do suburbanite or visit calamities upon the nation for its sins; fear that those at the bottom of society—sunk down, forced down, or kept down—would, one way or another, destroy society. Beecher did not, in his Mid-Victorian years, see this threat in terms of social revolution or Socialism, an attempt of the poor to take the property and power of the rich away from them; for him the threat was disintegration, anarchy, the dissolution of the ties that bind the social fabric together: "As ships built too long and not strong enough, [we] are in danger of breaking in the middle."[5]

Socially, the problem was the diversity of people (foreigners in the cities), economically, it was the poor growing too distant from the rich. But preeminently it was the prospect of sectional separation or secession—a diversity stemming from the immense land mass which now constituted the United States. In Beecher's lifetime the country had doubled in area and quadrupled in population. The westward movement was one of the most immense mass migrations in modern history. To a New-England-bred man, brought up in a tightly knit town-unit system which could trace its roots back two hundred years, this migration westward into the vastness of the plains and prairies was frightening—like the bottom dropping out of a bucket or like the staves of a barrel bursting asunder. The precious wine of "community" was gushing out to be lost in the sands of the great Western desert. And to this unbounded, migratory peril after 1840 the problems of sectionalism and of slavery and antislavery added an almost insuperable centrifugal movement toward national disunity. The nation was literally coming apart at the seams.

The response to this was, naturally enough, a desperate cry for unity, cohesion, order, the creation of national institutions which would put a new bottom in the bucket, new hoops around the barrel, new roots in the deracinated society. Naturally, too, those institutions which had served New England well for so long seemed the best suited to this purpose—if only they could somehow be adapted to fit the whole nation and developed in time. Here was an almost fatal danger. For traditions and institutions take years, centuries, ages to develop. They have to grow out of the spirit of a community or people and to grow up over many generations before their unitive power manifests itself in a deeply felt communal sense. Beecher, therefore, had to stretch the old New England values paper-thin (or voice-thin) to make them applicable to the whole nation—the Church, the home, the school, the arts. He had to fall back on rhetoric, emotional appeals, to hold the nation together. But what did these symbols mean to a floating, rootless population with a hundred and fifty forms of Christian denominationalism and an inveterate individualism and anti-institutionalism nourished by John Locke's atomistic theory of natural rights?

Searching desperately for some means of consolidation, Beecher found two emotion-laden concepts which might keep the ship from breaking asunder: nationalism (or patriotism) and organic natural laws. To these he added the self-sacrificing love of God which bound men together and absolved their guilt, a concept of overarching love such as a competitive, individualistic, exploitative society desperately needed: "Be not discouraged because you are sinful. It is the very office of Christ's love to heal your sin."[6]

As Christ died for the souls of all men, so all Americans should be willing to die for the life of the nation. As science revealed the marvelous laws of the natural world, so the preacher must demonstrate how a benevolent God had designed those laws to help His children find sustenance and grow to Christian manhood. In a system which seemed based upon selfishness and greed, Beecher preached love and sacrifice. In a period when change seemed only to presage chaos, Beecher tried to concoct order by amalgamating science and theology. Where some saw a jungle ethic, Beecher saw reciprocal dependence. What others saw as dissolution, he chose to call growth. Where some said God was dead and Nature was red-in-tooth-and-claw, he insisted that a loving God was in Nature and master of it.

John Higham, in a recent essay entitled *From Boundlessness to Consolidation*, has described the immense popularity of Herbert Spencer in Victorian America in terms which help to explain why Beecher seized upon his complex, dynamic view of the laws of Nature to replace the simple and stable order of eighteenth-century natural law theory:

> One of the principal attractions of Spencer to such men inhered in his reaffirmation of the old Enlightenment belief in a beneficent order of nature underlying the conflicts, the confusion, the cross-purposes of a competitive way of life. Americans, in rejecting the authority of history, had turned in part to the authority of nature; and now that a sense of intimacy with that tutelary presence was dissolving in an urban milieu, Spencer translated the old assurance into terms relevant to a complex society. By conforming to the methods of Nature, he insisted, man was evolving a more and more coherent, rational civilization. In short, Spencer succeeded where the romantics had failed: he reconciled the ideas of nature and civilization.[7]

But there was one great gap in Spencer's answer to the cultural shift taking place in Mid-Victorian America: He left out God. Spencer, like Darwin, was an agnostic who acknowledged God only as "the Unknowable." Such a philosophy, however, was anathema to evangelical Americans. It was Beecher's important and significant task to wed Spencerian science to evangelical Christianity. In order to make Spencer relevant, he had to make him palatable; he had somehow to give God and Jesus a place in the universe and to make room in Spencer's philosophical calculus for human feelings and yearnings, for conscience and moral sympathy, for throbbing hearts and exalted sentiments. If the deists had placed God outside of the world of natural law, they had at least left a proof for His existence in natural theology. Spencer deprived Him of even that. And Spencer in these terms was unacceptable to most Americans.

To make him acceptable, to amalgamate his outlook with that of evangelicalism, Beecher simply sloughed off all the dogmatic aspects of theology that might conflict with science and then moved God bodily back into the empty home in the universe from which Spencer had evicted Him. This he called establishing the harmony of religion and science, of Christianity and organic law. "The Unknowable" became "the Master of Nature" and, with a little refurbishing, took on most of the old familiar aspects of the God of evangelical Christianity, minus His Calvinist frown and thunderbolts.

To top off this theology of reassurance, of faith, charity, and hope, Beecher found in Romanticism—that is, in transcendental idealism—a concept of knowledge in whose terms every man could know, could discover experientially for himself, the ultimate truth of Christianized Social Darwinism. In Nature (and in art, Nature's surrogate) dwelt the living presence of God, not as symbol or form, not as mere design, but as a real, vibrant, throbbing, sentient Being. Wordsworth had put it best in those "sublime" lines written above Tintern Abbey:

> *. . . And I have felt*
> *A presence that disturbs me with the joy*
> *Of elevated thoughts; a sense sublime*
> *Of something far more deeply interfused*
> *Whose dwelling is the light of setting suns,*
> *And the round ocean, and the living air,*
> *And the blue sky, and in the mind of man;*
> *A motion and a spirit, that impels*
> *All thinking things, all objects of all thought,*
> *And rolls through all things.*

To the melodious strains of this great celestial harmony, Spencerian science and Liberal Protestantism walked hand in hand down the aisle of Plymouth Church. The marriage lasted almost a century. For most Americans the Liberal Protestant outlook ceased to be viable after World War II.

In creating a new theology based upon romantic feeling for God in Nature, yet buttressed by scientific laws, Beecher did much to relieve the religious strains brought about by the inadequacies of Calvinism. "The theology that is rising upon the horizon," he said in the 1880's, "will be a regenerated one, and I think far more powerful than the old—a theology of hope and of love which shall cast out fear."[8] Or, as he had said in 1866: "It is a period of the world when men should take courage and be glad. I thank God every morning and every night and ten thousand times a day that he permitted me to be born in such an age as this."[9]

What is difficult to accept in Beecher is not his Romanticism but his penchant for denigrating the Jeffersonian concept of natural rights. One could understand his pointing out that men are not really all equal, that the Declaration of Independence is a bit too simplistic in this regard. But why was it necessary for him to defend these inequalities in terms of race, of nationality, of social class? Beecher obviously felt that he had to counteract the excessive individualism and anti-institutionalism of the age which preceded him. But in seeking to bring order out of confusion and community out of disunity, he threw out not only the bad, but the good, aspects of Locke; he preferred to sacrifice minority rights to a myth of national purity, to sustain the old Yankee traditions in an increasingly pluralistic society. Though he never said so, it is a good bet that if he had been asked, he would have preferred Edmund Burke to John Locke (we know that one of the first purchases for his private library was a collection of Burke's works). But what a distortion of Burke to try to create by rhetoric a definition of Americanism which left out the greater part of its people!

Beecher's greatest talent was his facility with language (we obviously cannot evaluate such other aspects of his oratory as his use of inflection, gesture, dramatics in the pulpit). He did have a gift for imagery, for playing with words and popular ideas. It was also his great failing that he did not know when to stop playing with them. Sometimes the rhetoric seemed more important than the substance. In general, he lacked discipline with either language or ideas. It might be argued that he was a showman to whom dexterity was all, and that his most important talent was his ebullient optimism. "My usual frame of mind," he once said disarmingly, "is hopefulness. I am apt to look at the bright side of things and take a cheerful view of life."[10] Perhaps that was what Mid-Victorians needed most—not to be afraid of fear.

If he was a professional showman, he was one who knew

his job, who enjoyed doing it, and did it easily and well year after year. In his sphere he was as admirable as Garrison, Webster, or P. T. Barnum. For at least three decades Beecher was the high priest of American religion. His pulpit was the nation's spiritual center—at least for that vast body of solid, middle-class Protestant citizens who were the heart of the nation. By his sermons, his publications, and his public lectures he kept in constant touch with the public. Millions read him, millions heard him, millions believed in him. Perhaps his lawyer was right when he tried to prevent the adultery suit from coming to trial: "The scandal would tend to undermine the very foundations of social order."[11]

It was not the least of Beecher's accomplishments that he reversed a trend which had been developing for over forty years in the ministry—ever since the Jeffersonian Republicans had silenced the Federalist pulpits of New England by accusing them (and rightly) of meddling in politics. The clergy had taken the criticism to heart and confined their attention from 1800 to 1840 to the saving of souls (as Locke had long before urged them to do in his *Letters Concerning Toleration*). Estopped from direct political influence, they utilized the rapidly developing institutions of benevolent societies and mass revivalism to influence indirectly the moral life of the nation. In 1827, when the clergy began to campaign for the prohibition of the delivery of the United States mail on Sundays, and when Ezra Stiles Ely, a Presbyterian clergyman of Philadelphia, let drop a remark about the need for "a Christian party in politics," the wrath of Jacksonian anticlericalism intensified this trend. Not until Beecher did a clergyman dare to reassert the right of a minister to meddle in public affairs.

Perry Miller argues in his book *The Life of the Mind in America* that mass revivalism represented a search for a sense of community in the expanding nation between 1800 and 1840. But revivalism waned after that. It was too otherworldly, too ephemeral, too personal—even though enacted in periodic mass rituals—to serve this end. Others have argued that Fourth of July celebrations and presidential inaugurals have been significant means of uniting the country around a fixed set of ideas and principles; but Beecher was already noting in the 1850's that these ceremonies had lost their importance. Some historians have said that the creation of distinctive American forms of literary expression and of art and architecture after 1830 became decisive factors in developing America's sense of its own national character. And still others maintain that it was the Battle of New Orleans, the personality of Jackson, the jingoism of the Mexican War, and the concept of "Young America" that gave this patriotic nationalism firm outlines.

All of these were manifestations of the yearning for community, identity, ideology. All of them played a part in the development of what Ralph Gabriel describes in *The Course of American Democratic Thought* as "the American democratic faith." Robert Bellah, in a recent essay, has presented a sociological analysis of what he calls "America's civil religion," and has traced its origin to the early years of the nineteenth century.[12] But so far no one has given Henry Ward Beecher much credit for formulating and promulgating it.

Bellah describes America's civil religion as "a collection of beliefs, symbols, and rituals with respect to sacred things and institutionalized into a collectivity" which supplies "a strong moral consensus amidst continual political change." And he cites Seymour M. Lipset, another sociologist, who has shown that "American religion at least since the early nineteenth century has been predominantly activist, moralistic, and social rather than contemplative, theological or innerly spiritual." The fundamental principle behind this civil religion, Bellah writes, is its driving concern "that America be a society as perfectly in accord with the will of God as men can make it, and a light to all the nations."

Beecher was the first prominent exponent of this kind of unity of Church and State, of the sacred and the secular: "It is the duty of the minister of the Gospel to preach on every side of political life. I do not say that he *may*, I say that he *must*."[13] He demonstrated in his own career the impact a man driven by this aim and gifted with his talents could have upon the nation, especially when he minimized sectarian differences and stressed Christian ecumenicalism. With Beecher, American religion became an integral part of American nationalism.

Beecher was the first American clergyman to attain a national audience which acknowledged him as its spokesman; the first to make it part of his regular practice to speak out on every significant political and social issue; the first to make a point of being seen with Presidents, to campaign for Presidents, to make much publicly of his friendship with Presidents—in short, our first, self-appointed national chaplain. Before 1850 this would not have been possible; anticlerical sentiments, inherited from the long fight against an established church system, were too strong (Massachusetts did not disestablish its Congregational churches until 1833). A long heritage, from the English Reformation through the bitterness of the Puritan Revolution and its persecutory aftermath, had left an ingrained fear of mixing religion and politics which continued to Beecher's day. Furthermore, the perfectionist strain in American pietism which reached new heights in the 1830's and 1840's had developed a strong anti-institutional bent and an even stronger utopianism which made everyday politics seem irrelevant to true holiness.

Beecher changed all that; or at least he came at a moment when the anti-institutional swing of the pendulum had reached its farthest extreme and he helped to swing it back. He was, of course, as much a product of the triumph of evangelical Protestantism as he was an architect of its quasi-established position in Mid-Victorian America. But the movement needed a leader, and in Beecher it found one. True, he emphasized the Christian aspect of the national religion, but he was willing to welcome Jews, as well as Buddhists, Shintoists, or Confucianists, into the nation. Though he could not avoid the urge to call for the "Christianization" of all immigrants, there is no indication, at least after 1847, that he ever actively supported such a *Kulturkampf* as his father did against Roman Catholics. And in a sermon in which he spoke of the new urge of Americans to trace their ancestry "to colonial days and to the Mayflower," he added that other Americans liked "to trace it to Huguenot or Hebrew blood."[14] He was, as we have noted, no friend to the Know-Nothing movement; but, given his own doctrine of Anglo-Saxon supremacy, it is amusing as well as ironic that he coined the term "un-American" to describe it.[15]

There is one other problem in evaluating Henry Ward Beecher: how to explain why a man so conservative in his social outlook was such a liberal in his theological outlook. But the answer is not difficult. Theologically he represented the logical continuation of the line from Edwards to Emerson which Perry Miller has delineated—the line which emphasized the subjective, mystical side of Calvinism in relating man to God and Nature. But Beecher was able, unlike Emerson, to reject the rationalistic and doctrinal side of orthodoxy without rejecting the Church as well. He did so by applying his subjectivism to evangelical conversion: Man found God in Nature, but experienced a conversion so similar to that of the revival meeting that in effect his regeneration could be defined in orthodox terminology—loosely applied. (A later generation of Liberal Protestants called this interpretation of the conversion experience "progressive orthodoxy.")

Beecher's social and economic conservatism was merely the obverse side of his religious liberalism. For subjectivism in reverse was rugged individualism; science in reverse was intellectual elitism; progress was survival of the fittest; mystical experiences in art, culture, and Nature were aspects of social control. Only the highly endowed, the refined, the gifted were able to commune with God directly; only the intelligent could fathom the secret laws of the universe. The rest of mankind existed on lower rungs of the Great Chain of Being.

Beecher's father had fought to preserve, but had lost in 1818, the authority which the established Puritan clergy had exercised in maintaining an objective, doctrinal religion. When the churches were disestablished, the clergy lost their position as the intellectual elite who guarded Truth by virtue of their knowledge of classical tongues and theological doctrine, lost the status theretofore assured them by virtue of their learning and their membership in an entrenched upper class. With this institutional status gone and the anti-institutionalism of voluntary church membership triumphant in the Age of Jackson, Lyman Beecher and his semi-Calvinist colleagues had sought to retain clerical leadership in America by associational reforms leading prospectively to the formation of a Christian Party in politics. But this form of theocratic control, even when wedded to the new mass revivalism of the frontier, proved untenable. The spirit of individualism was too intense to permit concerted unity even in voluntary, associational Christian benevolence.

Henry Ward Beecher rejected the halfway measures of his father's generation and fought Jacksonian anticlericalism on its own ground. He accepted individual self-reliance, the subjective experience of the common man, and the romantic view of God in Nature. But he shrewdly erected a new kind of status and social control out of his exaltation of the finer or higher feelings of those truly in harmony with God and Nature. The highly endowed individual was the most perfect, the most sublime individual, for he felt and saw God more clearly than the average man. Self-cultivation, however much Emerson or Whitman may have intended it as the bulwark of democracy, nevertheless created its own hierarchy. Henry Ward Beecher, by virtue of his talent for words and feelings which at least appeared to support democracy and the common man, provided the last resting place for religious orthodoxy, the last pedestal for clericalism. With objective theology and philosophy dead or dying, with the establishment and its learned clergy gone, the only possible authority left for an elite lay in the cultivation of enlightened and refined individual sensitivity. Superiority, authority, control rested after 1850 with men like Beecher, whose cultivation, taste, refinement and aesthetic values were, by self-definition, the sublime evidence of divinity in mankind. Beecher made it possible for Mid-Victorian America to retain its faith in religion and its admiration for the clergy, because he demonstrated how the true man of God brought the sublime into harmony with the practical, everyday world.

It is illuminating to recall, in conclusion, the contemporary assessment of Beecher's work made by a Boston Unitarian. The Unitarians were hardly prone to be favorable to evangelicals ("the Orthodox") or to Beechers, yet they recognized a decided difference between Henry Ward and his father. Lyman Beecher had been a divisive force in

America, a polemicist who berated and damned every creed but his own. Henry Ward was an ecumenicist, a man who sought to unite Americans of all faiths in the love of God and country. "His orthodoxy hangs very loosely over his shoulders," wrote the Unitarian reviewer of one of his books in 1860. "To classify him is no easy task, for he is a cross between the 'Evangelical' and 'Liberal' Christian." (The Unitarians had hitherto considered themselves the only "liberals" in America, and this was quite a concession.) The important point about Beecher, said this reviewer, was that he was not a "bigot," nor did he exhibit those "prejudices against learning and philosophy which blinded and narrowed some of the most gifted among the earlier popular Methodist preachers [like Peter Cartwright]." Beecher was both "a man of the people" and a man who tried to "harmonize the advanced thought of the age with a working and living faith." In short, in a time of great spiritual and intellectual crisis, "there is not a man in the United States who is doing so much to 'Americanize' religion among the Orthodox as Mr. Beecher."[16]

Many people have described Beecher as a mountebank, a spiritual witch doctor holding up bright, feathery, rattling symbols and singing incantations of tribal wisdom to frighten away the evil spirits that were bedeviling a frightened community. A more sympathetic observer might call him a popular psychologist ministering to the neurotic anxieties of a troubled society. But I would prefer to describe him, as probably he would himself, as a creator of spiritual myths, a poet of the popular imagination, who managed for a time to capture and inspire an audience that the more profound literary and religious figures of his age—Emerson, Thoreau, Whitman, Hawthorne, Melville, Bushnell—were unable (often unwilling) to cater to.

These men saw deeper than he, and their works still

have meaning today. But Beecher had a different sociological function: that of contemporary interpreter, popularizer, prophet of the ordinary. A man never ahead of or behind his time but always perfectly in step with it. Pompous, vain, bombastic, sentimental, Beecher was not on the whole a likable character—though, of course it was always his paramount concern to be liked, to be popular, to attract and hold the crowd. Even one of his most eulogistic biographers acknowledged that "Mr. Beecher was an opportunist." But he did provide spiritual nurture and sustenance of a necessary kind to a very large number of Americans. And he at least had the grace occasionally to acknowledge his shortcomings, as when he admitted that he did "slop over" a bit sometimes. "I am impetuous. I know very well I do not give crystalline views."[17] It is significant that when he came to Plymouth Church, one of his first innovations was to take out the old carved oaken pulpit which lifted the preacher high above the crowd in lonely splendor. In its place he put an armchair and a small, plain table. When his church was rebuilt after a fire in 1849, he directed that the new platform project slightly out into the pews and that the pews themselves be arranged in a semicircular fashion surrounding the chair in which he sat. How he loved to meet with his congregation (all three thousand of them) for prayer meetings or informal Sunday services! He would sit talking, chiding, praising, comforting, uplifting them; they sat smiling, nodding, weeping back at him. It was difficult to decide who was deriving more nurture, the pastor or the flock. It was a mutual love feast. He fed them and they fed him.

It is a minor order of prophets to which Henry Ward Beecher belonged—the very American and mundane order of Saint Oral and Saint Aural. The path of our history is strewn with the remains of this priesthood, their numerous volumes (usually taken down verbatim as the words flowed endlessly from the prophet's mouth, so as not to lose a precious syllable) now unread and almost unreadable. George Whitefield was perhaps the first of them, Lyman Beecher surely belongs there, then Henry Ward Beecher, Phillips Brooks, Harry Emerson Fosdick, Norman Vincent Peale—to name only a few: American prophets of reassurance for a nation that desperately wants to be loved and to love itself.

NOTES

INDEX

NOTES

PROLOGUE

1 Walter E. Houghton: *The Victorian Frame of Mind, 1830–1870* (New Haven; 1957), p. 17.
2 Henry Ward Beecher: *Star Papers; Or, Experiences of Art and Nature* (New York; 1855), p. 309.

CHAPTER ONE

1 Walter E. Houghton: *The Victorian Frame of Mind, 1830–1870* (New Haven; 1957), pp. 18, 49, 50.
2 John Higham: *From Boundlessness to Consolidation* (William L. Clements Library: Ann Arbor; 1969).
3 George Frederickson: *The Inner Civil War* (New York; 1965).
4 Quoted in William C. Beecher and Samuel Scoville: *A Biography of Henry Ward Beecher* (New York; 1888), p. 50.
5 Ibid., p. 66.
6 Quoted in Paxton Hibben: *Henry Ward Beecher: An American Portrait* (New York; 1927), p. 19.
7 Henry Ward Beecher: *Norwood* (New York; 1868), pp. 268, 406.
8 Hibben: *Beecher*, p. 18.
9 Beecher and Scoville: *Beecher*, p. 604.

10 Ibid., p. 70.
11 See his essay "School Reminiscences," in *Star Papers* (New York; 1855), pp. 189–93.
12 Beecher and Scoville: *Beecher*, pp. 75–6.
13 Ibid., p. 164.
14 Quoted in Lyman Abbott: *Henry Ward Beecher* (Boston; 1903), p. 359. See also John D. Davies: *Phrenology: Fad and Science* (New Haven; 1955).
15 Beecher and Scoville: *Beecher*, p. 199.
16 Hibben: *Beecher*, pp. 108–18.
17 Abbott: *Beecher*, p. 157.
18 Ibid., p. 63.
19 Henry Ward Beecher: *Lectures to Young Men* (New York; 1850), p. 222.
20 Ibid., pp. 133, 213.
21 Ibid., pp. 250–1.
22 Ibid., p. 92.
23 Ibid., pp. 175–82.
24 Ibid., p. 224.
25 Hibben: *Beecher*, p. 243.
26 Ibid.
27 Abbott: *Beecher*, p. 395.
28 Henry F. May: *Protestant Churches and Industrial America* (New York; 1949), p. 67.
29 Abbott: *Beecher*, p. 394.
30 Beecher and Scoville: *Beecher*, p. 659.
31 Ibid., p. 158.
32 See Abbott: *Beecher*, p. 125.
33 Although he does not deal with Beecher's novel, *Norwood*, anyone interested in the early career of Beecher as a reformer should consult Clifford E. Clark, Jr.: "Henry Ward Beecher: Revivalist and Anti-Slavery Leader, 1813–1887" (unpublished doctoral dissertation, Harvard University, 1967). I regret that I did not become aware of this thesis until this book was in an advanced stage of editing, for it contains information and interpretations which would have modified some of the views I express here about Beecher's moral government theory and his concept of moral suasion and political coercion. Professor Clark has also kindly sent me a manuscript copy of his article "The Changing Nature of Protestantism in Mid-nineteenth Century America," which offers a rather different interpretation from mine of Beecher's *Lectures to Young Men*.

Notes

CHAPTER TWO

1 Henry Ward Beecher: *New Star Papers* (New York; 1859), p. 219.
2 R. V. Wells: *Three Christian Transcendentalists* (New York; 1943), pp. 11–12.
3 See ibid., pp. 15 ff.
4 Francis Wayland: *The Elements of Moral Science* (Boston; 1842), pp. 49–54.
5 Daniel D. Williams: *The Andover Liberals* (New York; 1941), pp. 20–1.
6 Henry Ward Beecher: *Norwood* (New York; 1868), p. 325.
7 See ibid., p. 326.
8 Ibid., p. 26.
9 Beecher: *New Star Papers*, p. 183.
10 Ibid., pp. 184–6.
11 For a comparison of Bushnell and Beecher as "liberators" of American theology see John W. Buckham, *Progressive Religious Thought in America* (Boston; 1919), Chapter I.
12 Ibid., p. 32.
13 *Christian Examiner*, Vol. LXVIII (March 1860), 183–6. The article was written by S. W. Bush.
14 See Beecher's article "Working with Errorists," *New Star Papers*, pp. 187–201, for his efforts to keep his skirts clear of excessive friendliness with Unitarians, and his article "Is Conversion Instantaneous?," ibid., pp. 213–18, as evidence of his unwillingness to get too far away from revivalism.
15 Beecher: *New Star Papers*, p. 223.
16 Ibid., p. 227.
17 Beecher and Scoville: *Beecher*, p. 353.
18 Henry Ward Beecher: *Eyes and Ears* (Boston; 1863), p. 23.
19 Ibid., p. 20.
20 John D. Davies: *Phrenology: Fad and Science* (New Haven; 1955), pp. 165–72.
21 Abbott: *Beecher*, p. 112.
22 Ibid., p. 317.
23 Hibben: *Beecher*, p. 185.
24 Ibid., p. 299.

25 Beecher and Scoville: *Beecher*, p. 608.
26 Beecher: *Eyes and Ears*, p. 265.
27 Henry Ward Beecher: *Freedom and War* (Boston; 1863), pp. 29, 31.
28 Ibid., p. 34.
29 Ibid.
30 L. B. Stowe: *Saints, Sinners and Beechers* (Indianapolis; 1934), p. 262.
31 F. H. Foster: *The Modern Movement in American Theology* (New York; 1939), p. 87.
32 Henry Ward Beecher: *Royal Truths* (Boston; 1866), p. 215.
33 Beecher: *Freedom and War*, p. 313.

CHAPTER THREE

1 On Beecher's editing activities, see Lyman Abbott: *Henry Ward Beecher* (New York; 1903), pp. 328–44.
2 Henry Ward Beecher: *Star Papers* (New York; 1855), p. 307.
3 Ibid., p. 310.
4 Ibid., pp. 310–11.
5 Ibid.
6 For similar early statements, see ibid., pp. 100, 234–5, 312; Beecher: *Eyes and Ears*, pp. 31, 35, 287; Beecher: *Royal Truths*, pp. 42–3, 121, 192, 214.
7 Beecher: *Royal Truths*, p. 214.
8 Beecher: *Star Papers*, p. 234.
9 Beecher: *Eyes and Ears*, p. 35.
10 Ibid., p. 37.
11 *Biblical Repertory and Princeton Review*, XL (October 1868), 639.
12 *Atlantic Monthly*, XXI (June 1868), 761–4.
13 *Nation*, VI (April 2, 1868), 274–5.
14 This letter is printed in the preface to the edition of *Norwood* published by Fords, Howard and Hulbert in 1887.
15 For a discussion of the book's popularity and its rendition as a play, see Marvin Felheim: "Two Views of the State, or the Theory and Practice of Henry Ward Beecher," *New England Quarterly*, XXV (September 1952), 314–26.

16 For this chapter in *Norwood*, see pp. 50–61.
17 For Barton Cathcart's conversion, see *Norwood*, pp. 265–75, 373–8.
18 Beecher: *Norwood*, p. 21.
19 Ibid., p. 133.
20 See H. Shelton Smith's introduction to *Horace Bushnell* (New York; 1965), pp. 29–35.
21 Beecher: *Norwood*, pp. 377–8.
22 Beecher: *New Star Papers*, pp. 336–7.
23 Beecher: *Norwood*, p. 318.
24 Ibid., p. 58.

CHAPTER FOUR

1 Frank H. Foster: *The Modern Movement in American Theology* (New York; 1939), pp. 85–6.
2 Henry Ward Beecher: *Royal Truths* (Boston; 1866), p. 90.
3 William C. Beecher and Samuel Scoville: *Henry Ward Beecher* (New York; 1888), p. 67.
4 Lyman Abbott: *Henry Ward Beecher* (New York; 1903), p. 24.
5 Beecher and Scoville: *Beecher*, pp. 67–8.
6 Ibid., p. 49.
7 Beecher: *Royal Truths*, p. 288.
8 Ibid., p. 2.
9 Henry Ward Beecher: *Norwood* (New York; 1868), p. 307.
10 Ibid., p. 155.
11 Paxton Hibben: *Henry Ward Beecher* (New York; 1927), p. 182.
12 Beecher: *Norwood*, p. 307.
13 Ibid., p. 171.
14 Ibid., p. 499.
15 Ibid., p. 307.
16 Ibid., p. 171.
17 Ibid.
18 Ibid., p. 270.
19 Ibid., pp. 175–6.
20 Ibid., p. 167.
21 Ibid., p. 72.

CHAPTER FIVE

1 *The New York Times*, July 23, 1877, p. 2.
2 Henry Ward Beecher: *Royal Truths* (New York; 1866), p. 139.
3 Henry Ward Beecher: *Lectures to Young Men* (New York; 1850), pp. 26–7.
4 Ibid., p. 98.
5 Ibid., pp. 225–6.
6 Beecher: *Royal Truths*, p. 79.
7 Ibid.
8 Ibid., pp. 40–1.
9 Henry Ward Beecher: *Star Papers* (New York; 1855), pp. 106–7.
10 Henry Ward Beecher: *Eyes and Ears* (Boston; 1863), p. 298.
11 Beecher: *Star Papers*, p. 305.
12 Beecher: *Norwood*, p. 187.
13 Beecher: *Star Papers*, pp. 300–1.
14 Beecher: *Norwood*, p. 158.
15 Ibid., p. 187.
16 Beecher and Scoville: *Beecher*, p. 615.
17 Beecher: *Norwood*, p. 158.
18 Ibid., p. 44.
19 Beecher: *Royal Truths*, p. 25.
20 Beecher: *Star Papers*, p. 199.
21 Beecher: *Eyes and Ears*, pp. 1–10.
22 Ibid., pp. 85–9.
23 Ibid., pp. 65–71.
24 Ibid., p. 70.
25 Beecher: *Royal Truths*, pp. 20–1.
26 Ibid., p. 203.
27 Beecher: *Star Papers*, p. 290.
28 Ibid., p. 297.
29 Ibid., p. 299.
30 Beecher: *Eyes and Ears*, p. 284.
31 Beecher: *Norwood*, pp. 209–14.
32 For the relationship between the new American interest in art and architecture after 1830 and the rise of a more conservative social outlook, see Neil Harris: *The Artist in American Society*

(New York; 1966), especially pp. 215, 310–12. This is discussed more fully in the following chapter.

33 Beecher: *New Star Papers*, p. 258.

CHAPTER SIX

1 Walter E. Houghton: *The Victorian Frame of Mind, 1830–1870* (New Haven; 1957), p. 17 and *passim.*

2 Neil Harris: *The Artist in American Society* (New York; 1966), p. 185.

3 Henry Ward Beecher: *Star Papers* (New York; 1855), p. 94.

4 Ibid., pp. 293–302.

5 Henry Ward Beecher: *Eyes and Ears* (Boston; 1863), pp. 225–8.

6 Ibid., p. 265.

7 Ibid., p. 229.

8 Ibid., pp. 265–6.

9 Ibid., p. 221.

10 Ibid., pp. 225–6.

11 Ibid., pp. 227–9.

12 Beecher: *Star Papers*, p. 294.

13 Beecher: *Eyes and Ears*, p. 228.

14 Ibid., p. 220.

15 Henry Ward Beecher: *Freedom and War* (Boston; 1863), p. 39.

16 Beecher: *Eyes and Ears*, p. 219.

17 Ibid., p. 219.

18 Beecher: *Star Papers*, p. 296.

19 Beecher: *Eyes and Ears*, p. 219.

20 Beecher: *Norwood*, pp. 300–1.

21 Ibid., p. 301.

22 However, he also warned that "Ruskin is full of wildness" and contains much that must be avoided: Ibid., p. 222.

23 Ibid., p. 221.

CHAPTER SEVEN

1 See John Higham: *From Boundlessness to Consolidation* (Ann Arbor; 1969), p. 5, for a perceptive analysis of Mid-Victorianism in terms of this statement by Spencer.
2 Henry Ward Beecher: *Norwood* (New York; 1868), p. 51.
3 Ibid., p. 84.
4 Ibid., p. 531.
5 On the democratic elements in the New Lights and the elitist elements in the Old Lights of the First Great Awakening, see Alan Heimert: *Religion and the American Mind* (Cambridge; 1966), especially pp. 47–8.
6 Beecher: *Norwood*, pp. 134–5.
7 Ibid., p. 531.
8 Henry Ward Beecher: *Freedom and War* (Boston; 1863), p. 265.
9 Beecher: *Norwood*, p. 2. For another remark about the Irish, see ibid., p. 286.
10 Ibid., p. 102.
11 Ibid., p. 362.
12 Ibid., p. 370.
13 Beecher: *Eyes and Ears*, p. 297.
14 See George Frederickson: *The Inner Civil War: Northern Intellectuals and the Crisis of Union* (New York; 1965), p. 199. I am much indebted to Frederickson's fine work throughout this and the next chapter.
15 Ibid., pp. 10–11.
16 Beecher: *Norwood*, pp. 213–14.
17 Beecher: *Star Papers*, pp. 293–306; Beecher: *Eyes and Ears*, pp. 281–4.
18 Beecher: *Star Papers*, pp. 294–5.
19 Henry F. May, *Protestant Churches and Industrial America* (New York; 1949), p. 69.
20 Beecher: *Freedom and War*, p. 285.

Notes

CHAPTER EIGHT

1 Henry Ward Beecher: *Freedom and War* (Boston; 1863), p. 280.
2 Ibid., p. 279.
3 Ibid., p. 251.
4 Ibid., p. 252.
5 Ibid., p. 253.
6 Ibid., p. 67.
7 Ibid., pp. 276–7.
8 Henry Ward Beecher: *Royal Truths* (Boston; 1866), p. 134.
9 Beecher: *Freedom and War*, p. 252.
10 Ibid., p. 255.
11 Ibid., pp. 158, 239.
12 Ibid., p. 255.
13 Ibid., p. 239.
14 Ibid., p. 350.
15 Ibid., p. 351.
16 See Henry Ward Beecher: *Royal Truths* (Boston; 1866), pp. 133–4.
17 Henry Ward Beecher: *New Star Papers* (New York; 1860), p. 271.
18 Beecher: *Royal Truths*, p. 25.
19 Beecher: *Freedom and War*, p. 313.
20 Beecher: *New Star Papers*, p. 267.
21 Beecher: *Royal Truths*, p. 90.
22 Ibid., p. 91.
23 Beecher: *New Star Papers*, pp. 253–7.
24 Lyman Abbott: *Henry Ward Beecher* (New York; 1903), p. 388. In college his idol had been Lord Nelson; L. B. Stowe: *Saints, Sinners and Beechers* (Indianapolis, 1934), p. 244.
25 Beecher: *Royal Truths*, p. 114.
26 Ibid.
27 Ibid., p. 27.
28 Beecher: *Star Papers*, p. 295.
29 Beecher: *Eyes and Ears*, p. 311.
30 Beecher: *Norwood*, p. 181.
31 Ibid., p. 143.

32 Ibid., pp. 26–7.
33 Ibid., p. 21.
34 Ibid., p. 183.
35 Ibid., p. 162.
36 Ibid., p. 77.
37 Ibid., pp. 92, 109, 369.
38 Ibid., p. 116.
39 Ibid., p. 70.
40 Ibid., p. 70.
41 Ibid., p. 91.
42 Ibid., p. 155.
43 Ibid., p. 198.
44 Beecher: *New Star Papers*, pp. 211–12.
45 Beecher: *Norwood*, p. 102.
46 Ibid.
47 Ibid., p. 137.
48 Ibid., p. 139.
49 Ibid., p. 406.
50 Ibid., p. 529.
51 W. G. McLoughlin: *Modern Revivalism* (New York; 1959), pp. 84–5.
52 Beecher: *Norwood*, pp. 263–6.
53 Ibid., p. 265.

CHAPTER NINE

1 Henry Ward Beecher: *Patriotic Addresses*, ed. J. R. Howard (New York; 1887), p. 748.
2 Henry Ward Beecher: *New Star Papers* (New York; 1860), p. 266.
3 Ibid., p. 274.
4 Henry Ward Beecher: *Freedom and War* (Boston; 1863), p. 141.
5 William C. Beecher and Samuel Scoville: *Henry Ward Beecher* (New York; 1888), p. 398.
6 Ibid., p. 283.
7 Henry Ward Beecher: *Lectures to Young Men* (New York; 1850), p. 25.

8 Beecher: *Freedom and War*, pp. 8, 10, 318.
9 Ibid., p. 10.
10 Ibid., pp. 6–7.
11 Beecher and Scoville: *Beecher*, p. 302.
12 Ibid., p. 267.
13 Beecher: *Freedom and War*, p. 15.
14 Ibid., pp. 96–7.
15 Lyman Abbott: *Henry Ward Beecher* (New York; 1903), p. 179.
16 Beecher and Scoville: *Beecher*, p. 242.
17 Beecher: *Freedom and War*, pp. 320–1.
18 Ibid., p. 44. This argument hardly squares with Beecher's practice of auctioning slaves to freedom from his pulpit.
19 Ibid., p. 12.
20 Ibid., pp. 14, 23.
21 Beecher and Scoville: *Beecher*, p. 254.
22 Beecher: *Freedom and War*, p. 11.
23 Ibid., p. 21.
24 Ibid., p. 22.
25 Ibid., p. 24.
26 Beecher: *Patriotic Addresses*, pp. 182–5.
27 Beecher: *Freedom and War*, p. 17.
28 Ibid., pp. 18–19.
29 Beecher and Scoville: *Beecher*, pp. 292–300.
30 Paxton Hibben: *Henry Ward Beecher* (New York; 1927), p. 133.
31 Beecher: *Freedom and War*, pp. 63–71.
32 Ibid., p. 71.
33 Ibid., p. 83.
34 This letter is printed in the preface to the edition of *Norwood* published in 1887 by Fords, Howard, and Hurlbert in New York.
35 Beecher: *Norwood*, pp. 277–86.
36 Quoted in Hibben: *Beecher*, p. 36.
37 Beecher: *Norwood*, pp. 305–6.
38 Ibid.
39 Ibid., p. 390.
40 See Hibben: *Beecher*, pp. 151–5.
41 Beecher: *Norwood*, pp. 405–6.
42 Ibid., p. 357.
43 George Frederickson: *The Inner Civil War* (New York; 1965), pp. 161–5.

44 Beecher: *Norwood*, p. 408.
45 Ibid., p. 459.
46 Ibid.
47 Ibid., p. 408.
48 Ibid., p. 409.
49 Ibid., p. 540.
50 On the "will to believe" of the English Victorians, see Walter Houghton: *The Victorian Frame of Mind: 1830–1870* (New Haven; 1957), p. 20.
51 Beecher: *Norwood*, p. 439. On the elitism of the Sanitary Commission itself, see Frederickson: *The Inner Civil War*, pp. 434–44.
52 Beecher: *Norwood*, p. 448.
53 Frederickson: *The Inner Civil War*, pp. 79–97.
54 Beecher: *Norwood*, pp. 493–4.

CHAPTER TEN

1 Henry Ward Beecher: *Patriotic Addresses*, ed. J. R. Howard (New York; 1887), p. 717.
2 Ibid., p. 718.
3 Ibid., p. 720.
4 Ibid., p. 718.
5 Ibid., p. 724.
6 Ibid., p. 741.
7 Lyman Abbott: *Henry Ward Beecher* (New York; 1903), p. 280 *n*.
8 Beecher: *Patriotic Addresses*, p. 732.
9 Ibid., p. 731.
10 Ibid., p. 733.
11 Henry Ward Beecher: *Freedom and War* (Boston; 1863), p. 425.
12 Beecher: *Norwood*, pp. 83–7.
13 Ibid., p. 78.
14 Ibid., p. 84.
15 Ibid., p. 89.
16 Henry Ward Beecher: *Royal Truths* (Boston; 1866), p. 134.
17 Beecher: *Freedom and War*, pp. 352–3.

18 Beecher: *Royal Truths*, p. 180.
19 Beecher: *Patriotic Addresses*, p. 730.
20 Beecher: *Freedom and War*, pp. 66–7.
21 Ibid., p. 68.
22 Ibid., p. 70.
23 Paxton Hibben: *Henry Ward Beecher* (New York; 1927), p. 311.
24 Henry Ward Beecher: *New Star Papers* (New York; 1860), p. 271.
25 Beecher: *Freedom and War*, p. 292.
26 Ibid., p. 268.
27 Ibid., p. 75.
28 Ibid., p. 391.
29 William C. Beecher and Samuel Scoville: *Henry Ward Beecher* (New York; 1888), pp. 412, 421–2, 432.
30 Ibid., p. 582.
31 Beecher: *Freedom and War*, p. 317.
32 Beecher: *Royal Truths*, p. 44.
33 Beecher: *Freedom and War*, p. 120.

EPILOGUE

1 Henry Ward Beecher: *Freedom and War* (Boston; 1863), p. 55; William C. Beecher and Samuel Scoville: *Henry Ward Beecher* (New York; 1888), p. 402.
2 Henry Ward Beecher: *Freedom and War*, p. 63.
3 Henry Ward Beecher: *Royal Truths* (Boston; 1866), p. 137.
4 Beecher: *Freedom and War*, p. 64.
5 Henry Ward Beecher: *New Star Papers* (New York; 1860), p. 271.
6 Beecher: *Royal Truths*, p. 281.
7 John Higham: *From Boundlessness to Consolidation* (Ann Arbor; 1969), p. 4.
8 Beecher and Scoville: *Beecher*, p. 609.
9 Beecher: *Royal Truths*, p. 242.
10 Beecher and Scoville: *Beecher*, p. 377.
11 Paxton Hibben: *Henry Ward Beecher* (New York; 1927), p. 243.

12 Robert Bellah: "America's Civil Religion," in W. G. McLoughlin and Robert Bellah, eds.: *Religion in America* (Boston; 1968).
13 Beecher: *Freedom and War*, p. 295.
14 Beecher: *Royal Truths*, p. 179.
15 Beecher: *Freedom and War*, p. 268.
16 S. W. Bush: "The Liberal Religious Movement in the United States," *Christian Examiner*, LXVII (March 1860), 183–6.
17 Beecher and Scoville: *Beecher*, pp. 591–2, 658.

INDEX

Abbott, Lyman, 9, 11, 19–20, 225
abolitionism, 26, 178, 189–200, 201
Adams, Henry, 166
Adams, John, 205
Africa, 18, 194, 221, 227, 234, 236; *see also* Negroes
agnosticism, 137, 151, 249
Alcott, Louisa May, 161
Alger, Rev. Horatio, 99, 147
American Colonization Society, 18
American Revolution, 4, 7
Americanization, 157; *see also* xenophobia
Amherst College, 15, 17, 63, 76, 96, 164, 232
Andover Theological Seminary, 37
Anglo-Saxons, 4, 10, 31, 138, 139–40, 181, 194, 215, 221–42, 255; *see also* racism
anti-Catholicism: *see* Roman Catholics
Antietam, Battle of, 216
antislavery cause, 10, 18, 26, 189–200; *see also* Negroes
aristocracy: *see* elitism
Arminianism, 174
Arnold, Matthew, 4, 57, 59, 63, 101, 120, 121, 122

Baptists, 36, 41, 51, 136, 177
barbarism, 6, 46, 54, 59, 121, 130, 137, 174, 181, 234, 235
Barnum, P. T., 252
Beecher, Catharine, 13, 16, 165
Beecher, Charles, 13
Beecher, Edward, 13, 165
Beecher, Harriet: *see* Stowe, Harriet Beecher
Beecher, Henry Ward: biographical sketch, 11–30; on Anglo-Saxons, 4, 10, 31, 139, 140; and antislavery cause, 10, 18, 19–20, 21, 26–7, 31, 189–200; on art and artists, 111–13, 119–33; on blacks, 18, 21, 31, 135, 221–42; and Horace Bushnell, 40–1, 74, 78, 82, 85, 143, 169; on business and businessmen, 10, 31, 47, 99–101, 114–18, 127, 130, 141–51; and Calvinism, 4, 9, 10, 12, 24, 31, 42, 56, 62, 64, 65, 71, 74, 78, 82, 115, 138; and Catholicism, 9, 12, 26, 86, 126, 148; on charity and philanthropy, 23, 101, 110, 113–18, 128, 140–8, 156, 245; on chauvinism and patriotism, 10, 31, 117, 158–9, 185–6, 241–2, 247; on cities, 23, 24, 25, 31, 101–7, 148–50, 154; and Civil

Beecher, Henry Ward (*cont.*) War, 29, 185–220; on class structure, 137–43, 148–51; as conservative, 9–33, 41–2, 98–9, 119, 129–33, 134, 142–51, 254–6; on conversion, 14–15, 74–80, 90–1; on culture, 4, 23, 109, 120, 121, 145–51, 181; on Darwin and Social Darwinism, 4, 10, 11, 49–51, 99, 134–51, 230, 233, 248–50; on democracy, 31, 51, 152–3, 154–5, 157, 170, 186, 237; on education, 31, 39, 53–4, 153–83; and Emerson, 32, 60–1, 72, 135, 143, 144, 149, 180, 217, 255, 257; and elitism, 4, 54, 93–4, 116, 118, 119, 121, 124, 128, 133, 134–51, 152, 162–4, 212, 215; on England, 29, 221, 239–40; and evolution, 5, 10, 30, 49–51, 52, 135, 138; on the family, 157, 176–7; on Charles G. Finney, 41, 178; on Fugitive Slave Act, 27, 192–3; and Genteel Tradition, 118, 119–33; and health, 35–6, 46–7; and heart religion, 39, 68, 175; on Heaven, 142; and the higher criticism, 10, 32, 35, 79; and immanentism, 10, 22, 43, 44–6, 52, 58–80; and Jews, 255; and Kansas, 10, 27, 188, 193; on labor and labor unions, 10, 98–101; *Lectures to Young Men* (1844), 20–4, 56, 85, 89, 189; on leisure, 109–11; and Liberal Protestantism, 6, 10, 38, 54, 56, 59, 65, 66, 80–2, 138, 158, 167, 168, 182, 217, 236, 250, 256, 258; as liberating force, 6–7, 9–33, 40–2, 54, 99, 132, 151, 254–6; on logic, 37–8, 40, 67–8, 73; on love, 21, 84–96; on luxury and wealth, 20, 23, 113, 114–18, 140–8; and the millennium, 51, 52, 53, 117, 118, 140, 182; on miracles, 41–4; on motherhood, 13–14, 76, 86–8, 95–7, 157, 176–7, 244–5; on Nature, 4, 5, 19, 35, 45–6, 58–80, 104–5; on New England, 21, 31, 140, 145, 171–3, 185–6, 202–7, 242, 246–7; *Norwood* (1867), 14, 34, 55–6, 62–83, 89–97, 114–18, 130–3, 134, 138, 140–8, 151, 164–75, 179–83, 202–19, 227–32; optimism of, 4, 5, 46, 51, 130, 215, 251; and phrenology, 17–18, 46–9; and predestination, 12, 14, 51, 74, 85; and progress, 4, 5, 51, 52, 117, 138, 148, 181–2, 183, 215, 244; and Protestant ethic, 21, 23, 30, 31, 98–118, 140–51; racism of, 4, 18, 21–2, 139–41, 193–201, 221–42; and Reconstruction, 29–30, 222–7; and Republican Party, 27, 29; and revivalism, 36, 39–41, 80, 177–83; and Romanticism, 4, 5, 25, 32, 40–1, 63, 66, 70, 241, 249–50; rural life, 23, 101–8; on the Sabbath, 170–3; and science, 5, 6, 21, 31, 34–6, 39, 41–4, 46, 48, 50, 52–3, 71–2, 107–9, 160–1; *Sermons to Preachers* (1872), 19, 34, 70; and slave auctions, 10, 199–201; and social control, 129–33, 140–51, 153–83, 257; social philosophy

Beecher, Henry Ward (*cont.*) of, 129–33, 137–51; and the South, 26, 29, 31, 93, 185–220; and Herbert Spencer, 4, 30, 134–51; on taste and refinement, 142–51; and Mrs. Elizabeth Tilton, 10, 27, 30, 92; on total depravity, 14, 17, 22, 24, 39, 42, 168–9; and transcendentalism, 4, 5, 32, 61–3, 67–8, 70, 74, 81, 133, 169; and Unitarianism, 12, 41, 62, 68, 81, 205, 257–8; on war, 186–7; and Whig Party, 19, 27, 128, 158; and women's rights, 10, 167
Beecher, Mrs. Henry Ward (Eunice Bullard), 18
Beecher, Lyman, 9, 11–15, 18, 28, 35, 38, 39, 50, 65, 66, 68, 69, 70, 72, 82, 116, 136, 177, 191, 256, 257, 260
Beecher, Thomas, 13
Beecher, William, 13
"Beecher's Bibles," 188
Bellah, Robert, 252–3
benevolent societies, 13, 101, 116
Bible, 5, 25, 32, 34–5, 43, 54, 71, 73, 77–9, 159; *see also* higher criticism
blacks: *see* Negroes
Bonner, Robert, 57, 63
Boston (Mass.), 15, 57, 64, 93
Brooklyn, 9, 10, 25–7, 56, 57, 64, 82, 130, 140, 172, 199
Brooklyn Armory, 157–8
Brown, John, 32, 153, 189
Brown University, 36
Brownson, Orestes, 62–3, 169
Bumppo, Natty, 229
Burke, Edmund, 251
Burns, Robert, 25, 37, 57
Bushnell, Horace, 40, 41, 74, 78, 82, 85, 143, 169
businessmen, 47, 99, 114–18, 141–8

Calhoun, John C., 10, 192, 224, 225
Calvinism, 4, 6, 9, 10, 12, 24, 25, 34, 36, 37, 39, 42, 51, 56, 59, 62, 64, 65, 68, 71, 74, 78, 82, 84, 115, 136, 138, 164, 180, 249, 250; *see also* predestination; total depravity
camp meetings, 35, 177
Carnegie, Andrew, 99, 151
catechism, 168
charity, 23, 158; *see also* philanthropy
Chinese, 237
Christian democracy, 154, 186
Christian evolution: *see* evolution
Christian Examiner (Boston), 41
Christian nurture, 40, 74, 96, 145, 167
cities: *see* urbanism
Civil War, 6, 7, 14, 29, 51, 143, 144, 155, 164, 175, 185–220
civilization, 51, 153, 230
Clay, Henry, 10, 19
Coleridge, Samuel Taylor, 4, 36, 57, 67, 74, 143, 204
Comte, Auguste, 25
Congregationalism, 10, 12, 30, 65, 72, 82, 136–7, 159, 205
conversion, 14–15, 21, 74–80, 142, 177, 255
Conwell, Rev. Russell H., 117

culture, 4, 23, 26, 56, 59, 145–51, 181

Darwin, Charles, 30, 49, 215, 249
Darwinism: *see* Social Darwinism; Spencer, Herbert
deism, 12, 25, 35, 70
democracy, 31, 51, 152–3, 154–5, 157, 170, 186, 237
Devil, 15, 180
Dewey, John, 16, 182, 183
Douglas, Stephen A., 192
Dwight, Timothy, 12

earnestness, 206
Eddy, Mary Baker, 47, 97
Edwards, Jonathan, 12, 37, 38, 60, 65, 78, 92, 135–7, 138, 177, 180, 255
election, doctrine of, 14, 128
elitism, 4, 54, 72, 93–4, 116, 118, 119, 121, 124, 128, 133, 134–51, 152, 162–4, 212, 215
Ely, Rev. Ezra Stiles, 252
emancipation, 221
Emerson, Ralph Waldo, 25, 32, 36, 57, 60–1, 68, 72, 73, 135, 143, 144, 149, 180, 217, 255, 257
Episcopal Church, 205–6
established church, 12, 136–7, 256
evangelicalism, 6, 23, 24, 25, 29, 38, 54, 64, 72, 79, 81, 91, 94, 132, 147, 212, 249
evolution, 4, 5, 10, 30, 46, 49–51, 52, 135, 138, 215; *see also* Social Darwinism

family, 157, 176–7; *see also* home; motherhood
Federalists, 12, 28, 128, 158, 186, 209, 241, 252
Finney, Charles Grandison, 13, 41, 82, 178
Fort Sumter, 29, 208, 241
Fosdick, Harry Emerson, 260
Fowler, Orin S., 17
Franklin, Benjamin, 30
Frederickson, George, 143–4, 186, 212, 216
Frémont, John C., 27
frontier, 154, 235, 256; *see also* barbarism; sectionalism
Fruitlands (utopian community), 161
Fugitive Slave Act, 27, 192–3
fundamentalism, 22, 24, 79–80

Gabriel, Ralph, 253
Galton, Sir Francis, 238
Garrison, William Lloyd, 32, 41, 190–1, 201
Genteel Tradition, 118, 119–33
Gettysburg, Battle of, 213, 217–20
Gilded Age, 6, 49, 99, 127, 131
Graham, Billy, 183
Grant, Ulysses S., 30
Greeley, Horace, 57

Harris, Neil, 121–2
Harvard University, 36, 66, 68, 72, 165–6
Heaven, 142
Hedge, Frederick H., 36
Hegel, Friedrich, 4, 216, 219
Hell, 15, 22–3, 180
heresy trial, 12, 82

Hibben, Paxton, 28
Higham, John, 248–9
higher criticism, 10, 25, 32, 79; *see also* Bible; science
Hofstadter, Richard, 210
Holmes, Oliver Wendell, Sr., 29, 34, 37, 62, 82, 83, 125
Holy Spirit, 21
home, 176–7; *see also* family; motherhood
Houghton, Walter, 215
Howe, Julia Ward, 216
Hughes, Bishop John, 157

ideality, 21, 38, 66, 169
immanentism, 10, 22, 44, 52, 58–80, 138, 166–8
immigration: *see* Chinese; Irish; xenophobia
Indianapolis (Ind.), 9, 19, 66
Indians, 22, 53, 234–5
industrialism, 11, 150; *see also* businessmen; urbanism
intuition, 50, 67, 121; *see also* Coleridge, Samuel Taylor; Emerson, Ralph Waldo; transcendentalism
Irish, 26, 140, 212, 224–5, 238, 239
irresistible conflict, 210, 214; *see also* Civil War

Jacksonian Era, 3, 6, 10, 11, 40–1, 51, 99, 122, 128, 137, 144, 151, 160, 240, 252, 253, 256, 257
James, William, 5
Jefferson, Thomas, 7, 28, 35, 136, 163, 171, 205, 241, 250, 252
Johnson, Andrew, 29, 225; *see also* Reconstruction

Kansas, 10, 27, 188, 193
Kant, Immanuel, 4, 54, 57, 67
Kingdom of God: *see* millennium; Second Coming
Know-Nothings, 255

labor unions, 10, 30, 98–9
laissez-faire, 31, 147; *see also* Social Darwinism
Lane Seminary, 13, 18
Lawrenceburg (Ind.), 18–19
Lee, Robert E., 224
leisure, 109–11
Liberal Protestantism, 6, 10, 30, 34, 40–1, 56, 59, 65, 66, 67, 80–2, 89, 97, 138, 139, 158, 167, 168, 182, 183, 185, 217, 236, 250, 256, 258
Lincoln, Abraham, 29, 175, 189
Lipset, Seymour M., 253
Litchfield (Conn.), 11, 63, 112
Locke, John, 4, 36–7, 67, 89, 151, 164, 247, 251, 252
London, Jack, 230
love, 21, 84–96
luxury, 20, 140–8, 176–7, 201; *see also* suburbia; wealth

Manifest Destiny, 239–40, 242, 243; *see also* progress
Marsh, James, 36
Marx, Leo, 107
materialism, 6
Mather, Cotton, 137

Index

Methodists, 41, 82, 85, 136, 137, 177
Mexicans, 235, 236
millennium, 51, 53, 117, 118, 140, 181, 182, 243
Miller, Perry, 252, 255
miracles, 41–4, 74, 151, 177; *see also* Bible; science
missions, 13, 18, 101, 128, 195, 233–4, 237, 245
Modernism: *see* Liberal Protestantism
Moody, Dwight L., 24, 183
moral reform, 13, 20–4
moral suasion, 196–7
motherhood, 13–14, 76, 86–8, 95–7, 157, 176–7, 244–5

natural law, 43, 46, 49, 52, 54, 139–40, 181–2, 247; *see also* science
Nature, 4, 5, 25, 37, 43, 45, 58–80, 122–3, 138; *see also* Romanticism; science; transcendentalism
Nature (Emerson), 134–5
Negroes, 18, 21, 135, 168, 189–200, 221–42; *see also* antislavery cause; racism; slavery
New England, 21, 31, 140, 145, 158, 171–3, 177, 185–6, 212
New Haven Theology: *see* New School Theology
New School Theology, 12, 37, 84
New York City, 9, 25, 100, 127, 157
Norris, Frank, 217, 218
Norwood (H. W. Beecher), 14, 55–6, 62–83, 89–97, 114–18, 130–3, 134, 138, 140–8, 151, 164–75, 179–83, 202–19, 227–32

Octopus, The (Norris), 217
Onesimus, 194

Paine, Thomas, 35
Paley, William, 4, 73
Park, Edwards A., 37, 85
Parker, Theodore, 41, 42, 81
Pater, Walter, 5
patriotism, 10, 158–9, 185–6, 202, 213, 233, 241–2, 247
Peale, Norman Vincent, 47, 260
philanthropy, 13, 23, 113–18, 128, 156, 245
Philemon, 194
phrenology, 17, 46, 47–8
pietism, 136, 137, 243, 254
Platonism, 4; *see also* ideality
pluralism, 11
Plymouth Congregational Church, 25, 188, 259
poverty, 23, 31, 147–51, 152, 154
prayer, 44, 174–5
predestination, 12, 14, 51, 74, 85
Presbyterians, 10, 19
progress, 4, 5, 26, 138, 148, 181–2, 183, 215, 244
prostitution, 20
Protestant ethic, 21, 25–6, 30, 98–118, 140–51, 204, 213
Providence, Divine, 41–4, 95, 139, 175, 211, 216, 219
psychology, 5, 46–7, 160–1, 178–80
Puritanism, 31, 60, 74, 88, 128, 137, 138, 145, 157, 158, 176, 239

Quakers, 136, 138

racism, 4, 18, 21–2, 139–41, 193–201, 221–42; *see also* Anglo-Saxons; Irish; Negroes
railroads, 107–8
Rauschenbusch, Walter, 100
reconstruction, 29–30, 206, 214, 222–7
Republican Party, 27, 29
revelation, 5; *see also* Bible
Roman Catholics, 9, 12, 26, 86, 126, 148, 157, 255
Romantic Christianity, 19, 32, 40, 54, 63, 66, 187
Romanticism, 4, 5, 25, 32, 63, 66, 70, 241, 249–50; *see also* transcendentalism
Ruskin, John, 57, 101, 120, 121, 122

Sabbath, 13, 158–9, 170–3, 252
Salvation Army, 151
schools: *see* education
science, 3, 5, 6, 21, 25, 41–3, 45–6, 47–50, 52, 53, 107–9, 160–1, 166
Scottish philosophy, 5, 25, 36–7, 67; *see also* Locke, John
secession, 29, 186, 206–7, 213, 246; *see also* Civil War
Second Coming, 51, 52; *see also* millennium
sectionalism, 210–11, 213, 246; *see also* Civil War; New England
Shakespeare, William, 23, 37, 56, 132
slaveholders, 194–8; *see also* Negroes
slavery, 10, 21, 189–200; *see also* antislavery cause; Negroes; racism
Social Darwinism, 4–5, 10, 11, 49–50, 99, 134–51, 230, 233, 248–50
Social Gospel, 99, 100
Socialism, 26, 246
Spencer, Herbert, 4, 30, 49–50, 134–51, 181, 183, 215, 233, 248–9
states' rights, 208–9
stewardship: *see* businessmen; Carnegie, Andrew; philanthropy
Stowe, Harriet Beecher, 13, 15, 62, 87
suburbia, 25–6, 40, 56, 100, 114, 130, 140–51, 246; *see also* urbanism; wealth
Sumner, William Graham, 149
Sumter: *see* Fort Sumter
Sunday, Billy, 183
survival of the fittest, 45, 99, 118, 147, 152, 216, 248

Taylor, Frederick W., 160–1
Taylor, Nathaniel W., 12, 39, 65
Taylor, William R., 203
technology, 106–9; *see also* science
temperance, 12, 13, 20
Thoreau, Henry David, 57, 133
Tilton, Mrs. Elizabeth, 10, 27, 30, 92
total depravity, 14, 22, 24, 39, 42, 85, 168–9; *see also* Calvinism
trade unions: *see* labor unions
transcendentalism, 4, 5, 6, 25, 32,

transcendentalism (*cont.*) 48, 54, 57, 61, 62, 67–8, 74, 81, 85, 92, 122, 133, 134–51, 168, 217, 232; *see also* Coleridge, Samuel Taylor; Emerson, Ralph Waldo; Romanticism

Unitarianism, 12, 15, 18, 29, 35, 36, 41–2, 48, 62, 64, 68, 69, 81, 82, 205, 257–8
Universalism, 48
urbanism, 11, 23, 25–6, 31, 45, 100–7, 148–50, 154, 201; *see also* suburbia

Veblen, Thorstein, 146, 149
Virgin Mary, 14, 86, 176
voluntarism, 12

Washington, Booker T., 225
Washington, George, 186
Watson, John B., 160
Wayland, Francis, 36–7
wealth, 23, 114–18, 140–8, 245–6
Webster, Daniel, 10, 186, 241, 252
Weld, Theodore Dwight, 13, 18, 41
Westminster Confession, 168
Whig Party, 19
white supremacy, 221–42; *see also* Anglo-Saxons; Negroes; racism
Whitman, Walt, 30–1, 32, 60, 133, 216, 257
Wilberforce, William, 191
Wordsworth, William, 25, 54, 57, 69, 143, 168, 250; *see also* Romanticism

xenophobia, 140–1, 224–5, 237, 238, 239, 240

Yale College, 12, 15, 19, 34, 65

Zola, Emile, 218

A NOTE ABOUT THE AUTHOR

William G. McLoughlin is professor of history at Brown University, where he has taught since 1954. Born in Maplewood, New Jersey, he was graduated from Princeton in 1947 and received his M.A. (1948) and Ph.D. (1953) from Harvard. He was a Guggenheim Fellow in 1960–1, a Fellow of the Center for the Study of the History of Liberty at Harvard in 1960–2, and the recipient of a Senior Fellowship from the National Humanities Foundation in 1968–9. He is the author of Billy Sunday Was His Real Name *(1955),* Modern Revivalism from Charles Grandison Finney to Billy Graham *(1958),* Billy Graham: Revivalist in a Secular Age *(1959), and* Isaac Backus and the American Pietistic Tradition *(1967). Mr. McLoughlin lives in Providence with his wife and three daughters.*

A NOTE ON THE TYPE

This book was set on the Linotype in Janson, a recutting made direct from type cast from matrices long thought to have been made by the Dutchman Anton Janson, who was a practicing type founder in Leipzig during the years 1668–87. However, it has been conclusively demonstrated that these types are actually the work of Nicholas Kis (1650–1702), a Hungarian, who most probably learned his trade from the master Dutch type founder Kirk Voskens. The type is an excellent example of the influential and sturdy Dutch types that prevailed in England up to the time William Caslon developed his own incomparable designs from them.

The book was composed, printed, and bound by The Haddon Craftsmen, Inc., Scranton, Pennsylvania. Typography and binding design by Betty Anderson.

209.73
M226m
40938